D1304705

Spiritual Strength

FOR EACH DAY

All Scripture quotations in this book are taken from the King James Version of the Bible unless otherwise noted.

Spiritual Strength for Each Day
Copyright © 2011 By Midnight Call Ministries
Published by The Olive Press, a subsidiary of Midnight Call, Inc.
West Columbia, South Carolina 29170

Translated from the original German edition, *Andachten für jeden Tag*, by Ann Fankhauser

Copy Editor: Kimberly Farmer
Proofreaders: Kimberly Farmer, Kathy Roland and Lynn Jeffcoat
Layout/Design: Michelle Kim
Cover Design: Michelle Kim

Library of Congress Cataloging-in-Publication Data

Malgo, Wim
          Spiritual Strength for Each Day
          ISBN #9780937422670

          1. Bible Study/Christian Living/Devotional

Printed in the United States of America

CONTENTS

FOREWORD

"Be ye holy; for I am holy" (1 Peter 1:16).

*W*im Malgo, the man I was married to for 43 happy years, was a blessed servant of the Lord. Since he was 27 years old—the day, in fact, after our wedding—until the last day of his life, he was in the service of his great Master. This time could be divided into three phases:

First, he was an evangelist, through and through, with one burning passion: to save souls for the Lamb. In the 1950s, God gave him the task of radio ministry, from which the ministry of the "Midnight Call" proceeded in the year 1955. Later on, he received a further burden on his heart, namely the message of holiness, as the Lord demands of His children, "Be ye holy; for I am holy" (1 Peter 1:16). The question of why this "holiness" was lacking in the daily lives of many Christians gave him much cause for concern. On the grounds of the proclamation of "holiness" in his teaching, came the third part of his ministry: the proclamation of the Maranatha message and the expounding of biblical prophecy. He was simultaneously a voice in the night calling, "The Lord is coming! Prepare yourselves!" For, "...holiness, without which no man shall see the Lord" (Hebrews 12:14).

Wim Malgo left us a great treasury of literature, from which this devotional book has been compiled. I would like to emphasize that it must never take the place of the Bible. It is rather to serve to awaken in its readers the love of the Word of God, so that they read more of the Holy Scripture and study it for themselves.

The daily devotions have consciously been kept brief and were compiled with much prayer. Much hidden work is behind it. My heartfelt thanks goes to all those who helped in some way toward the completion of this devotional book.

We, as the Midnight Call Ministry, are publishing this devotional book in remembrance of Wim Malgo, and we are also reminded of the words of the Bible, "...by it he being dead yet speaketh" (Hebrews 11:4).

–Annie Malgo
Pfäffikon, Switzerland, December 1994

Spiritual
Strength
FOR EACH DAY

JANUARY

9

1 JANUARY

"Even to your old age I am he; and even to hoar hairs will I carry you: I have made, and I will bear; even I will carry, and will deliver you"
(Isaiah 46:4).

*H*ow unsure this year that lies ahead of us is! Insecurity makes us restless and nervous. What may lie in store for you? But most important to ask is, do you want to be eternally safe? Then be prepared to fulfill the two conditions which the Bible names. The one is, "Whoso hearkeneth unto me shall dwell safely" (Proverbs 1:33), and the other, "He that walketh uprightly walketh surely" (Proverbs 10:9). To be obedient means to be prepared to follow the Lord Jesus at all costs. To be upright in God's eyes is to believe in the cleansing power of the blood of Jesus, and in true, heartfelt repentance claim it for your sins.

Perhaps you ask fearfully, how much hardship will I have to bear in this coming year? As soon as you begin to know the power of Jesus that bears you, your cares will subside. What did He have to bear? He bore a crown of thorns, His cross and the sins of the world. What does He bear now? He bears all things by the word of His power. He will also bear you. Therefore, you have no justifiable reason to worry!

2 JANUARY

"He that taketh not his cross, and followeth after me, is not worthy of me" (Matthew 10:38).

You may ask, what suffering will this year bring? But listen, those who suffer most speak the least of their suffering. They find that suffering, for a child of God, is nothing other than the loving hand of the Father, the hand that tenderly frees us from all that is temporal and transitory. Through suffering, God prepared us as partakers of an eternal, indescribable glory. If you have to suffer as a child of God during this coming year, then look to Jesus who went before you; His path attained to utmost glory. As great as His suffering and humiliation were, so great was His glory, "...the sufferings of Christ, and the glory that should follow" (1 Peter 1:11).

Most Christians try to avoid the sufferings of Christ, of which Paul speaks in 2 Corinthians 1:5-7. But if you want to enter into glory rejoicing one day, then decide before God to "follow the Lamb whithersoever he goeth" from now on. Then Romans 8:17 will be fulfilled in your life, "...[We are] heirs of God, and joint-heirs with Christ; if so be that we suffer with him, that we may be also glorified together."

3 JANUARY

"But they that wait upon the LORD shall renew their strength; they shall mount up with wings as eagles; they shall run, and not be weary; and they shall walk, and not faint" (Isaiah 40:31).

Many people sigh, "How weary I am at the beginning of this new year!" There are indeed many weary people. However, the more Christ is the only and primary goal in your life, the less you will be weary in your spirit. What gives you the greatest encouragement to walk in faith? The goal, the purpose. Those who have no eternal purpose become tired of life. So the question, what is your highest goal? Your business, money, family, or success? And then Christ? No wonder you are always in need of a rest! Your will is divided because your purpose is concentrated on many material things. You are drawn to temporal things. For this reason you are no longer able to set your eyes on the highest, best and eternal things. What should you do? Turn your eyes in the other direction. Do it now. Let your life's motto be, "For me to live is Christ" (Philippians 1:21). Then your heart will be glad, and unceasing strength will flow into you from the sanctuary. The Lord says, "Look unto me, and be ye saved, all the ends of the earth: for I am God, and there is none else" (Isaiah 45:22).

4 JANUARY

"Remember ye not the former things, neither consider the things of old. Behold, I will do a new thing; now it shall spring forth; shall ye not know it? I will even make a way in the wilderness, and rivers in the desert"
(Isaiah 43:18-19).

We have crossed the threshold into the New Year, and at the beginning I want you to ask yourself, how many opportunities to witness did you fail to take advantage of in the past year? How many things did you neglect to do which you ought to have done? How many times were you disobedient? You probably have good reason to be despondent upon looking back over the past year. But that's not final; you can come to the Lord with your failures. What a God we have who forgives our sins! Regardless of the many things you failed to do, He will not reject you. The blood of Jesus Christ guarantees you today complete cleansing and renewal; you only need to truly humble yourself, for He says, "Remember ye not the former things, neither consider the things of old." Those who have experienced this forgiving grace will hate sin and go from strength to strength, as it says in Psalm 84:7: "They go from strength to strength, every one of them in Zion appeareth before God."

5 JANUARY

"... In the which the heavens shall pass away with a great noise, and the elements shall melt with fervent heat, the earth also and the works that are therein shall be burned up" (2 Peter 3:10).

*H*ow many things have changed in the past year! People change. Good friends become enemies; healthy people become ill and die. The world changes and passes away; natural catastrophes and climate changes alter the world. The Word of God says, "They shall perish, but thou shalt endure: yea, all of them shall wax old like a garment; as a vesture shalt thou change them, and they shall be changed: but thou art the same, and thy years shall have no end" (Psalms 102:26-27).

We are approaching a great and terrible time of judgment. Blessed are they who have taken refuge from the "wrath to come" in the eternal and unchanging Rock, Jesus Christ. He says, "Because I live, ye shall live also" (John 14:19). If all else perishes, He will not perish; He will remain, and we with Him. Again He said, "...They shall never perish, neither shall any man pluck them out of my hand" (John 10:28). Nothing will "...be able to separate us from the love of God, which is in Christ Jesus our Lord" (Romans 8:39), and "Jesus Christ the same yesterday, and to day, and for ever" (Hebrews 13:8).

6 JANUARY

"But he answered her not a word" (Matthew 15:23).

From the Scriptures we know how this woman cried to the Lord for her sick and tormented daughter—and He did not answer a word. A few days of the New Year have passed already, but maybe the cry in your heart has not been answered, the cry for visible, tangible help. It seems as though the Lord is not answering you a word. But persist and you will receive the comfort you have been waiting for. Why didn't the Lord answer the Canaanite woman immediately who had such great faith? Isn't it hard and puzzling to read, "He answered her not a word"? Was there something the matter with her prayer? Was her request not urgent enough? Jesus Himself answers these questions in the affirmative when He says, "O woman, great is thy faith" (Matthew 15:28). And yet at first, He did not answer her a word. It is the Lord's way to reveal to you His wonderful help in spite of His apparent immediate silence to your prayer. It may seem incomprehensible that the Lord is silent, especially during times of great need. But why is He silent? Answer: So in faith you may even more cling to the promises of your Lord. The moment is not too far when the Lord will no longer be silent, but will answer you, "with good words and comfortable words" (Zechariah 1:13).

7 JANUARY

"For the Lord himself shall descend from heaven with a shout, with the voice of the archangel, and with the trump of God: and the dead in Christ shall rise first" (1 Thessalonians 4:16).

*N*ow for a long time we, the Church, in unison with the Holy Spirit, yearningly exclaim, "Come soon, Lord Jesus." Many may ask, why are you waiting, Lord? Let me, my dear reader, give you words with great confidence. His silence is nothing but the revelation of the fact that He will come soon in the clouds of heaven to take us into His presence. Therefore, be of good courage, dear brother and sister, those who are in great tribulation, even persecution. While He may be silent, He nevertheless hears your cry. He is waiting for your faith to be fully grounded. Then you will call and He will answer you personally, "Behold, here I am." Then the dark night of temptation and tribulation will be overpowered by His unspeakable grace. Therefore, I beg you, do not cease to search and yearn for the Lord, even if you have not received the answer as yet. In the end, you will joyfully understand all that has occurred in your life. Cling even closer to His Word, for the waiting of the righteous results in utter joy. Jesus Himself answers, "Surely, I come quickly."

8 JANUARY

"Strengthen ye the weak hands, and confirm the feeble knees. Say to them that are of a fearful heart, Be strong, fear not: behold, your God will come with vengeance, even God with a recompence; he will come and save you" (Isaiah 35:3-4).

*T*his is a very concrete promise for all who realize that they are tired. "Behold, your God will come...." Usually, physical tiredness is soon overcome, but spiritual tiredness is often quite insidious. We read in the book of Jeremiah, "For I have satiated the weary soul, and I have replenished every sorrowful soul" (31:25). A plainer translation of this verse reads, "I will refresh the weary and satisfy the faint." This promise of God may be fulfilled now in our lives. How can we say this with such certainty? Because God wants to fulfill His promises always. We must learn to take note of what God wants to do and what He does not want to do. He not only wants to refresh the weary and worried soul, but He will also do it! There are no limits to the power of our God. This is written so wonderfully in Isaiah 40:28, "Hast thou not known? Hast thou not heard, that the everlasting God, the Lord, the Creator of the ends of the earth, fainteth not, neither is weary? There is no searching of his understanding."

Those who have fellowship with the living God through the Lord Jesus Christ are connected to an inexhaustible source of power.

9 JANUARY

"According as his divine power hath given unto us all things that pertain unto life and godliness, through the knowledge of him that hath called us to glory and virtue" (2 Peter 1:3).

*T*he words "all things" mean that the power of God is there for all situations in our lives. If this power of Jesus Christ lives in us, then it also shines out of us. God's children should have a little more radiance in their eyes, for the eye is the light of the body. There are light switches with which we can regulate the brightness of a light bulb. In many Christians, this switch seems to have been turned down so far that the light is very dim. What is the reason? The power of Jesus does not dwell in them by faith, and therefore is not effective in their weakness. It is a terrible thing when everything in our lives remains theory because we do not really know Him or the power of His resurrection. This wonderful spiritual power, which also overcomes physical tiredness, must become effective in us. We need not be excluded from this power of God that is revealed in Jesus Christ, but we may be directly included in it. Let us, therefore, give thanks for the power that He has given us.

10 JANUARY

"If we walk in the light, as he is in the light, we have fellowship one with another, and the blood of Jesus Christ his Son cleanseth us from all sin"
(1 John 1:7).

When we come into the light, everything becomes clear. The truth is revealed, even if it is painful. But in the same measure, our innermost being is cleansed in the precious blood of Jesus, according to the above text. The trouble with many people, Christians too, is their attempt to embellish things. This is evident in their daily lives. Everybody tries to put himself in a good light. If you attempt to embellish yourself and make yourself out to be better than you are, you are excluding yourself with such action from the presence of God. The emotional complexes, dark entanglements and feelings of powerlessness come from your lack of self-knowledge; subsequently, you try to make yourself look better before God than you are. The Lord rejects these attempts at renovation, however. The breakthrough to a truly new life will become reality when you are willing to surrender your old life completely into the death of the Lord Jesus.

11 JANUARY

"Therefore if any man be in Christ, he is a new creature: old things are passed away; behold, all things are become new"
(2 Corinthians 5:17).

*N*ostalgia, this sentimental longing for former things, is a trend in our day. We want things to be as they used to be. In Christian circles, we find an increasing tendency toward spiritual nostalgia. The old man with his tendencies and bad habits, his faults, is to be upheld. The old, decaying ego is to be kept alive at all costs. What is missing is this, "Behold, all things are become new." Paul cries, "Put off..the old man, which is corrupt...put on the new man, which after God is created in righteousness and true holiness" (Ephesians 4:22, 24). Don't stop halfway! Take the decisive step that is long overdue, "Lift up the hands which hang down, and the feeble knees" (Hebrews 12:12). Leave the old life and enter into the new life of fellowship with the Father and the Son!

12 JANUARY

*"Hereby know ye the Spirit of God: Every spirit that confesseth that
Jesus Christ is come in the flesh is of God"
(1 John 4:2).*

The zealous study of the Word of God, and therewith the prophetic Word, is of immense importance for our spiritual lives. Peter says that we should take heed of it until "...the day star arise in your hearts" (2 Peter 1:19). But the door of the Word of God can only be opened with the key of diligence. The Holy Scriptures demand earnest study. They bear the divine seal of authenticity. Who can dare to treat them with indifference? Those who despise them despise God, who caused them to be written, inspired through His Holy Spirit. May the Lord keep each of us from turning away from His Word in indifference. The Holy Scriptures "grow" under quiet contemplation. They are full of surprises. I am always conscious of the fact that the pace of our time would keep us from Bible study. So we call all the more, "Search in the Scriptures!"; then the mystery of the victory of Jesus will be revealed to you to a much greater extent. David recognized the necessity of this searching in the Scriptures, and he exclaimed, "Thy word have I hid in mine heart, that I might not sin against thee" (Psalm 119:11).

13 JANUARY

"He that dwelleth in the secret place of the most High shall abide under the shadow of the Almighty. He is my refuge: my God; in him will I trust" (Psalm 91:1-2).

Just as man-made and so-called natural catastrophes take place, there are also inward (spiritual) catastrophes. Most of us are oblivious of this. Even many Christians are unaware inwardly. It is striking how the Lord always spoke of the inward things first. When Noah had to build the ark, for instance, the Lord commanded him to, "Pitch it within and without with pitch" (Genesis 6:14). This goes against our logic. We would say, "First it must be sealed from the outside, so that if there is a danger of water, it will be watertight." But here it says expressly that it must be done first "within" and then "without." We all take great care that our outward appearance is in order, but we take less care that our inner being is protected and kept by the blood of Jesus. Thus, as children of God, we often go through unnecessary suffering that is not for Jesus' sake.

14 JANUARY

"But thou, when thou prayest, enter into thy closet, and when thou hast shut thy door, pray to thy Father which is in secret; and thy Father which seeth in secret shall reward thee openly" (Matthew 6:6).

I would like to say to all those who serve the Lord Jesus behind the scenes, do not be envious of those who serve the Lord in public, who are in the spotlight. These have many more battles than those who serve the Lord in the background and are not seen by men, but are seen by God. It is a gift of God if you are allowed to serve the Lord in the background. Not many people desire this, for we all like recognition, but serving the Lord in secret is pleasing to Him. "Man looketh on the outward appearance, but the Lord looketh on the heart" (1 Samuel 16:7). This will be read by many whose inner battles are unknown to men but known to God, for He sees our hearts. He sees that we come under the discipline of the Holy Spirit so we can serve the Lord with joy in spite of inner conflicts, tears and suffering, of which the world around us sees nothing. That is serving the Lord in "secret."

15 JANUARY

"Shall your brethren go to war, and shall ye sit here?"
(Numbers 32:6).

*A*s members of the Church of Jesus Christ, we are intimately related to one another, bought by the same precious blood. Blood relationship brings obligation, however. We have received untold blessings through the many battles and sufferings of the saints of past times. Many had the true pioneer spirit of faith; they did not doze away in self-complacency. Through their faith, we are mightily spurred on to follow the Lord even more decisively. It is said of those in Hebrews 11:40 that they will not be made perfect without us. The Lord says through the prophet Jeremiah, "Cursed be he that doeth the work of the Lord deceitfully" (48:10). There is a note in the margin of the Scofield Bible, giving the alternative reading, "Cursed be he that doeth the work of the Lord negligently."

I know the fear of trials is a great drawback for those who sit at home in peace and look down on the arena of the kingdom of God instead of entering it, but we are called to battle!

How can you receive a crown if you avoid the cross? If even the best Christians are purified through the fire, you will hardly be able to avoid testing. Arise today, for we are living in a serious time. The Lord of the vineyard wants to find us watching and praying when He comes.

16 JANUARY

"But ye, beloved, building up yourselves on your most holy faith, praying in the Holy Ghost..." (Jude 20).

*P*rayer in the Holy Spirit is a mystery. This prayer has the guarantee of being heard, because its origin is not in us but in the heart of God. When we begin to contemplate on this and grasp it with our understanding and our spirit, we will no longer dare to be negligent in intercession and worship. Samuel, the servant of the Lord, realized this when he said to the people of Israel at the end of his service, "God forbid that I should sin against the Lord in ceasing to pray for you" (1 Samuel 12:23).

Praying in the Holy Spirit is something so great, so tremendous, that the apostle Paul described it in the following words, "...We know not what we should pray for as we ought: but the Spirit itself maketh intercession for us with groanings which cannot be uttered" (Romans 8:26).

If it is really the case that it is not we who are praying but the Spirit of God through us, then we understand that true prayer comes from God and, by means of His Spirit, goes through the one who prays to the object of his prayer, and then returns to God. That is "praying in the Holy Spirit."

17 JANUARY

"And every man that hath this hope in him purifieth himself, even as he is pure" (1 John 3:3).

I believe that many temptations that are attributed to Satan, in reality come from a heart that has not been cleansed of all sin. Much nervous tension and irritability would be overcome in your life if you had not forgotten the cleansing of your former sins (see 2 Peter 1:9). The purification crisis is caused by your not keeping in step with the Lord. Enoch was not raptured by chance. It says of him, "Enoch walked with God: and he was not; for God took him" (Genesis 5:24). In other words, Enoch kept in step with the Lord. Do you know what it means to run ahead of the Lord and not keep in step with Him? It means plunging yourself into religious activity without deeper cleansing in His presence. If we say, sing and pray things that do not conform with our inner self, we are only fooling ourselves. If you testify of something you have not experienced, it has no credibility, because the shadow of a purifying crisis has fallen upon your life. That is a demonstration of Christian powerlessness. Therefore, come to the light and permit Him to purify you today!

18 JANUARY

"And the very God of peace sanctify you wholly"
(1 Thessalonians 5:23).

Sanctification of children of God is an important issue. Of God the Father it says in 1 Thessalonians 4:3: "This is the will of God, even your sanctification...." So whoever resists sanctification is rebelling against the will of God and finds himself in an inner crisis. Sanctification is also the urge of the Holy Spirit, for He is called in Romans 1:4, "...the spirit of holiness." Whoever says "no" to sanctification, therefore, finds himself in a crisis of sanctification. The Son, Jesus Christ, has paved the way to sanctification for us. Hear His high-priestly prayer, "For their sakes I sanctify myself, that they also might be sanctified through the truth" (John 17:19).

Sanctification is so important that God the Father, God the Son and God the Holy Spirit are concerned with it. This is what Peter meant when he said, "Elect according to the foreknowledge of God the Father, through sanctification of the Spirit, unto obedience and sprinkling of the blood of Jesus Christ: Grace unto you, and peace, be multiplied" (1 Peter 1:2).

19 JANUARY

"But avoid foolish questions, and genealogies, and contentions, and strivings about the law; for they are unprofitable and vain"
(Titus 3:9).

*M*any Christians have burning questions which they do not understand and to which they receive no answer. I am convinced there are such among my readers who have often cried to God, "Why me?" And God is silent. Why does He not answer? Because He loves you. It says in Zephaniah 3:17 (Amplified), "In His love He will be silent." The Son of God cried on the cross, "My God, my God, why hast thou forsaken me?" (Matthew 27:46). But God was silent. Why was He silent? It was His beloved Son who was suffering the pangs of death, beladen with the sins of the world. Why did He not answer? Because He loved us, you and me, so very much (John 3:16). The singer of the Song of Solomon says, "Love is strong as death" (8:6). God loved His Son so much that He once called from heaven, "This is my beloved Son, in whom I am well pleased" (Matthew 3:17).

Jesus Christ had to taste being forsaken by God for your sake and mine, and when He cried to His Father, God was silent. Why? I repeat, because He so loved you. This love was stronger than the death of His Son.

20 JANUARY

"And ye now therefore have sorrow: but I will see you again, and your heart shall rejoice, and your joy no man taketh from you. And in that day ye shall ask me nothing" (John 16:22-23).

Why do you receive no answer to certain questions in your prayers? It is because God loves you, because He has planned great things for you, and because He wants to do glorious things through you. We must have the courage to give God the glory when He is silent. We should hold on to the fact then that He is silent because He loves us. It does not matter that we do not understand His love. That will come later. When we see Jesus, all our questions will be answered. When we see Him as He is, we will cover our face with our hands, bow down before Him in worship and confess, "O Lord, I had no idea that You meant so well with me! Forgive my indignant questions, my persistent impatience." Truly, what the Lord Jesus said, "In that day ye shall ask me nothing" will be fulfilled. Bow before Him and do not ask "why" or "how come" any longer. The answer is hidden in the unfathomably great love of the Lord for you personally.

21 JANUARY

"Our conversation [citizenship] is in heaven; from whence also we look for the Saviour, the Lord Jesus Christ"
(Philippians 3:20).

The Bible says that we who believe on the Lord Jesus Christ are already in heaven while we still live on earth. We do not have to strive after citizenship because we already have it. What does this mean in actual practice, though? We find the answer in Colossians 2:6: "Walk ye in him." I must be in Christ, and He in me. In this way I walk in Him. This is the heavenly life. Jesus ascended into heaven, where He now sits at the right hand of God. But He is simultaneously on earth and in heaven. While He sits at the right hand of the Father, He dwells in our hearts through the Holy Spirit, as it says in Ephesians 3:17, "That Christ may dwell in your hearts by faith."

In this way we see this wonderful work in action. While you live on earth—body, soul and spirit—the spirit that dwells in your heart by faith is already in heaven. The inevitable result is written in 1 John 2:6, "He that saith he abideth in Him ought himself also so to walk, even as He walked."

22 JANUARY

*"My people are bent to backsliding from me: though they called them to
the most High, none at all would exalt him"
(Hosea 11:7).*

What is the reason for the fact that so few Christians
lead a really godly life? First of all, spiritual slug-
gishness is an obstacle. Such believers do not keep in step
with the Lord, where they should walk with Him and in Him.
They remain behind, lazy and sluggish in prayer and in their
willingness to serve. Through this, the organic union with the
Lord Jesus is interrupted. Spiritual circulatory problems are
the result. In Hebrews 12:3 we are told not to become wearied and faint in our minds. Such weariness results in our becoming insensitive and unresponsive to the Word. We hear
the Lord lament in Isaiah 42:20, "Seeing many things, but
thou observest not; opening the ears, but he heareth not."

These words describe spiritual weariness. Let us, therefore,
give our all. In 2 Peter 1:3, we are assured that we have been
given the best conditions for such a walk, "According as his
divine power hath given unto us all things that pertain unto
life and godliness, through the knowledge of him that hath
called us to glory and virtue."

23 JANUARY

"Why do the heathen rage, and the people imagine a vain thing?"
(Psalm 2:1).

The present world-political situation looks like a tornado. Everything is in motion. If we were to look at a tornado from the inside, we would be confused to a state of panic. The raging of the nations and individual people is becoming louder and louder. People are crying for social justice, yet remaining selfish themselves. They are calling for peace and demonstrate, yet they themselves do not have peace with God. This is the fatal contradiction. They are saying, "Peace, peace," yet there is no peace.

Is this the contradiction in your heart? Do you demand of others what you lack yourself? The desperate striving to create a better world by human means is becoming more and more intense, but is doomed to failure because the nations are turning against the people who, through Jesus Christ, brought the peace of God to this earth. This is in essence the world in crisis today. But hidden in this world-political tornado is the still, gentle moving of God. True peace—the Kingdom of Peace and the Prince of Peace—will come, literally and physically in and through Israel. Satan is trying to mimic prophecy, anticipating this, which is why everything that looks like peace is in reality a pseudo peace.

24 JANUARY

"And, having made peace through the blood of his cross, by him to reconcile all things unto himself; by him, I say, whether they be things in earth, or things in heaven" (Colossians 1:20).

The whole world is in contradiction to Israel, because God made peace through the blood of Jesus Christ on Calvary's cross in Israel. This is ultimately the reason that the world rejects Israel and thereby says "no" to the Son of God. But the Son will return, and He will install the peace of God. Jesus is not only our peace, but also the light of the world. Peace without light is impossible. Word, light, peace—all three are united in Jesus Christ. He is the incarnate Word. He is the light. He is our peace. "Thy word is a lamp unto my feet, and a light unto my path" (Psalm 119:105).

It exposes and convicts you, but in this way you come to the cross at Calvary. There you will be cleansed by the blood of the Lamb from all sin. Only in the light of the Word of God, can you find the peace of God that will fill your heart. Around you there will still be storms, but you can be filled with the peace of God in the midst of increasing unrest.

33

25 JANUARY

"Blessed is the man that trusteth in the Lord,
and whose hope the Lord is"
(Jeremiah 17:7).

We must learn to trust in the Lord completely and unconditionally. "He is a shield unto them that put their trust in him" (Proverbs 30:5).

Disappointment in people should not lead to bitterness, but to correction and your recognition: I did not trust in the Lord. Even if everything you have built up through years of work collapses, do not resign. The Holy Scriptures tell us, "Cast not away therefore your confidence, which hath great recompence of reward" (Hebrews 10:35).

The Lord will break down more and more of the earthly supports on which we lean so that we have only Jesus to lean on. Abraham did not become the father of all believers automatically. The Lord took away everything on which he relied, little by little, but he believed. In these ever darker end times, we have all the more opportunity to honor the Lord through complete trust in Him. Let us pray, therefore, "Help Lord, for the godly man ceaseth; for the faithful fail from among the children of men" (Psalm 12:1).

26 JANUARY

*"Jesus said unto her, I am the resurrection, and the life:
he that believeth in me, though he were dead, yet shall he live"
(John 11:25).*

What a wonderful promise for God's children! The believer lives forever, because he has eternal life abiding in him. Even when he takes his last breath on earth, he will not see death, according to the express promise of the Lord Jesus. Only Jesus has the power to ignore death as though it does not exist. Of Jairus' daughter He said, "She is not dead, but sleepeth" (Luke 8:52). And of His dead friend Lazarus He said, "Our friend Lazarus sleepeth" (John 11:11).

Of the born again Christians who are waiting for the Rapture, but are no longer here on earth at the time of the Rapture, Paul says that they are asleep. This means that as far as their earthly existence is concerned, they are asleep, but they are alive before the throne of God. Jesus Christ guaranteed us this through His resurrection. "Death is swallowed up in victory. O death, where is thy sting? O grave, where is thy victory?" (1 Corinthians 15:54-55). Jesus Christ is truly risen again, so that we may say of a child of God who dies, he or she is not dead. They are alive in Paradise in unspeakable bliss!

27 JANUARY

"Be sober, be vigilant, because your adversary the devil, as a roaring lion, walketh about, seeking whom he may devour"
(1 Peter 5:8).

We as believers all have inner and outer battles to endure every day. If these battles become fiercer and fiercer, although we have received forgiveness of our sins, we should know that these battles are often indefinable temptations from our mortal enemy, Satan. We who have the Lord Jesus in our hearts can resist Satan, victoriously in faith. What about when I am weak and miserable, when I can hardly believe, when I feel nothing and it is all darkness around me? Then James gives you a wonderful answer, "Resist the devil, and he will flee from you. Draw nigh to God, and he will draw nigh to you." You may draw near to God, then, in resisting the devil, for the way to Him in the inner sanctuary is free, "Having therefore, brethren, boldness to enter into the holiest by the blood of Jesus...and having an high priest over the house of God; let us draw near with a true heart in full assurance of faith" (Hebrews 10:19, 21-22).

28 JANUARY

"Sing aloud unto God our strength...the pleasant harp with the psaltery"
(Psalm 81:1-2).

The Word of the Lord is so timeless, so topical, because it is the eternal Word for all times. In the above Scripture, Israel is told to sing joyfully and to play all kinds of musical instruments. There are many Bible verses that continually remind us of the redemption that took place. In Psalm 81:7, the Lord reminds His people how He hears prayer, "Thou calledst in trouble, and I delivered thee; I answered thee in the secret place of thunder: I proved thee at the waters of Meribah."

Why does the Lord continually remind us? Why did He command Israel to tell their children and grandchildren of His miracles, and to write His commandments on the doorposts of their houses? Because He knows how forgetful we are. This is why He reminds His people today that He hears our prayers. The fact that we do not pray more proves how forgetful we are. Letting ourselves go without prayer gives the enemy the opportunity to outwit us. Because the Lord is the eternally unchanging One, He wants to hear our prayers now. He hears the cries of the righteous and fulfills the desire of them that fear Him.

29 JANUARY

"Hear, O my people, and I will testify unto thee:
O Israel, if thou wilt hearken unto me"
(Psalm 81:8).

God's twofold demand to Israel at that time and to us today is first to "Hear!" and then to "hearken." Why does the Lord say this twice? Parents often experience that children of a certain age have difficulty in listening to them because the children think they know everything better in any case. Somehow, this is also the case in a child of God's relationship to his or her heavenly Father. When the Lord says, "Hear" and "if thou wilt hearken unto me," He is not yet speaking of obedience, but of listening to Him. If we would learn to listen more, the fullness of God could break through in us to a much greater extent. Becoming inwardly still and listening is extremely important. Then we experience what we cannot achieve through effort or activity. In Isaiah 55:2-3 it says, "Wherefore do ye...labour for that which satisfieth not? hearken diligently unto me, and eat ye that which is good, and let your soul delight itself in fatness. Incline your ear, and come unto me: hear, and your soul shall live." If the Lord emphasizes this, it must be of great importance to listen. How long have you listened to Him today?

30 JANUARY

"If we walk in the light, as he is in the light, we have fellowship one with another, and the blood of Jesus Christ his Son cleanseth us from all sin" (1 John 1:7).

During my ministry, I was required to travel often. When flying overseas, particularly from the West to the East, I was always fascinated by flying toward the light, leaving behind the darkness. It always was a moving demonstration of spiritual reality, because we who believe are approaching the light of eternity. How important it is for a child of God that his or her path is directed toward the light and not in the other direction. It is just as necessary in your and my faith-lives to escape the darkness.

"Follow peace with all men, and holiness, without which no man shall see the Lord" (Hebrews 12:14).

Flee from darkness. The Lord said of His servant Job, "He is blameless and upright, a man who fears God and shuns evil" (Job 1:8, NIV). This is the secret of victory: shun evil, flee from it, and come into the all-illuminating presence of the Lord Jesus. Hasten toward the light. Flee form the darkness, for Jesus is coming soon!

31 JANUARY

*"In all these things we are more than conquerors
through him that loved us"
(Romans 8:37).*

*M*any years ago, a postage stamp was issued in Israel in remembrance of the soldiers fallen in the wars. One depicted an Israeli soldier with his battle gear and *tallit* (prayer shawl). Can the power of prayer be portrayed better? Hardly. The fighter prays. If your prayer life does not keep up with the battle to which you have been assigned, you will be overcome. Woe betide us if we proclaim the Word of God without having wrestled on our knees beforehand! All children of God are kings and priests, but in their service, which should be kingly and priestly, there is often a bitter lack of holy influence. I fear that in our activity for the Lord, there is too much of the business-like planning of a manager. Whoever has anything at all to say or proclaim in the kingdom of God, can only be a servant of Christ and not a servant of man if he prays. So pray, therefore. Pray then when you are full of despondency over your unfortunate plight, for it says, "In the day when I cried thou answeredst me, and strengthenedst me with strength in my soul" (Psalm 138:3).

Spiritual
Strength
FOR EACH DAY

FEBRUARY

41

1 FEBRUARY

"Rest in the Lord, and wait patiently for him"
(Psalm 37:7).

Those who are continually being tossed to and fro because they do not cast all their cares upon the Almighty God, cannot wait for the Lord in the right manner. Let all other voices become silent in you now. We must not let ourselves be influenced and distracted from our goal, which is to wait for the Lord. Do not rely on any measure based on emotion or feelings. If you have truly turned away from "idols" to serve the Lord, it cannot be other than that you are waiting for Him. Is it not high time for you to lay aside everything that clouds your expectation of the appearance of Jesus? We only have a short time left, for the Lord will come soon. All the accompanying signs of His return are here already. Everything around us is being dissolved. And the Lord calls to us through 2 Peter 3:11 with great earnest, "Seeing then that all these things shall be dissolved, what manner of persons ought ye to be in all holy conversation and godliness."

John writes the same thing to us in other words in 1 John 2:28, "And now, little children, abide in him; that, when he shall appear, we may have confidence, and not be ashamed before him at his coming."

2 FEBRUARY

"Wherefore henceforth know we no man after the flesh"
(2 Corinthians 5:16).

I want to say with great earnest and assurance that, just as the individual child of God must claim the power of the death of Jesus for his or her being, so we as the Church of Jesus Christ must also put on the death of Jesus for us all collectively, for it is written, "…if one died for all, then were all dead" (2 Corinthians 5:14).

If we are living members of the Body of Jesus, we have all passed through His death. Herein lay the authority of the first Church. All conflicts and tension found their immediate solution in their being crucified with Him. For this very reason we no longer know any man after the flesh, because we have all died with Christ. The flesh has been crucified. The Lamb of God died on the cross so that you and I—our old man— should and could die with Him. If we say, "Jesus died for my sins," we are limiting the glorious victory of Jesus. The main object of the death of Jesus for you and me is defined in Romans 6:4: "Therefore we are buried with him by baptism into death: that like as Christ was raised up from the dead by the glory of the Father, even so we also should walk in newness of life."

3 FEBRUARY

"He sent his word, and healed them, and delivered them from their destructions" (Psalm 107:20).

We often underestimate the miraculous power of the Word of God. It has an eternal, healing, renewing effect. "Being born again, not of corruptible seed, but of incorruptible, by the word of God, which liveth and abideth for ever" (1 Peter 1:23).

If this Word is able to generate new life, is it not also capable of refreshing, healing and renewing our tiny, temporal lives? What did the centurion say to Jesus? "Speak the word only, and my servant shall be healed" (Matthew 8:8).

In times of sickness, we often get things the wrong way around. We seek healing for our bodies without our souls being healed first through the Word. If the soul is not healed, however, you have put the cart before the horse, and the torment will begin anew. You sought only to remove the effect and not the cause. We must seek the healing of our soul first; that is done through His Word: "Speak [thy] word...and...servant shall be healed." Jacob cried as the sun arose at Peniel, "I have seen God face to face, and my life is preserved" (Genesis 32:30).

Has your soul been healed? Before you seek physical healing, seek the healing of your soul through the Word in faith. Then you will also experience miracles where your body is concerned.

4 FEBRUARY

"Cast not away therefore your confidence...
ye might receive the promise" (Hebrews 10:35-36).

To do the will of God consistently, to be constantly obedient, is the key to discovering that He fulfills His promises. The key to experiencing the fulfillment of His promises lies in Jesus Christ alone. Every promise, however, has its own particular key. Take, for instance, the well-known words of Psalm 37:4-5, "Delight thyself also in the Lord...and he shall bring it to pass." In these two verses, we have two promises and three keys belonging to them. The will of God, the key to the promise in verse 4, says, "Delight thyself in the Lord."

He, the Lord, must be our highest priority, and only after Him do we come. By delighting in the Lord, however, our desires are sanctified. When this is the case, He fulfills our desires gladly, "He shall give thee the desires of thine heart."

Let us consider verse 5 now, whose promise is, "He shall bring it to pass." What are the two keys necessary so that He can "bring it to pass"?

- "Commit thy way unto the Lord," and
- "Trust also in him."

5 FEBRUARY

*"I am crucified with Christ: nevertheless I live;
yet not I, but Christ liveth in me"
(Galatians 2:20).*

*H*as your faith life been without authority up till now?
Is it without impact? Perhaps you have to admit that
this is the case. The reason for this is your self-assertion. Surrender your pride and your dishonest, selfish ego into the death of Jesus. You must reckon with the fact that you are crucified with Christ. This is not a theory but is based on solid assurance, just as it is a historical fact that Jesus died on the cross. The Lord will try you in this attitude of faith. People around you in your daily life will provoke you, challenge you, appeal to your pride and ambition, betray you, despise you, slander you. But these are all tools in God's hand to prove whether you really are crucified with Christ. It must be revealed whether you will react as Jesus did, who, when He was provoked to come down from the cross, was silent and remained on the cross. This is the secret. Then your family will change, your whole environment, because you yourself have changed. Your Christianity is no longer powerless and colorless, for it is no longer a miserable theory but a living reality. Self-renunciation means Jesus-affirmation. Surrendering yourself into the death of Jesus leads to true life eternal.

6 FEBRUARY

*"Awake thou that sleepest, and arise from the dead,
and Christ shall give thee light"
(Ephesians 5:14).*

I am afraid, although the Bible frequently says, "Fear not!" There is one thing I am afraid of. I am afraid of the terrible sign of the end times, "The love of many shall wax cold" (Matthew 24:12). Much is spoken of brotherly love, of love for one's neighbor, but I am thinking of the wonderful, fervent first love for the Lord Jesus. You were once converted, found forgiveness of your sins, rejoiced in the Lord, were zealous in witnessing for Him, sought to win souls for the Lamb, bowed your knee together with other children of God—and today? Everything has died down. The love in you has grown cold. Paul says that the love of Christ binds us together. Hear what the exalted Lord says, "I have somewhat against thee, because thou hast left thy first love" (Revelation 2:4).

I am afraid of this, and I continually seek the face of the Lord, to let Him search me and to ask Him, "Lord, am I still in my first love for you?" Don't you feel this end-times, deadly frost threatening over us? "The love of many shall wax cold." I admonish you from the depths of my heart, don't let this happen to you!

7 FEBRUARY

"The devil, as a roaring lion, walketh about, seeking whom he may devour" (1 Peter 5:8).

In these end times, in which Satanic activity, as described in Ephesians 6:12, is increasing enormously, we can only survive unharmed as children of God if we watch and pray perseveringly. Nothing is so dangerous as when members of the body of Jesus start to fall asleep. Then the enemy pounces. Then we are already in his clutches. The Lord Jesus warns us, "And what I say unto you I say unto all, Watch" (Mark 13:37). Turning to Peter, He said in the night when He was betrayed, "Simon, Simon, behold, Satan hath desired to have you, that he may sift you as wheat" (Luke 22:31).

If the Lord Himself says this, why don't you take it seriously? Wake up, you who are asleep! Put on the whole armor of God. Practice the victory of Jesus in your daily life. But you may respond, don't we have to fear that one day we will be overcome, if we are so attacked? Not at all! The One who is with us is greater and infinitely stronger than those who are against us. Nobody will be able to pluck us out of His hand.

8 FEBRUARY

"Be not rash with thy mouth, and let not thine heart be hasty to utter any thing before God: for God is in heaven, and thou upon earth: therefore let thy words be few" (Ecclesiastes 5:2).

"Never again!" you have probably said before the face of the Lord in prayer, and yet a short time later you were in the same situation again. "I never want to commit this sin again, Lord," you pray, but perhaps you have never let go of it, and you remain bound to it. Why do we often promise the Lord so much, and yet we do not keep our promises? It is because our decisions are made on an emotional level. Nothing is so changeable as our feelings. We soon forget the Lord and what we promised Him. "Well," you may say, "I can't help it. That's just the way I am." This is no excuse, however. You may be weak, but you don't have to remain weak. The Lord has given you a mighty, miracle-working weapon so that you can become free of your emotional nature: the sword of the Word of God, which divides spirit and soul. Yet one thing must be clear: a theoretical agreement with the Word does not produce this division between soul and spirit. If this division really does take place, however, our vows take on eternal validity before the face of the Lord.

9 FEBRUARY

"All that the Lord hath said will we do"
(Exodus 24:7).

*I*srael vowed to do everything the Lord had said on Mount Sinai, but very soon the whole nation became apostate. God takes our decisions seriously, and He adds to our spiritual will also the ability to do His will (see Philippians 2:13). Everything remains theory in our lives, however, if we refer to the Word but do not lead a prayer life. In other words, the Word of God only has its powerful, abiding effect on our emotional hang-ups when we talk with the Lord. Through the Bible God speaks to you, and in prayer you speak to Him. In spirit I want to take you by the hand and ask you to stop for a moment and answer the following question: Are you still a prayer warrior, in spite of all your activity and stress? How much time did you spend before the Lord today? Did you get through to Him? Or did you plunge yourself into your daily routine, after a quiet time? Was the fire of your first love rekindled in your heart? It is my heartfelt plea that after reading these lines, you will humble yourself before God and say, "Lord, I will never again neglect to put my devotion to You into daily practice; I want to keep my vow to You from now on."

10 FEBRUARY

"The Lord on high is mightier than the noise of many waters . . .
holiness becometh thine house, O Lord, for ever"
(Psalm 93:4-5).

Why is it that we are humbled through inner and outer controversies? It is so that we become more and more rooted in Him. If only we would understand better why we are often subjected to storms of increasing wind velocity in our life. The divine perspective is, the more a person is rooted in Jesus Christ, the more unshakable he will be in all the storms that he encounters. It is vital for us to be rooted in the Lord. Especially in our day, when the signs of the end times are becoming clearer, and we hear the hurricane of tremendous temptations approaching, the question arises, are you rooted in the Lord Jesus? We can only be rooted in the Eternal One in the measure that we have let ourselves be uprooted from the things of this world. When the mighty storms of temptation come, you cannot survive with theories. Only being grounded in the Lord Jesus will help us then. With this attitude, you will rejoice in the midst of the storms, "Nevertheless I am continually with thee" (Psalm 73:23).

11 FEBRUARY

"Behold, I have prepared my dinner...come unto the marriage"
(Matthew 22:4).

*O*ften this invitation is given us in the Word of God, "Come!" It is the simplest thing in the world to respond to the call of the Lord. You worry and sigh and find no answer to your problems, but the Lord is simply calling you, "Come!" You who are lonely, come to the marriage feast, for everything is prepared. Fellowship with the Father and the Son is a reality for those who believe. John wrote in his first letter, "Our fellowship is with the Father, and with his Son Jesus Christ" (1 John 1:3).

Come, therefore, especially you, my weary brother and burdened sister. What does the Lord Jesus say that you should do? Does He speak of particular spiritual exercises, keeping days of silence, seeking new, better retreats? No, the Lord says quite simply, "Come unto me, all ye that labor and are heavy laden" (Matthew 11:28). Then He adds to His call to come to Him the promise, "I will give you rest." I am aware that Satan wants to bring you into such stress that you simply cannot find the time to come to Jesus. Hear what He says, Come! And those who come to Him He will not cast out (see John 6:37). Remember, there is much forgiveness with Him (see Psalm 130:4).

12 FEBRUARY

*"This they said, tempting him, that they might have to accuse him.
But Jesus stooped down, and with his finger wrote on the ground"*
(John 8:6).

*A*n adulteress is brought before Jesus by her accusers.
The Lord appears to be in an irresolvable dilemma,
because the righteousness of God must be completely satisfied. If your conscience accuses you and says you are guilty
before the holy face of God, accept it to be true, for God is
holy. But see the wonderful solution Jesus had for this adul-
terous woman. "Jesus stooped down, and with his finger
wrote on the ground." It is as though He wanted to say, "Yes,
this woman has sinned, but I am stooping, bending down,
humbling down in her place." Did He write words of grace
on the ground? We suspect this is the case, for immediately
after His statement He said, "He that is without sin among
you, let him first cast a stone at her." As a result, they all went
away, convicted. Jesus got up and said, "Hath no man con-
demned thee?" She answered, "No man, Lord." "Neither do
I condemn thee: go, and sin no more." This woman found
forgiveness and was able to rejoice: Jesus had made all things
well.

13 FEBRUARY

"Having a form of godliness, but denying the power thereof"
(2 Timothy 3:5).

*W*hy do Christians today pursue more and more what is not genuine? Why is the façade passionately accepted and defended, while the essence, the true thing, withers? Clinging to what only appears to be real, to a deception, is increasing daily. This is all the more the case because the revelation of the pseudo-Christ, the Antichrist, is no longer far off. The more we walk in the light, in prayer and with the Word of God, the more we will be able to distinguish between the genuine and the false, the real thing from the apparently real. Those who have the Spirit of God have the Spirit of truth, have the anointing, and do not need anyone to teach them. This means that when such a person enters a church, he or she feels instinctively whether Jesus Christ really is at the center, or merely an appearance that is maintained. In this connection, I would like to pronounce an earnest warning. In the indivisible point of time when the Rapture will take place, the genuine will be divided from the false, the truly born-again person from the nominal Christian. Therefore, my question is, is being crucified with Jesus Christ a reality in your daily life?

14 FEBRUARY

*"Without controversy great is the mystery of godliness: God was manifest
in the flesh, justified in the Spirit, seen of angels, preached unto the Gentiles, believed on in the world, received up into glory"*
(1 Timothy 3:16).

The desperate plight of many Christians is that they do
not know Jesus. They know Him by name, from hear-
ing Him proclaimed, but they do not know Him by nature.
Those who know the Lord Jesus Christ, the Son of God, in
His innermost being, find discipleship sheer joy and glory,
even if they experience tribulation. We even find this tragedy
in some of the disciples, that they did not really know Him.
To Philip He says, "Have I been so long time with you, and
yet hast thou not known me, Philip?" (John 14:9). Let us take
more note in our personal lives of the Lord's statement,
"Where I am, there shall also my servant be" (John 12:26).

Where was He when He first came to this earth? In Bethlehem. His life began in humility. And where did His earthly
life end? In the deepest humiliation and suffering on Calvary's
cross. There nobody wants to seek Him and find Him, but it
is there that you will come to know Jesus, and there He will
reveal Himself to you.

15 FEBRUARY

"Remember that Jesus Christ of the seed of David was raised from the dead" (2 Timothy 2:8).

*E*verything is subject to death. All human efforts ultimately lack the power of order. We see this clearly. The progress of the human mind, knowledge, has brought the world unprecedented chaos. Although technological progress has virtually exploded, leading to more comfort, man has actually become a slave to his own inventions. Now the Word tells us, "Remember that Jesus Christ of the seed of David was raised from the dead." The reality of His resurrection restores divine order to everything. The reality of His resurrection makes every person new who believes on Him. The historical fact of His resurrection also guarantees a new heaven in the future and a new earth. Yes, the truth of His resurrection proves His divine sonship.

"In him was life; and the life was the light of men" (John 1:4). In Him is renewal, power, eternal life, joy, divine order, and victory. Without Him, chaos rules. What shall we do now? Remember Jesus Christ who is risen from the dead. Praise be to His holy name that He really is risen again.

16 FEBRUARY

"But the path of the just is as the shining light, that shineth more and more unto the perfect day" (Proverbs 4:18).

*T*he power of light impressed me anew recently when I saw streetlights that shine brighter the darker it gets. They adjust automatically. Before the sun goes down, they hardly shine at all, but the more darkness falls over the town, the brighter they shine. When I saw this I thought, this is our situation in these end times, which get darker and darker. Our calling is, "Ye are the light of the world" (Matthew 5:14).

Light is power. If the "bright light of the Gospel" has been lit in your heart, then the more the night comes upon us, the brighter it will shine. This does not apply to Christendom collectively. Religious Christianity can only produce synthetic light, which illuminated the darkness of heathenism. People are then "Christianized" but not evangelized. We as children of God today, more than any generation of the Church before us, have the task of letting our light shine brighter, for the darkness is increasing.

17 FEBRUARY

"And beside this, giving all diligence, add to your faith virtue; and to virtue knowledge; And to knowledge temperance; and to temperance patience; and to patience godliness" (2 Peter 1:5-6).

These are all fruits of the divine nature in you, if you belong to Jesus, and know Jesus. Peter knew Him. He knew that he would soon have to die, but because he knew Him, he was filled with a radiant and living hope. Do you know Jesus? If you really accept Calvary, this diligence, this first love for Jesus, will burn in you. To those who love Jesus first and foremost and above all else, with all their hearts and souls, He will reveal Himself. He promised, "He that loveth me shall be loved of my Father, and I will love him, and will manifest myself to him" (John 14:21). Then you will know Jesus and will be more than a conqueror in your daily life. If you know Jesus now, then He will also know you on that great day when you stand before Him. Then He will take you by the hand and lead you into His heavenly kingdom, where you will be eternally blessed.

18 FEBRUARY

"Therefore, behold, I will allure her, and bring her into the wilderness, and speak comfortably unto her" (Hosea 2:14).

The Lord wants to speak to us. A true child of God is conscious of this and is not annoyed when from time to time, the Lord holds up a red light in front of him saying, "Stop. Stand still for a moment." "Be still, and know that I am God" (Psalm 46:10). In other words, contemplate. O, the reverent, blessed hours spent at Jesus' feet! The impatience we have toward unexpected circumstances and people shows how little we are capable of being inwardly still before the Lord. How long does our patience last? Usually, until we need it. The Bible speaks of patience with joy. In the above verse we read that the Lord leads His people into the wilderness to speak kindly to them. In the wilderness it is quiet. "Study to be quiet," says 1 Thessalonians 4:11. Only in this way can we get through to the sanctuary. Do you have the necessary patience? Be honest, when you spend time in prayer, are you not drawn back to your work, instead of continuing in prayer? How long were you still in the presence of the Lord today? Has everything in you become still so He can speak to you? Let this message be a stop sign from the Lord for you, for He wants to speak to you. Then all stress and nervousness will disappear and you will go out into your daily life as a person who can cope.

19 FEBRUARY

". . . Thou shalt be called by a new name, which the mouth of the Lord shall name" (Isaiah 62:2).

Whoever uses the name of the Lord Jesus with a cleansed and believing heart, will experience that through this Satan is driven away like lightning. No enemy power can withstand this precious and wonderful name. Abram was alone with his wife Sarai for a long time. They believed God's Word. He had promised to make a great nation out of them. They waited for decades and remained obedient. They trusted in their God. Then came the moment when God could renew them: "Neither shall thy name any more be called Abram, but thy name shall be Abraham" (Genesis 17:5).

In other words, now you are an individual, but I will multiply you million-fold. When the Word of God can penetrate our hearts; when we believe against all odds, like Abraham, and are obedient to God's demand, "Walk before me, and be thou perfect" (Genesis 17:1), the Lord will renew our name so that we do not remain alone. The wonderful thing, however, is that God did not just take Abram's name and change it to Abraham: for God a married couple is an entity. The divine structure of a marriage is that the husband keeps in step with his wife and the wife with her husband. Genesis 17:15: "And God said unto Abraham, As for Sarai thy wife, thou shalt not call her name Sarai, but Sarah shall her name be." So the wife's name was changed too.

20 FEBRUARY

"And God said unto Abraham, As for Sarai thy wife, thou shalt not call her name Sarai, but Sarah shall her name be. And I will bless her, and give thee a son also of her: yea, I will bless her, and she shall be a mother of nations; kings of people shall be of her" (Genesis 17:15-16).

After the Lord gave Abram his new name, in the same chapter He turns to Sarai. In other words, "Abraham, your wife is also included!" The name Sarah has a lovely meaning: "princess." The wonderful thing is that Abraham and Sarah were satisfied with the Word of God alone, without seeing, without feeling and without experiencing. This is the faith we need in our day. His Word, His promise, should be enough for us. Abraham and Sarah believed, the Lord renewed them, and they became father and mother of many nations. The Lord wants to do this in your life also. What good is the name "Christian" if you do not want to bear the cross of Christ? You must obey the Word and take your discipleship seriously, and then you will be fruitful and your spiritual life will be multiplied.

21 FEBRUARY

"And he said unto him, 'What is thy name? And he said, Jacob. And he said, Thy name shall be called no more Jacob, but Israel: for as a prince hast thou power with God and with men, and hast prevailed"
(Genesis 32:27-28).

There is a third person whose name was renewed here on earth. This took place on that mysterious night in Peniel. We can hardly fathom this mystery. When Jacob was alone, a man wrestled with him. It is often taught that Jacob wrestled with God, but we read that God wrestled with Jacob until the breaking of the dawn. It says clearly, "There wrestled a man with him" (verse 24). How long? Until the Lord had broken him, because he did not want to humble himself. Only then did Jacob begin to wrestle. He clung to the Lord and cried, "I will not let thee go, except thou bless me" (verse 26). We must note that the Lord did bless him after his change of name, after Jacob had confessed what he really was. Jacob wept, fought and cried, "I will not let thee go, except thou bless me." He wanted the Lord to bless him immediately. But the Lord asked him, "What is thy name?" and he answered, "Jacob." This was his confession of sin, for Jacob means, "supplanter." After he had confessed this, the Lord said, "Thy name shall be called no more Jacob, but Israel."

22 FEBRUARY

"He answered him nothing"
(Luke 23:9).

This silence of the Lord is strange and moving. Why didn't He answer the false accusations? There can only be one reason: Jesus knew. My Father knows! Moses also, when he was attacked by his own sister and brother, was silent and did not open his mouth. But the Lord justified him. We are called to follow Jesus in this also; that means not returning insult for insult, but being silent. How much can be destroyed by one single word! Never fight flesh with flesh. You do not need to worry about your reputation, nor how your character is judged, for the Lord knows you and He judges you. You do yourself great harm if you attempt to build up your prestige. Be still! One violent response causes the quiet voice of the Holy Spirit to be silent. Are you misunderstood? Are your good intentions wrongly interpreted? This will not harm you. God Himself says to you in His Word, "No weapon that is formed against thee shall prosper; and every tongue that shall rise against thee in judgment thou shalt condemn" (Isaiah 54:17).

23 FEBRUARY

". . . Being reviled, we bless; being persecuted, we suffer it: being defamed, we intreat" (1 Corinthians 4:12-13).

*I*f you are wronged and your good name is defiled, you have in Jesus Christ the chance to remain meek and humble and not to say a word. He wants to keep you in perfect peace. Trust Him instead of fighting, debating and arguing. Not a word is necessary on your part. But the opposite also applies: "Judge not" (Matthew 7:1). This means, do not judge or condemn anyone you have not heard personally. A sharp word, indirect slander, an unkind look, or even a wrong thought harms the stillness of the soul. "Be still and know that I am God" (Psalm 46:10), says the Lord. Another text says, "When words are many, sin is not absent" (Proverbs 10:19, NIV).

Give Him the lordship over your life, and the peace of God which passes all understanding will keep your heart and mind through Christ Jesus (see Philippians 4:7). While your heart is still, you will be blessed and refreshed by Him. When the old indignation threatens to break out over all the negative and untrue things that are said about you and the wrong that is done to you, then think of the practical words, "The Lord will perfect that which concerneth me" (Psalm 138:8).

24 FEBRUARY

"Every spirit that confesseth not that Jesus Christ is come in the flesh is not of God: and this is that spirit of antichrist, whereof ye have heard that it should come; and even now already is it in the world"
(1 John 4:3).

The lordship of Christ or anarchy. Just as Satan said at the beginning, "I will be like the most High" (Isaiah 14:14), so he is already attempting in these end times to be like Christ, i.e. to replace Christ. The lordship of Jesus in your personal life makes you capable of fulfilling the actual purpose of your conversion: to serve the living God. The choice is the lordship of Christ or anarchy, to serve or to rule. What does serving mean? Nothing other than self-surrender in favor of others. What does ruling mean? Self-assertion at the expense of others. The pseudo-ruler was overcome by the Servant. The Lord Himself told us this, "Whosoever will be chief among you, let him be your servant" (Matthew 20:27).

All pride, all self-assertion is a degradation of your personality. What is the power of serving? It is in the practice of the victorious lordship of Jesus. We see this revealed in the cross of Calvary. The Servant attained victory over the cruel rule, or ruler, through the surrender of His life.

25 FEBRUARY

"How much more shall the blood of Christ, who through the eternal
Spirit offered himself without spot to God,
purge your conscience from dead works to serve the living God?"
(Hebrews 9:14).

What was the purpose of Jesus' service for the living God? He poured out His life in His blood so that we could become capable of serving. The unlimited, victorious power of the service of Jesus is the source of the power of your and my service. In Jesus Christ, we have everything. How foolish it is, therefore, to surrender to anarchy and through it come under the rulership of the enemy.

Let us consider the nature of Jesus' service. It had the element of complete free will. There is no compulsion to serve God. The Lord Jesus said of Himself, "No man taketh it [His life] from me, but I lay it down of myself" (John 10:18). Even in Joshua's time, at the end of his life, we see this voluntary nature, "As for me and my house, we will serve the Lord" (Joshua 24:15). It takes only a free-will decision on your part, "I want to declare myself free of Satan's power and live and serve under the King—and lordship of Jesus Christ."

26 FEBRUARY

"Let this mind be in you, which was also in Christ Jesus"
(Philippians 2:5).

Service for God means to consciously allow the lordship of Jesus Christ in our lives. That in time testifies that the element of the fullness of His Spirit is at work. In Hebrews 9, we read that the Lord Jesus sacrificed Himself to God through the eternal Spirit, and not out of emotional sentimentality: "But into the second went the high priest alone once every year, not without blood, which he offered for himself, and for the errors of the people" (Hebrews 9:7). This is why Paul says so clearly, "We are the circumcision, which worship God in the spirit" (Philippians 3:3). That is the mind of Christ.

Very few Christians have learned to worship and serve the Lord in the Spirit! Most Christians are full of emotions or feelings. Such can never experience the living reality of the mind of Christ in their life.

27 FEBRUARY

"Blessed is the man that trusteth in the Lord,
and whose hope the Lord is"
(Jeremiah 17:7).

We can say "Amen" to this. "Amen" means, "So let it be." "Amen" confirms what has been said. Jesus is the great, unchanging Confirmer, for all the promises of God in Him are "Yea" and "Amen." The natural man is full of contradictions. All contradictions in our lives are in accordance with the nature of the Antichrist, who will portray the greatest contradiction: an apparent Christ, yet not the real Christ. But the risen Lord is "Yea" and "Amen." He is "Amen" in the full atonement of His precious blood. He is "Amen" in His righteousness. This holy, glorious robe of "Amen" is beginning to shine in the fallen world all the brighter. He is "Amen" in every name that He bears, the Bridegroom of the Church, who will never be separated from her again. The Friend who loves more than a brother. Your Shepherd who is with you in the valley of the shadow of death. Your Helper and your Redeemer, your Rock and your Guarantor, your confidence, your joy, your everything, your "Yea and Amen" in all things. If only I could engrave this on your heart in golden letters: Jesus alone is your confidence, the divine "Amen" in your soul!

28 FEBRUARY

"Man goes to his eternal home"
(Ecclesiastes 12:5, NJV).

We are all hastening toward a goal: the Lord Himself. What does this mean, to hasten toward the Lord? It means progressive sanctification, and nothing other than concerning ourselves more and more exclusively and concretely with the person of Jesus Christ. Paul is a shining example in this, for he pursued this goal. He was so one with his goal that he and Jesus were almost inseparable. This is why he could say, "For me to live is Christ" (Philippians 1:21). And in another place he testifies, "I am crucified with Christ" (Galatians 2:20). Therein lay his immense power. He was indeed one with Jesus, toward whom he hastened. Progression in sanctification can never be separated from hastening toward the Lord. The tragic tension in which many believers live is that they want to separate these two inseparable things. Whoever does this, however, falls prey to a great self-deception. Whether you like it or not, you are hastening toward the Lord timewise, but inwardly you are lagging behind. Examine yourself, in whether you are separating the inward from the outward.

29 FEBRUARY

*"For the weapons of our warfare are not carnal, but mighty through God
to the pulling down of strong holds"
(2 Corinthians 10:4).*

If our thoughts are pure and full of love, we will create a blessed, beneficial atmosphere around us. If they are evil, however, it is better for us to be alone, for then we spread a depressing, tense atmosphere, and one day the fellowship in which we live and work will be destroyed. It is said that this is due to suppressed aggression, but it is actually the suppressed evil thoughts against your brother and your sister. If the devil has power over your thoughts, flee into the protection of Jesus Christ. Then be of good comfort, because the promise of the Lord will apply, "Behold, I give unto you power…over all the power of the enemy" (Luke 10:19).

Sins of thought and sins of the tongue are brothers. Woe betide us if they are ignited by hell. But Jesus is Victor. He won eternal life for us all by surrendering His life. He did not let Himself be provoked. He did not accept the challenge to assert His right. He stayed on the cross as the Lamb of God, and overcame the enemy who oppresses you, once and for all.

Spiritual
Strength
FOR EACH DAY

MARCH

1 MARCH

"Above all, taking the shield of faith, wherewith ye shall be able to quench all the fiery darts of the wicked. And take the helmet of salvation, and the sword of the Spirit, which is the word of God" (Ephesians 6:16-17).

It certainly gave Paul great joy to write to the Thessalonians, "Your faith groweth exceedingly" (2 Thessalonians 1:3). Why had their faith grown? Through their continual "drawing near to the Lord." The nearer we come to Him inwardly, the more our faith will grow. Of course, the path will be steep, and naturally, it will grow darker, but by losing our hold on the world, we will hold on to Him all the more. Abraham became strong in faith and gave God the glory. He was fully persuaded that what God had promised, He was also able to perform (Romans 4:21).

Or think of David. David experienced terrible disappointments and persecution in his life, but for this very reason he could also say, "I will love thee, O Lord, my strength. The Lord is my rock, and my fortress" (Psalm 18:1-2). Where did the prophet Elijah get his authority? Solely from his attitude to the Lord, for he said, "I, even I only, remain a prophet of the Lord" (1 Kings 18:22). He was uprooted from all, but all the more rooted in the Lord.

2 MARCH

"As ye have therefore received Christ Jesus the Lord, so walk ye in him: rooted and built up in him, and stablished in the faith, as ye have been taught, abounding therein with thanksgiving" (Colossians 2:6-7).

With the increase of the hope of faith, something else also increases in us: His love. This is very often lacking in us. By coming nearer to the Lord, however, this most worthy goal will also manifest itself. The love of Jesus in you is one of the clearest signs of whether you are inwardly hastening toward the Lord, whether the actual nature of the Lord is taking on contours in you, or not. The love of God in the heart of a Christian expects nothing from others, but gives continually, just as the Lord Jesus gave Himself out of pure love. What did Paul pray in his unfortunate plight in the Roman prison? Did he pray that he would soon be liberated? No, he prayed, "And this I pray, that your love may abound yet more and more in knowledge and in all judgment" (Philippians 1:9).

This was his primary desire, which he often spoken of. It is a very important point of utmost urgency, for in our day love is decreasing instead of increasing. The same Paul also challenged us, "Above all these things put on charity [love], which is the bond of perfectness" (Colossians 3:14).

3 MARCH

"He that is void of wisdom despiseth his neighbour: but a man of understanding holdeth his peace" (Proverbs 11:12).

It is a wonderful thing when we see ourselves as we are. We come to know ourselves through continual, prayerful reading of the Bible. This leads, of a necessity, to deeper knowledge of the Lamb of God. The more I see my own, corrupt nature in the light of the Word, the more I am able to see the Lamb, in spirit and not just with my intellect, "Behold the Lamb of God, which taketh away the sin of the world" (John 1:29).

This makes us inwardly still, so that we learn to be careful with our words, particularly concerning others. We can become and remain still, even in the greatest storms of life, but only in union with Jesus. This union with Him is in the spirit, "He that is joined unto the Lord is one spirit" (1 Corinthians 6:17). That is divine wisdom. In Proverbs 9:10 it says, "The knowledge of the holy is understanding." Through ever deeper knowledge of the Lamb, we will become capable of being silent where the natural man so loves to talk and speaks evil of his neighbor. Are you a wise man who has put on wisdom in person in Jesus Christ? I call you today to heed the words, "Put ye on the Lord Jesus Christ" (Romans 13:14).

4 MARCH

"I know thy works: behold, I have set before thee an open door, and no man can shut it: for thou hast a little strength, and hast keep my word, and hast not denied my name" (Revelation 3:8).

To whom did the Lord give an open door? To those who had little strength. This is a message of hope for all those who are hopelessly weak. It is God's nature to glorify Himself in weakness. Remember this, you who so yearn for power and the feeling of strength. How often we ask for the opposite of what God wants to give us. He said, "My strength is made perfect in weakness" (2 Corinthians 12:9). Why doesn't the Lord need our strength? Because our strength only accomplishes temporal things, but His strength works eternal things. This is why we must become weak, because our own strength holds up and diverts God's strength. He gives this open door to those who keep His Word. How few remain standing on the foundation of the whole Bible. What does the Lord say, however? "To this man will I look, even to him that is poor and of a contrite spirit, and trembleth at my word" (Isaiah 66:2). Are you willing to let this Word judge you ever deeper? God does not expect strength of you but obedience.

5 MARCH

"By the which will we are sanctified through the offering of the body of Jesus Christ once for all" (Hebrews 10:10).

What is sanctification? We find the deepest meaning of sanctification or holiness in Hebrews 13:12 (NKJV), "Therefore Jesus also, that he might sanctify the people with His own blood, suffered outside the gate." Then follows the demand, "Therefore let us go forth to Him, outside the camp, bearing his reproach" (verse 13).

Jesus went out to sanctify us. We must go out to Him to be sanctified. The question is, are you willing to be sanctified, that is, to be set apart with Jesus? Is it your desire to let go of people, possessions and things in order to be completely united with Him? The path of sanctification is a lonely one, for it leads outside to Jesus. It leads there where Jesus was; not just to the cross but on the cross. Sanctification is vital, for if we do not want to go where Jesus was, we cannot come to where He is now. This is why it says in Hebrews 12:14, "Follow peace with all men, and holiness, without which no man shall see the Lord."

Time is pressing; the hour of our meeting with Jesus in the clouds of heaven is approaching rapidly. Let us therefore continually bear in mind, "God hath not called us unto uncleanness, but unto holiness" (1 Thessalonians 4:7).

6 MARCH

"And God shall wipe away all tears from their eyes; and there shall be no more death, neither sorrow, nor crying, neither shall there be any more pain: for the former things are passed away"
(Revelation 21:4).

The best is yet to come! The most glorious things lie ahead of us. The Lord has prepared unimaginable bliss for all those who love Him. This bliss cannot be described, for the words of 1 Corinthians 2:9 are true, "Eye hath not seen, nor ear heard, neither have entered into the heart of man, the things which God hath prepared for them that love him."

But the Lord has told us certain things about our eternal glory in His Word. We read in the book of Isaiah, for instance, "And the voice of weeping shall be no more heard in her" (Isaiah 65:19). This means that the glorified will weep no more, as the cause for sadness has been taken away. No suffering grieves them, nor do thoughts of death or any kind of loss make them sad. There they will weep no more, for there their sanctification is complete. No evil heart of unbelief will keep the blood-bought ones from the face of the living God (see Hebrews 3:12). There we will stand before His throne without blemish and will be completely transformed into the image of His Son. All whose sins have been washed in the blood of the Lamb will cease to grieve.

7 MARCH

"And there shall be no night there; and they need no candle, neither light of the sun; for the Lord God giveth them light: and they shall reign for ever and ever" (Revelation 22:5).

God's victorious children will weep no more because, among other things, all fear of change will have disappeared. They will know then that they are safe forever. Sin is excluded and they are included in glory.

They also will weep no more because all their longings have been stilled and all their dreams fulfilled. They cannot wish for anything more, because they already have everything. Their eyes, ears, hearts, hopes and imaginations are completely satisfied. And as imperfect as our present knowledge is about what God has prepared for those who love Him, we know enough through the revelation of the Holy Spirit: we will be unspeakably happy there. Such joyous rest is prepared and ready for us in heaven. Perhaps it is very near already. One thing is sure. One day we will exchange the willows on which we hang our harps with the palm branches of victory. The dewdrops of care will be changed into pearls of eternal bliss. This we know: Jesus is coming soon. That will be glory for me.

8 MARCH

"Him that cometh to me I will in no wise cast out"
(John 6:37).

The Lord Jesus spoke this tremendous, ever-valid Word. It is embedded in His great speech about what He is. "I am the bread of life: he that cometh to me shall never hunger; and he that believeth on me shall never thirst" (verse 35). Then in the following verse, the Lord laments over the fact that they do not want to believe Him. Finally, He refers to His Father and utters that mighty promise, "Him that cometh to me I will in no wise cast out."

The validity of this promise is unlimited. It does not say, "The sinner who comes to Me for the first time, I will not cast out," but, "Him that cometh to me I will in no wise cast out." He is saying here that He will not cast out any person who comes to Him, either for the first time or at any time after this. He will never do it. What about the Christian who has come to Jesus and then sins again? This promise still applies, for the same John writes in his first letter, "If any man sin, we have an advocate with the Father, Jesus Christ the righteous" (1 John 2:1).

9 MARCH

"Come now, and let us reason together, saith the Lord: though your sins be as scarlet, they shall be as white as snow; though they be red like crimson, they shall be as wool" (Isaiah 1:18).

The Lord washes me through His blood so that I am as white as snow. He further states, "I will cleanse them from all their iniquity, whereby they have sinned against me" (Jeremiah 33:8). Jesus Himself said, "My sheep hear my voice, and I know them, and they follow me" (John 10:27).

It is as though He is putting a divine seal on His promised, "He that cometh to me I will in no wise cast out," by adding, "neither shall any man pluck them out of my hand" (John 10:28).

Why do you fear, then? Is it not overwhelming grace that when you come to Jesus, you find in Him the One who receives you and incorporates you in His Church, and says to you, "You are Mine for all eternity"? So, resist the spirit of fear and bow to the Spirit of adoption, through whom you can say, "Abba, Father" (Romans 8:15).

What immeasurable grace is in this short but mighty promise, "He that cometh to me I will in no wise cast out."

10 MARCH

"I have yet to speak on God's behalf"
(Job 36:2).

We should never boast over our spiritual gifts in order to receive praise from people, or so that our zeal for the Lord's work is publicly acknowledged. At the same time, it is a sin of omission if we continually attempt to hide what the Lord has given us for our fellow men. The glorious purpose of conversion is that we become something, "To the praise of the glory of his grace" (Ephesians 1:6). Christians should not be like a village in a valley, but as a city on a hill. As a child of God, you should not be a candle hidden under a bushel, but you must be a light that is placed upon a candlestick, so that it illuminates everyone who comes into the house. But true light-bearers disappear in the light, and only the light they bear is seen. It is, therefore, true self-denial when we withdraw so as not to be seen. But it is never justified when we hide Jesus Christ, the truly risen Lord, who has taken up residence in our hearts. What a tremendous task we have in these end times, especially now as we draw ever closer to the Rapture.

11 MARCH

"And God is able to make all grace abound toward you; that ye, always
having all sufficiency in all things, may abound to every good work"
(2 Corinthians 9:8).

Time is short! Try, therefore, in the name of Jesus who is
not ashamed of you, to overcome your very human disposition and proclaim to others the salvation that Christ proclaimed to you. If you cannot speak with a voice like a
trumpet, then speak with a soft voice! If you are not called to
preach, then pray in stillness. If you cannot write books or
tracts to spread your testimony, then say with Peter, "Silver
and gold have I none; but such as I have give I thee" (Acts
3:6).

Speak at Jacob's well in Shechem with the Samaritan
woman, if you cannot preach to the people on the mountain.
Praise the Lord Jesus in your house if you cannot glorify Him
in the temple. Or do it in the field if the market is not the
right place for you. Witness of Him in your family, if the family of mankind seems too vast for you. Do not bury your tal-
ent, but use it! Then you will gain a lot of interest for your
Lord and Master. And by speaking about the Lord's business,
we ourselves are refreshed, the saints are quickened, sinners
are comforted and the Savior is honored.

12 MARCH

"Before I was afflicted I went astray: but now have I kept thy word"
(Psalm 119:67).

*W*e see this blessed result of affliction in our own lives. It teaches us to obey the Word. What Word? The Word of our Lord, of which He Himself said, "The words that I speak unto you, they are spirit, and they are life" (John 6:63).

This Word imparts to us the whole fullness of God, seeing Jesus Christ Himself is the incarnate Word, and, "In Him dwelleth all the fullness of the Godhead bodily" (Colossians 2:9). The prophet Ezekiel was told to eat the Word. In Ruth 2:14 we read, "And she did eat, and was sufficed."

Every time we eat of the Bread that the Lord gives us, we are refreshed as after a hearty meal. This is because we are satisfied by the Lord's truth, which Christ reveals to us through His Word. Our hearts find peace through the words of Jesus. He Himself is the unspeakable, lovely object of our longing. Our hope is fulfilled, for in whom could we hope other than in Him who speaks to us? What can we who are afflicted wish for more than that we learn to obey His Word through it and win Christ?

13 MARCH

"Then shall the dust return to the earth as it was: and the spirit shall return unto God who gave it"
(Ecclesiastes 12:7).

We are all on the way to the one goal, the eternal God. Innumerable people have attempted to escape this inevitable goal, but in vain. Those who are reconciled to the eternal God through the Lord Jesus Christ, however, hasten toward this goal with great joy and purpose. The following are examples of this:

Abraham: The Lord said of him, "Your father Abraham rejoiced to see my day: and he saw it, and was glad" (John 8:56). Abraham's strong faith made him walk toward the Lord unswervingly.

Jacob: Shortly before his death, he suddenly exclaimed, "I have waited for thy salvation, O Lord" (Genesis 49:18). Jacob hastened toward the Lord, although it seemed as though he was farther away from the goal than ever, for he was in Egypt at that time.

Job: This severely tested man saw the goal he pursued in spite of the greatest suffering. In all his terrible distress, he rejoiced, "I know that my redeemer liveth" (Job 19:25). From these examples we learn that the more we are liberated from the things of this world through suffering, the more clearly we will see the goal, and the better we can hasten toward the Lord.

14 MARCH

*"Wherefore in all things it behoved him to be made like unto his brethren,
that he might be a merciful and faithful high priest in things pertaining to
God, to make reconciliation for the sins of the people"*
(Hebrews 2:17).

*I*f you follow Jesus, you will have the desire to pass on
this saving message to your neighbor. Your efforts to win
others for Jesus often encounter hard hearts and strong rejection, however. Why is this? Perhaps it is because you are
not walking enough in Jesus' footsteps to identify yourself
with the sinner. We must come down to them, like the Lord
Jesus came down to us. Sin in us severs the connection to the
Lord, and from this comes our powerlessness where the sinner is concerned. Only when we are one with the person of
the Lord Jesus are we able to be one with the lost. This unity
with Jesus results in an increasingly priestly attitude. In this
way we stand in the gap for such miserable people who are
on their way to eternal damnation, and weep for them before the Lord. How wonderful it is when there is nothing between the Lord and your soul, nothing that prevents complete
unity with Him. In unity with the Lord, you will receive a
heart full of compassion for the lost, and your neighbor will
be deeply moved by your true love for Him.

15 MARCH

"And the very God of peace sanctify you wholly; and I pray God your whole spirit and soul and body be preserved blameless unto the coming of our Lord Jesus Christ" (1 Thessalonians 5:23).

Here God's call to you is clearly described. This call is actually a personal one: He is calling you to be sanctified, to be set apart for His holy service. In other words, to walk in the good works which God has ordained for you (cf. Ephesians 2:10). This is why Paul says that to be "wholly" sanctified is God's calling to give yourself wholly to Him. In other words, sanctification means an intensive, complete concentration on the will of God for your life, so that all the powers of the body, soul and spirit are prepared for God's goal and purpose. We generally take the expression "sanctification" far too lightly. I want to ask you, are you ready to pay the price of sanctification? It will cost you a great narrowing down of your earthly interests, but an immense enlarging of all your interest in God's cause.

16 MARCH

"For me to live is Christ, and to die is gain"
(Philippians 1:21).

As I considered these words, the thought struck me anew: Christ must have priority. Theoretically, as children of God we all affirm this, but what counts is whether it really is so in our personal lives. Is it my service, my family, my interests, or really Jesus Christ alone? If He really does have first place in my life, everything else has its rightful place. If we consider this text further, we come to the word "is," "For me to live IS Christ."

We have the tendency to put this off till later, and say, "Well, one day my life will be Christ." This is wrong, however, for right now, at this moment, He, to whom all power is given in heaven and on earth, is our life. If this really is so, no negative or dark things, no unbelief, will have room in our lives. Then we will not be influenced by emotions and impulses, for our innermost being is filled with Christ. We will be able to say in truth, "For me to live is Christ."

17 MARCH

"It is a faithful saying: For if we be dead with him,
we shall also live with him"
(2 Timothy 2:11).

Where our ego is concerned, with its emotional out-bursts, its inclinations and desires, Paul had another text that he had experienced in his own life, "To die is gain" (Philippians 1:21). This means that every opportunity the Lord gives us to prove that we are crucified with Him is our gain. Every insult, every misinterpretation of our motives, every time we are left out or set aside, is the time for the application of the death of Jesus on our personal life. We are certainly all in agreement that the death of the Lord Jesus, the fact that the "Lord of glory" was crucified, was the greatest injustice in all of history. But the death by crucifixion was the revelation of God's justice. This goes against our way of thinking. But this is God's way for us too, if we are following in Jesus' footsteps. By suffering injustice (and we all do if we are servants of the Lord), the death of Jesus is revealed in our lives. "For me to live is Christ, and to die is gain."

18 MARCH

"I thank my God upon every remembrance of you, always in every prayer of mine for you all making request with joy, for your fellowship in the gospel" (Philippians 1:3-5).

Although Paul was in a desperate situation, his thoughts of his brethren in the faith were unclouded and good. The reason for this was their "fellowship in the gospel." This fellowship, this working together, produces mutual, blessed thoughts. It is good for us to ask ourselves regularly, how do I think of others? Thoughts are powerful. Although they cannot be heard, they can be felt. This is why the devil is always attempting to make Christians disunited, so that this power, these blessed thoughts of one another, the mutual love for one another, is lacking. Do you think blessed thoughts of all those around you? Do you really love them all? The carnal Christian is absorbed with thoughts of his own situation, but the blessed thoughts of the spiritual Christian of his neighbors produce inner independence from his personal needs. Blessed are those people who bless their fellow man in their thoughts, regardless of their own troubles. Therein lies the mysterious authority of the body of Jesus Christ.

19 MARCH

"And there was a cloud that overshadowed them: and a voice came out of the cloud, saying, This is my beloved Son: hear him"
(Mark 9:7).

*A*m I waiting for the Lord Jesus alone, or is my expectation divided? If we really are waiting only for Him, it results in our being able to see Jesus alone in faith in our daily lives, in spite of all trials, tribulations, disappointments and darkness. This is what the three disciples experienced at the transfiguration of the Lord Jesus. The more we are waiting for Him alone, the more His power will be effective in us and through us. This is written in the well-known words of Isaiah 40:31, "They that wait upon the Lord shall renew their strength; they shall mount up with wings as eagles; they shall run, and not be weary; and they shall walk, and not faint." Notice the word "walk." Walking is going at a steady pace, not hurrying or jumping. It is the test of our endurance in waiting. To walk and not faint is the highest we can achieve. The word "walk" is not used as a verb here but to signify a character. The Bible is not abstract; it is always real and alive. God does not say, for instance, "Be spiritual," but "Walk before me" (Genesis 17:1). Do this today!

20 MARCH

"The hope of the righteous shall be gladness"
(Proverbs 10:28).

If we are in poor health, physically or spiritually, we look for something new. There has to be something going on all the time; the louder the better. This leads in the physical sphere to betrayal of the Holy Spirit, whose temple is our body. In our emotional life, it leads to disorderly passions and the destruction of our spiritual expectation. If we persist in our spiritual life on continually experiencing new excitements, instead of waiting for Him, it ends ultimately in the destruction of our living hope. If we are waiting for the Lord, we must have the absolute assurance that He is alive and He will surely return. The reality of the presence of God does not depend on a certain place, but on our decision to keep the Lord in mind at all times. If you have the Lord in mind continually, you will walk carefully in thinking, looking, speaking and acting. Problems arise when we refuse to rely on the reality of His presence and future coming. The Psalmist testifies, "Therefore will not we fear, though the earth be removed, and though the mountains be carried into the midst of the sea" (Psalm 46:2). This fearlessness will be ours when we build on the foundation of the reality of His presence. He was and always is present.

21 MARCH

"Thou art wearied in the greatness of thy way"
(Isaiah 57:10).

The reason that we are so often incapable of putting on the victorious power and strength of the Lord in our weakness is that we have a divided heart, with divided expectations. We are waiting in our daily lives for many things, just not for Jesus alone. And because He does not have highest priority in your life, much of what you had such high hopes for fails. I am reminded of the Word of the Lord here through the prophet Haggai, "Ye have sown much, and bring in little; ye eat, but ye have not enough; ye drink, but ye are not filled with drink; ye clothe you, but there is none warm; and he that earneth wages earneth wages to put it into a bag with holes" (Haggai 1:6).

This is because your own ego has priority and the Lord takes second or even third place. Let me point out that the Lord is examining you right now to see where your priorities lie. He is examining the depths of your heart. Whoever tries to keep from Him what belongs to Him proves that his heart is divided where the Lord is concerned. Such a person is not blessed.

22 MARCH

"Having spoiled principalities and powers, he made a show of them openly, triumphing over them in it"
(Colossians 2:15).

We are not wrong in thinking that our trials and temptations are increasing in these times, both physically and mentally. It cannot be otherwise, for with the approaching of the return of Jesus, currents of heavenly atmosphere are coming down to this earth. Therefore, the "rulers, authorities, powers of this dark world and spiritual forces of evil in the heavenly realms" (see Ephesians 6:12, NIV) find themselves in great distress. They desperately try to maintain their foothold in the heavenly realms. This movement in the invisible world is realized particularly by the saints in Christ. More than ever, we need to direct our eyes upon our Lord Jesus. As members of the Church of Jesus Christ, we stand today directly before our transformation. The Rapture is a definite reality now more than ever. Satan is resisting this, and therefore true children of God are exposed to increasing trials and temptations. Be of good cheer, however, for the eternal enlarging of our spiritual personality is imminent. The Lord says, "He that shall endure unto the end, the same shall be saved" (Matthew 24:13).

23 MARCH

"It is vain for you to rise up early, to sit up late, to eat the bread of sorrows: for so he giveth his beloved sleep"
(Psalm 127:2).

his verse not only says that it is better to sleep soundly than to be awake and idle, but also something quite different. I don't know if you have ever noticed what the Bible says about sleep. It is not true that sleep only serves to restore our bodies. In this text, "so he giveth his beloved sleep," we see a much deeper, more significant function of sleep than exclusively physical restoration. Sleep is a heavenly gift. It softly turns off our consciousness. Simultaneously, God comes to the unconscious soul as a place where only He and His angels have access. It is, therefore, recommendable that you take to heart the words of Psalm 63:6 when you lie down to sleep, "When I remember thee upon my bed, and meditate on thee in the night watches."

In other words, let your soul be with the Lord. Commit your life to Him, coupled with the request for His peace in the hours of your sleep. Then the friendly Creator's hand will do a deep and far-reaching work of regeneration in your soul, in your spirit and in your body.

24 MARCH

"For we are members of his body, of his flesh, and of his bones"
(Ephesians 5:30).

*T*he deepest concerns of our hearts, whether they are good or bad, are furthered when we sleep. We often say, "I'll sleep on it." Adam, the first man, had a great problem. He was a person alone. And what did God do?

"And the Lord God caused a deep sleep to fall upon Adam, and he slept: and he took one of his ribs, and closed up the flesh instead thereof" (Genesis 2:21).

Through this, Adam's problem of being alone was solved. This is also a wonderful prophetic pointer to the "last Adam," Jesus Christ. On the cross at Calvary, He sank into the sleep of death. One of the soldiers pierced His side, "and forthwith came there out blood and water" (John 19:34). The Bride of the Lamb came out of this. It is written, "This is he that came by water and blood, even Jesus Christ" (1 John 5:6). The water points to the "washing of water by the word" and the "washing of regeneration" spoken of in Ephesians 5:26 and Titus 3:5. And from the blood of Jesus Christ, His poured out life, came the Bride of the Lamb.

25 MARCH

"For the eyes of the Lord run to and fro throughout the whole earth, to show himself strong in the behalf of them whose heart is perfect toward him"
(2 Chronicles 16:9).

The increasing need in our day is not in the first place on account of the spectacular catastrophes like earthquakes, famines and floods everywhere, but in my opinion on account of our end-times Christianity, which is torn between Jesus and sin, and is in a perilous condition. The exalted Lord describes this with the following lament, "So then because thou art lukewarm, and neither cold nor hot, I will spue thee out of my mouth" (Revelation 3:16). To be lukewarm is the dangerous "neither...nor." This spiritual condition is inspired by the antichristian spirit and is spreading more and more; in the same measure, the return of Jesus and the judgment of the world draws near. Are you a child of God? You may say, "I hope so," or "I would like to be." If you cannot give a clear answer to this question, you are neither one nor the other. You are what the Lord Jesus called "neither cold nor hot"; that is, neither an unbeliever nor a fervent, burning Christian. If you are not saved, then come to Jesus today, because you do not have much time!

26 MARCH

"Better is the end of a thing than the beginning thereof"
(Ecclesiastes 7:8).

We are approaching the conclusion of our fight of faith. Look to Jesus. He was the most despised of all men, "full of sorrows and acquainted with grief." He was so despised that people hid their faces from Him. What was the end of His way, though? He now sits at the right hand of His Father, and everything is in subordination to Him. Just as He was, we are also despised in this world. This is what the Scriptures teach us. You must bear your cross if you want to receive a crown. You must go through the swamp, or you won't be able to walk the golden streets. Whoever says yes to Jesus, the crucified One, experiences the end of his old life and a new life breaks through, for, "if we be dead with Christ, we believe that we shall also live with him" (Romans 6:8). "The end of a thing is better than its beginning."

You may rejoice over the fact that you have found Him, for when you awake you will be like Him, conformed to His image. An uncut diamond looks unattractive and worthless, but in the hands of the diamond cutter, it is transformed into a glittering, valuable diamond. You may compare yourself to such a diamond. As a believer, you will be set in the crown of the King of all kings, because you are a member of the body of Jesus.

27 MARCH

"In whom we have boldness and access with confidence by the faith of him" (Ephesians 3:12).

God cannot be experienced through feelings but through faith in Jesus Christ.

I would have given up long ago if I had relied on my feelings, which are sometimes positive, other times negative. But through faith I can live in uninterrupted fellowship with Him without feelings, even in the greatest trials and storms. Faith is a mystery, yet it is so wonderfully simple: namely, to surrender in spirit to the strong Lord. Then the words of the songwriter will become your living experience, "Safe in the arms of Jesus, safe on His gentle breast." This will only become a continual experience, however, through reading the Bible and praying. Through the Bible God speaks to us, and through prayer we speak to Him. It is actually very simple. We receive everything that God offers us through Jesus Christ in childlike faith, not with our minds but with our hearts. The Lord says, "My son, give me thine heart" (Proverbs 23:26). If you have not yet done this, then do it today.

28 MARCH

"And Elijah said unto him, Tarry I pray thee, here; for the Lord hath sent me to Jordan. And he said, As the Lord liveth, and as thy soul liveth, I will not leave thee. And they two went on"
(2 Kings 2:6).

The Jordan harbors a secret: it is the secret of authority. When the Lord wanted to take the prophet Elijah to heaven, Elisha followed him. Elisha desired to have authority for his great task at all costs. The way for him led to the Jordan, through the Jordan actually. Elijah said to him, "The Lord hath sent me to Jordan" (verse 6).

The enemy tried everything to keep Elisha from following Elijah decisively through the Jordan. The sons of the prophets tried to distract him, but he answered them twice, "Yea, I know it; hold ye your peace" (verse 5).

Have you realized how the enemy tries to make you leave the narrow way, even by religious means? Have you noticed how he tries by all manner and devices to distract you from your decision to go through the Jordan of death with the heavenly Elijah, Jesus Christ? Do what Elisha did. Tell the tempter to be quiet, and cling to the Lord, even if the others do not come with you. Elijah and Elisha both stood by the Jordan. Many remain standing afar, but the true believer follows the heavenly Elijah, Jesus, through the Jordan of death.

29 MARCH

"And Elijah took his mantle, and wrapped it together, and smote the waters, and they were divided hither and thither, so that they two went over on dry ground" (2 Kings 2:8).

*E*lijah suggested the "way of least resistance" to Elisha three times, in verses 2, 4 and 6, with the words, "Tarry here." But Elisha answered each time in holy determination, "As the Lord liveth, and as thy soul liveth, I will not leave thee." Will you not also say, "I will not let Thee go except Thou bless me. I want to be united with You in Your death. I want to go through the Jordan with You. I want to remain on the cross with You." If you say this decisively, you will experience the wonderful thing that He, the heavenly Elijah, has already paved the way for you. This means practically that it is possible to go with Him "through the Jordan," for He is going ahead of you. And when you reach the other side, make the holy decision to go the whole way, the straight and narrow way, the way of dying, with Him. Then He will open up to you all His fullness, "And it came to pass, when they were gone over, that Elijah said unto Elisha, Ask what I shall do for thee" (verse 9). What an immeasurable fullness the acceptance of the death of Jesus opens up to us! If you will say yes to it, He will say to you, "Ask what I shall do for you."

30 MARCH

"For the life of the flesh is in the blood: and I have given it to you upon the altar to make an atonement for your souls: for it is the blood that maketh an atonement for the soul" (Leviticus 17:11).

*W*hat tremendous words! Here the Spirit of God explains in what way God reconciled and reconciles us to Himself, and how we can claim before the holy face of God that we are reconciled to Him in spite of our sins: through the shed blood of Jesus. The blood of Jesus Christ is a tremendous power. Let us attempt now in spirit to imagine what an eternal power was (and is up to the present day) in His blood, when the Son of God poured out His eternal life. In Matthew 27:50-52, this overwhelming event is described, "Jesus, when he had cried again with a loud voice, yielded up the ghost. And, behold, the veil of the temple was rent in twain from the top to the bottom; and the earth did quake, and the rocks rent; and the graves were opened." What actually took place under the impact of the shedding of the blood of the eternal Son of God is ultimately inconceivable. God is induced to do the greatest thing of all for us when we claim the blood of Jesus in faith: He forgives; he blots out our sins. He acknowledges the atoning blood of His Son.

31 MARCH

"God was in Christ, reconciling the world unto himself, not imputing their trespasses unto them; and hath committed unto us the word of reconciliation" (2 Corinthians 5:19).

What does the blood of Jesus mean to you? We may not merely consider this abstractly. Our hearts must be moved, for, "without shedding of blood is no remission" (Hebrews 9:22). The first and basic statement of this verse refers without question to the atoning sacrifice of our Lord Jesus, but it is simultaneously directed at us too. Have we actually realized what the Bible means by the blood of Jesus Christ? Blood and life are inseparable. We understand the blood of Jesus to be a means that works wonders, but in reality, Jesus made complete atonement through the pouring out of His precious blood on Calvary's Cross.

Do you realize the responsibility we have when we realize the wonderful power of the blood of Jesus, and do not follow Him decisively? Remember, the Lord through His death caused the unbridgeable gap between God and your soul to be reestablished. Have you fully walked across this bridge by calling out with all of your heart: "My God, I have decided eternally that I am yours!"?

Spiritual Strength
FOR EACH DAY

APRIL

1 APRIL

"Forasmuch as ye know that ye were not redeemed with corruptible things, as silver and gold, from your vain conversation received by tradition from your fathers; But with the precious blood of Christ, as of a lamb without blemish and without spot" (1 Peter 1:18-19).

Why is Jesus called the Lamb of God?

1. He is called the Lamb of God to reveal His nature to us. We know that a lamb is a picture of innocence and purity. Jesus was true man in all things, "...tempted like as we are, yet without sin" (Hebrews 4:15).

2. He is called the Lamb of God to show us His way. He came to this earth with a very clear divine purpose, namely to be slain for our sins. "Worthy is the Lamb that was slain" (Revelation 5:12). He was not taken by surprise at His execution, for He said in holy determination, "For this cause came I unto this hour" (John 12:27).

3. Jesus is called the Lamb of God to reveal the nature of His victory. The victory of Jesus is the victory of the Lamb. What is more helpless and dependent than a lamb? One of the weakest of all creatures does the greatest thing of all! The Lamb in its fragility bears the greatest burden of all. Jesus accomplished the victory apart from all human effort. Surely He was "crucified through weakness" (2 Corinthians 13:4), but He rose in power. This is why the words, "Behold the Lamb of God, which taketh away the sin of the world" (John 1:29) are so tremendous in their divine contradiction.

2 APRIL

"When Jesus therefore had received the vinegar, he said, It is finished:
and he bowed his head, and gave up the ghost"
(John 19:30).

The death of Jesus is an unfathomable event that can never be described in all its depth in human words. It was not a man who had a mortal, limited lifespan who died then, but He who alone possessed immortality. God died at that time in Jesus Christ. Eternal life died. As eternal life cannot actually die, for this would be a contradiction in itself, an even greater power must have been behind it. This power was love, the all-overpowering and conquering love of the Father and the Son. We read of this prophetically in Song of Solomon 8:6, "Love is strong as death." When eternal life cried, "My God, my God, why hast thou forsaken me?" (Mark 15:34), God was silent. Thus, the preaching of the cross is indeed for us who are saved the power of God, as 1 Corinthians 1:18 says.

For the world it is foolishness, however, for the natural man does not know what to make of a crucified Christ. Our Lord gave His life voluntarily. It was not taken from Him; this was clearly demonstrated when He first bowed His head, and then when He died.

3 APRIL

"For Christ also hath once suffered for sins, the just for the unjust, that he might bring us to God, being put to death in the flesh, but quickened by the Spirit" (1 Peter 3:18).

In the moment that Jesus died and breathed His last breath, He brought us back to God. That is the tremendous significance of Matthew 27:50-51, "Jesus, when he had cried again with a loud voice, yielded up the ghost. And, behold, the veil of the temple was rent in twain from the top to the bottom." This means nothing other than that in the same moment that Jesus died, God Himself opened His dwelling place, His sanctuary, which until then had been closed to us on account of sin. This opening was brought about through the death of Jesus Christ. His last cry and the tearing of the veil in the temple took place at the same time, so that the writer of the letter to the Hebrews rejoices, "Having therefore, brethren, boldness to enter into the holiest by the blood of Jesus, by a new and living way, which he hath consecrated for us, through the veil, that is to say, his flesh; and having an high priest over the house of God; let us draw near with a true heart in full assurance of faith" (Hebrews 10:19-22). This applies to us who believe on the Lord. Through the death of Jesus, the dividing veil was opened, and now we may come into the sanctuary.

4 APRIL

"Wherefore in all things it behoved him to be made like unto his brethren,
that he might be a merciful and faithful high priest in things
pertaining to God, to make reconciliation for the sins of the people"
(Hebrews 2:17).

This verse shows a second effect of the death of Jesus. It refers to Satan, the great enemy. Satan is the mortal enemy of man, for he tempted man to sin. Because death is the wages of sin, however, Satan was the prince of death and had the power of death until the Lamb died. I say expressly "until" Jesus died, for through His death He redeemed us from a threefold death:

• From a cruel eternal death. For without Jesus' sacrificial death, we would fall into Satan's hands after our death.

• From the terrible fear of death. A person dies several times during his life through fear of death, but we read in Hebrews 2:15, "And deliver them who through fear of death were all their lifetime subject to bondage."

• From the terrible death of eternal separation with God. When the Lamb of God died, everything came into place: children of Satan, children of death, became children of God, children of life. Let us thank the Lord who reconciled us with God, redeemed us from Satan's power, and liberated us from the hold which he had on us through sin.

5 APRIL

"And you, that were sometime alienated and enemies in your mind by wicked works, yet now hath he reconciled" (Colossians 1:21).

*H*ere we have the third effect of the death of Jesus: the effect on our guilt. When Romans 5:10 says that we are reconciled with God through the death of His Son, we ask ourselves, what about our innumerable sins? I am unspeakably grateful that 1 Corinthians 15:3 says that "Christ died for our sins"—plural! So you may know with certainty that His death, His shed blood, has blotted out your whole great guilt. We read in this connection in Colossians 2:13-14, "...having forgiven you all trespasses; blotting out the handwriting of ordinances that was against us." Isn't that wonderful? His blood, the blood of the sinless Son of God, blots out your sins and mine, as though they had never existed! God Himself paid the price for them with the blood of His own beloved Son.

This is why the Bible says so often that He died for us, "For when we were yet without strength, in due time Christ died for the ungodly" (Romans 5:6).

6 APRIL

"Love not the world, neither the things that are in the world. If any man love the world, the love of the Father is not in him. For all that is in the world, the lust of the flesh, and the lust of the eyes, and the pride of life, is not of the Father, but is of the world" (1 John 2:15-16).

When we consider the fourth effect of the death of Jesus on this world, we have to ask ourselves who the ruler, the god of this world is. The god of this world is Satan. But it was in this world, at the central point of the earth, that the Son of God died on the cross and overcame Satan, the god of this world. So whoever believes on the crucified Lord and His death, has died to the world and is shielded from the spirit of this world. This is the purpose of the death of Jesus, as Galatians 1:4 says, "Who gave himself for our sins, that he might deliver us from this present evil world." Isn't it a terrible thing, then, when children of God reject their deliverance from the world? All deliberate entanglement with the spirit of this world is crucifying Jesus anew. A child of God has come into a new dimension through the new birth, for it says, "Our conversation [citizenship] is in heaven; from whence also we look for the Saviour, the Lord Jesus Christ" (Philippians 3:20). On the grounds of the death of Jesus, we are in the world, but never of the world.

7 APRIL

*"O death, where is thy sting? O grave, where is thy victory? The sting of
death is sin; and the strength of sin is the law. But thanks be to God,
which giveth us the victory through our Lord Jesus Christ"*
(1 Corinthians 15:55-57).

As the fifth effect of the death of Jesus, we will consider its effect on death itself. Death is a cruel reality. Many of you have experienced this when you stood by the grave of a loved one. The Lord Jesus never ignored the reality of death. When He came to raise His friend Lazarus, who had been lying in his tomb for four days, He wept. But there is another wonderful reality; namely, the overpowering of death through the death of the Lord Jesus. Although you are getting older every day, you have the promise of Psalm 92:14: "They shall still bring forth fruit in old age; they shall be fat and flourishing." According to the words of the apostle Paul, you are getting younger all the time inwardly, "Though our outward man perish, yet the inward man is renewed day by day" (2 Corinthians 4:16). Such a person has eternal youth, for in Psalm 103:5 it says that one's youth is renewed like the eagle's. This is the wonderful part: Jesus Christ has reconciled us with God through His death. He has delivered us from the power of Satan. He has saved us from the nature of this world and has given us eternal life.

8 APRIL

"For in that he died, he died unto sin once: but in that he liveth, he liveth unto God. Likewise reckon ye also yourselves to be dead indeed unto sin, but alive unto God through Jesus Christ our Lord"
(Romans 6:10-11).

A sixth effect of the death of Jesus concerns our sinful nature. We sigh beneath our nature, because in the light of the majesty and holiness of God, we realize that we are corrupt by nature. We groan beneath this burden, until the mystery of the death of Jesus and its effect on our nature, our self, is revealed. The effect of the death of Jesus on our nature is described very clearly in the above verse. This means quite practically, when you feel your sinful nature, its evil desires, you may stand in faith on the grounds of the cross of Jesus: He died and I died with Him, whether I feel it or not. When you adopt this attitude, you are "freed from sin" according to Romans 6:7, for whoever is dead is freed from indwelling sin, from his sinful nature. God does not see this sinful nature any more, because you have died to your sinful nature in Christ Jesus: "For if we have been planted together in the likeness of his death, we shall be also in the likeness of his resurrection" (Romans 6:5).

9 APRIL

*"Other foundation can no man lay than that is laid,
which is Jesus Christ" (1 Corinthians 3:11).*

The harvest day, the day of judgment, the day on which we, as the Church of Jesus Christ, will stand before the judgment seat of Jesus Christ, is very near. Redeem the time, therefore. See that you build on the foundation of your salvation, Jesus Christ, gold, silver and precious stones. This means in practical terms, let everything in your life be a means to the end of the glorifying of the name of the Lord. Let your first love for Jesus be the driving force behind the use of your time, for then your time will be given eternal value. In this way, your life's harvest will be a triumph before the judgment seat of Christ. Such a life will be under attack from the enemy, but the Scriptures say, "They that sow in tears shall reap in joy" (Psalm 126:5). Redeem the time, because suddenly it will be over. "Lay up for yourselves treasures in heaven, where neither moth nor rust doth corrupt, and where thieves do not break through nor steal" (Matthew 6:20). Maybe you are asking, how should I begin to redeem the time for eternity? Pray more! Read more in the Word of God! Talk with God! That is the beginning.

10 APRIL

"We are not ignorant of his [Satan's] devices"
(2 Corinthians 2:11).

Notice the small, even minute, footprints of the enemy in your life. It is the little foxes that spoil the vines. Catch them. The heedless passing by of the footprints of the enemy can have fateful effects on your faith life. Do not avoid the victorious confrontation with the enemy; face your temptation head on. Jesus is Victor! What does the Lord Jesus say in the parable of the tares among the wheat? He answers the question of the servants about the origin of the tares, "An enemy hath done this" (Matthew 13:28). Suddenly you notice that within your church, in your own family, tares have grown among the wheat. This is the work of the enemy; these are his footprints. He is active everywhere. You must abide in Jesus! We are in the world, it is true, but we are not of the world. We are surrounded by demonic powers, but they are not in us as long as the Lord remains in us and we in Him. Then He, the Victor, works in you and through you. Then you are not only able to recognize the enemy, but you can also withstand him victoriously so that he is powerless and you can overcome him.

11 APRIL

"Let both grow together until the harvest: and in the time of harvest I will say to the reapers, Gather ye together first the tares, and bind them in bundles to burn them: but gather the wheat into my barn"
(Matthew 13:30).

*W*e are not told here to remove the enemy, because he is not in us but outside our hearts. So we are apparently passive and do nothing, as the Lord said. This passivity, however, is greatest activity of faith. Footprints of the enemy? Yes, but if you are secure in Jesus, he can do nothing to you. Eradicate these prints through the power of the blood of Jesus. Begin anew to lead a faithful prayer life. Seek a deeper relationship with the Bible. See that the prints you leave behind are prints of light. Do works of love for Jesus' sake. Sow the seed of the Word of God. Give a clear testimony. These footprints of light are indelible. They will remain. They lead to eternity, so that it will be read of you afterwards in golden letters, "Their works do follow them" (Revelation 14:13). Walk like the Lord Jesus and walk with Him, and then you will leave prints behind that remain for eternity.

12 APRIL

*"Though he slay me, **yet** will I trust in him"*
(Job 13:15).

*L*ittle words are often of great significance. They are of infinitely greater significance, however, where the Word of God is concerned. One of these words is "yet," which expresses the unshakable faith of a person who is being tried and tested, yet who reckons with the Lord in all his trials. When everything goes wrong in your life, when everything collapses around you, and if you are getting older and weaker, then cling to Jesus so that you can say with the prophet Habakkuk, "**Yet** will I rejoice in the Lord, I will joy in the God of my salvation. The Lord God is my strength, and he will make my feet like hinds' feet, and he will make me to walk upon mine high places" (Habakkuk 3:18-19).

How often have you experienced this, that you received help when everything threatened to overwhelm you on account of your sins? We forget all too soon that darkness and trouble are often the result of our own disobedience. And yet, in His grace the Lord forgave us and we experienced the words of Lamentations 3:31-32, "The Lord will not cast off for ever: but though he cause grief, **yet** will he have compassion according to the multitude of his mercies. For he doth not afflict willingly nor grieve the children of men."

13 APRIL

*"**But** God is faithful. . ." (1 Corinthians 10:13).*

*T*he word "but" often occurs at turning points in the Bible. Where the Lord is concerned, it often means glory. When Joseph was in great distress in Egypt, we read of him, "**But** the Lord was with Joseph, and shewed him mercy, and gave him favour in the sight of the keeper of the prison" (Genesis 39:21). This fact turned his cell into a palace, for where the Lord is it is light and clear; it cannot be dark.

When the children of Korah turned against Moses, it says, "But if the LORD make a new thing, and the earth open her mouth, and swallow them up, with all that appertain unto them, and they go down quick into the pit; then ye shall understand that these men have provoked the LORD" (Numbers 16:30).

The same thing applies to us. When we lived under the power of darkness and were children of wrath, hopelessly caught in the claws of the enemy, God's almighty "But" sounded through the universe, "**But** God, who is rich in mercy, for his great love wherewith he loved us, even when we were dead in sins, hath quickened us together with Christ" (Ephesians 2:4-5). Should not our lives be lived to the praise and worship of our Lord?

14 APRIL

"Yea, though I walk through the valley of the shadow of death, I will fear no evil: **for** *thou art with me" (Psalm 23:4).*

*H*ere we have the insignificant little word "for," which connects to unspeakable glory. David sings of this and expresses his faith very vividly in Psalm 23. He should have collapsed in fear and trembling because he was surrounded by enemies, but he clung to the Lord, "**For** thou art with me." This "for" emphasizes the exalted person of God. If the Lord has greater, all-overpowering room in your life, you can always exclaim a victorious "for." You have reason to fear and worry, but dare to say, "I will fear no evil: **for** thou art with me." This little word also solves the acute question of powerlessness. You may say, "I have no strength. I want to serve the Lord better, but I find closed doors everywhere." Be of good courage, for the Lord accepts your weakness. The Psalmist testifies, "He weakened my strength in the way" (Psalm 102:23). But hear the Lord's promise, "I have set before thee an open door, and no man can shut it: **for** thou hast a little strength" (Revelation 3:8). Because you are weak, He is mighty in you. Because you can do nothing, He can!

15 APRIL

"He leadeth me in the paths of righteousness for his name's sake"
(Psalm 23:3).

Those who know the depths of this promise become strong and comforted and are not discouraged. If He is leading you in the paths of righteousness for His own name's sake, how can anything be wrong in your life? All your fears, all discontent, despondency and complaining come from unbelief. Let me tell you again personally: the Lord will only be honored and praised through your taking His promises for you seriously. When it says here, "He leadeth me in the paths of righteousness for his name's sake," it means for Jesus' name's sake. The promises of the Bible are guaranteed, sure and certain in the precious name of Jesus. Second Corinthians 1:20 says, "All the promises of God in him [Jesus] are yea, and in him Amen, unto the glory of God by us." This assurance of being led in the paths of righteousness comforts our hearts. The same David who had this assurance also exclaimed, "I will run the way of thy commandments" (Psalm 119:32). It is like we are entering a blessed divine circle; then it is so easy to be obedient, because we are in His way.

16 APRIL

"Yea, though I walk through the valley of the shadow of death, I will fear no evil: for thou art with me; thy rod and thy staff they comfort me"
(Psalm 23:4).

When your heart is encouraged through faith in His promises, you will run the way of His commandments, i.e. you will be healed—as the prophet Jeremiah puts it—from your disobedience. Temptations will still come, of course. It will often be dark on this path, but "though I walk through the valley of the shadow of death, I will fear no evil." In other words, the path of righteousness often leads through a dark valley. Perhaps you are in this valley now. The valley is dark; you cannot see ahead or behind you. You can only look upwards. But that is sufficient, for the Bible says, "Looking unto Jesus the author and finisher of our faith" (Hebrews 12:2). In this way, we experience the opposite of what the devil wants. He wants you to be afraid in the dark valley and despondent. But the Lord wants to give you fellowship with Himself in the midst of the dark valley. He is your light and your salvation in that moment. Especially then, you have every reason to rejoice instead of being afraid.

17 APRIL

"Thou anointest my head with oil; my cup runneth over. Surely goodness and mercy shall follow me all the days of my life: and I will dwell in the house of the Lord for ever"
(Psalm 23:5-6).

The 23rd Psalm is a wonderfully rounded-off promise, which the enemy cannot destroy. This is tremendous: although we are in the valley of the shadow of death, we need not fear evil because we are walking in paths of righteousness. We even have fellowship with the Lord because He has prepared a table for us. I want to tell you with great assurance, that the Lord also wants to lead you in His paths of righteousness for His name's sake. You only have to let Him lead you. It is often the case, however, that we are led in paths of righteousness through dark valleys where we do not want to go, "Another shall gird thee, and carry thee whither thou wouldest not" (John 21:18). These dark valleys are increasing, because we children of God are being led through the dark valley of the end times. It is becoming darker and darker. Isaiah said, "The morning cometh, and also the night" (Isaiah 21:12). Let us not be surprised if it is often dark for a long time on the paths of righteousness. At the end it will be light, for on the other shore our exalted, blessed Lord Jesus Christ is waiting. He is our goal, and we will see Him soon—very soon!

18 APRIL

"Watch ye, stand fast in the faith, quit you like men, be strong. Let all your things be done with charity" (1 Corinthians 16:13-14).

What is a car without an engine? What is a body without a spirit? What is a born-again person without a victorious faith? It is important to ask these questions, for in our day we are not only experiencing inflation of all values in the material realm, but also the inflation of faith is a terrible fact. Faith is no longer victorious. The Bible emphasizes the indivisibility of these two facts, however, "This is the victory that overcometh the world, even our faith" (1 John 5:4). It does not say, "Our faith wins the victory," but "our faith *is* the victory." We must admit to ourselves that faith divided from victory is in vain. This is the reason that Paul admonishes, "Examine yourselves, whether ye be in the faith; prove your own selves" (2 Corinthians 13:5). In other words, where is the engine of your faith? Nothing is moving; victory, power and joy are lacking. Why is everything at a standstill? My friends, this question is vital. This is also the reason that Paul says, "Watch ye, stand fast in the faith, quit you like men, be strong."

19 APRIL

"For in Jesus Christ neither circumcision availeth any thing, nor uncircumcision; but faith which worketh by love"
(Galatians 5:6).

We have to acknowledge that the testing of our faith is vital because God Himself tests our hearts. David said at the end of his life, "I know also, my God, that thou triest the heart, and hast pleasure in uprightness" (1 Chronicles 29:17). As far as the future is concerned, the great test is still ahead of us when we appear before His face at His judgment of reward. If you test your faith today, honestly and truthfully, you may see that everything is lacking: power, victory, joy, fruit. You might have to admit, "My faith has no results; it is not active." Let the Word of God reveal unto you that the actual engine of your faith is not working. What engine? Love. "Faith which worketh by love." Only such faith is valid before God. Paul admonishes us, "Let all your things be done with charity [love]" (1 Corinthians 16:14). He knew that strong faith can only become active and steadfast through our first love for the Lord. Is your faith active through your love for Jesus Christ, or is your faith actually dead?

20 APRIL

"Little children, it is the last time" (1 John 2:18).

It concerns me that we as the Church of Jesus Christ do not realize enough the seriousness of the times in which we are living, namely the last time. Why do we not behave accordingly? It is because the deception—and thereby the attempts of the enemy to lull us to sleep—is the greatest in the end time. The words of the Lord Jesus are so clear, "What I say unto you I say unto all, Watch" (Mark 13:37). My brothers and sisters, we really are living in the end times. The time is imminent of which the prophetic Word says, "There shall be a time of trouble, such as never was since there was a nation even to that same time" (Daniel 12:1). The "superhuman" Satan incarnate, is wreaking havoc through his spirit with a great force that is almost physically perceptible. The hour of temptation that will come over the whole earth before the dawning of the Great Tribulation, is already in operation. I urge you, therefore, to say a determined and decisive "No!" to every compromise with the spirit of this world. The Lord wants to bring all of us through this temptation unblemished, for we are hastening toward the most holy One of all: Jesus. We shall see Him as He is, "And every man that hath this hope in him purifieth himself, even as he is pure" (1 John 3:3).

21 APRIL

"Neither be ye sorry; for the joy of the Lord is your strength"
(Nehemiah 8:10).

*O*f what does joy consist here? Of power and strength. But we must not take these words of Nehemiah out of their context, for the joy of the Lord is never an isolated thing. Something must precede it. Here too it is a secret, namely inner joy in great distress. The people had returned outwardly from their exile to the land of Israel. Everything seemed to be all right, but inwardly there was no true joy. This is the situation of many Christians in our day. Outwardly everything is in order, but not inwardly. What was lacking then and is lacking now? Distress! What distress? Distress through the living Word of God. When we are in great distress through the deep conviction of the Word of God, this great, overpowering joy of the Lord is born in us because the Word has convicted us. There is no other way to obtain the joy of the Lord. Conviction through the Word of God is needed. Then the joy of the Lord will be born out of inner distress. This is the secret of real joy in the Lord.

22 APRIL

"And he read therein before the street that was before the water gate from the morning until midday, before the men and the women, and those that could understand" (Nehemiah 8:3).

*T*he sequence of events in Nehemiah 8 is very clear. In verse 1, we read that Ezra fetched the book of the law of Moses. He got hold of the Bible. In verse 2, it says that he gathered the people together, and in verse 3, he began to read aloud to them. Then it says something important, "And the ears of all the people were attentive unto the book of the law" (verse 3). In verse 8, it is even emphasized that they, "...read in the book in the law of God distinctly, and gave the sense, and caused them to understand the reading." This reciprocal action/mutual effect between the preacher and the Church is vital. This means, however, that simultaneously the hearts of the hearers are willing to receive the Word. In Nehemiah 8, the key to overpowering joy in the Lord is shown us, "For all the people wept, when they heard the words of the law" (verse 9). Because they were willing to hear the Word and receive it, it had its effect. The people were convicted in their hearts: they came into inward distress, but out of this inward distress the joy of the Lord was born.

23 APRIL

"I rejoice at thy word, as one that findeth great spoil"
(Psalm 119:162).

The joy of the Lord is independent of our feelings, for nothing is more changeable and unreliable than our feelings. Feelings are the expression of emotional joy or sadness. This imperfect, inconsistent joy must become perfect and consistent through the unchanging joy of the Lord. Everything changes, but He does not change. It is written of Him, "Jesus Christ the same yesterday, and to day, and for ever" (Hebrews 13:8). If we do not reject the sword of the Word, then we do not reject Jesus Christ either. Then we will abide in Him and our joy will be complete—perfect. Your soul will lift itself up to the Lord and His joy. His unchanging, eternal joy will be so strong in you that you can rejoice, "The joy of the Lord is my strength." Those who have this joy in the Lord are regally independent of their own feelings, whether these are joyful or sad. The joy of the Lord is only born out of inward distress; thus, it is completely independent of outward circumstances.

24 APRIL

". . . Redeeming the time, because the days are evil"
(Ephesians 5:16).

This is a great contradiction: modern man wrestles with time and laments over lack of time, although he can produce significantly more with available technology. Time is a relative term. One person can accomplish in minutes that which for others takes hours. When Paul says we should redeem the time, he wants to emphasize that we should give our brief, appointed time eternal value. How can we do this? First, by leading a faithful prayer life. We should not pray occasionally but faithfully and regularly. Daniel redeemed his time properly during his life. The eternal value of his life is striking. Why? Because he was a man of prayer. He prayed three times a day, at regular times. That is why eternity and infinite things broke through in his life.

A person who prays can also be still. The devil fears this, which is why Paul says, "Study to be quiet." When we are still, the Spirit of God speaks to us, convicts us, and judges us, and we may claim the blood of Jesus over past sins that we have forgotten. That's part of redeeming the time, our time, before it is too late.

25 APRIL

"Be not hasty to go out of his sight"
(Ecclesiastes 8:3).

I am convinced that the hectic lives of many Christians makes them blind to the importance of the present spiritual hour. Satan does not want to leave us time to contemplate about eternity. He wants us to be busy more and more. The apostle Paul was very aware of this and exclaimed with great authority, "We are not ignorant of his devices" (2 Corinthians 2:11).

To have time does not mean gaining more time to work, but to pray more. Prayers create miracles. I have read the words of Jesus in Matthew 7:7 a thousand times perhaps, but they burn into my soul anew each time I read them, "Ask, and it shall be given you; seek, and ye shall find; knock, and it shall be opened unto you." How simple, and yet so exalted! How rich, powerful and blessed your life could be if you were a prayer warrior. Those who have time for the Lord find immeasurable things that remain for eternity. The Word of God challenges us, "See then that ye walk circumspectly, not as fools, but as wise, redeeming the time, because the days are evil" (Ephesians 5:15-16); and, "For yet a little while, and he that shall come will come, and will not tarry" (Hebrews 10:37).

26 APRIL

"I have not spoken in secret, in a dark place of the earth: I said not unto the seed of Jacob, Seek ye me in vain: I the Lord speak righteousness, I declare things that are right" (Isaiah 45:19).

"Seek ye me"! This is a repeated command of the Lord. If God demands that we seek Him, then it must be possible to find Him. How can we find Him? Our Lord names the only condition for finding Him in Jeremiah 29:13-14, "Ye shall seek me, and find me, when ye shall search for me with all your heart. And I will be found of you, saith the Lord." There is no point in praying or holding prayer meetings if we do not do it with all our hearts. In Jeremiah 48:10, the Lord says, "Cursed be he who doeth the Lord's work negligently" (Luther). Prayer is a wonderful thing but also dangerous, for if we do not seek the Lord with all our hearts, it is all in vain. We only receive precise directions and the necessary clarity in the presence of the Lord when we seek Him sincerely, "with all our hearts."

27 APRIL

"Seek ye the Lord while he may be found, call ye upon him while he is near" (Isaiah 55:6).

*L*et us ask ourselves the question, why should we seek the Lord? After His command, "Seek ye me" in Isaiah 45:19, He Himself gives us the answer to this question: "I the Lord speak righteousness, I declare things that are right." I know of the terrible satanic temptation to be excessively busy all the time. All sorts of things combine to make us become absorbed by our work; thus, we have no time to seek the Lord with all our hearts. Even while we are praying, we suddenly find we are thinking of other things. The Lord admonishes us to listen to Him. When we seek Him sincerely, we do not necessarily find what is important to us, the answer to our prayers, but that may not be of primary importance to the Lord. The important thing is that we find Him. When we find Him, we have found everything. We have also found the answer to our prayers. When we find Him, our problems, questions and difficulties may not be solved perhaps, but we have become free of them. When we find Him, He is able to act. The Lord says, "Whoso findeth me findeth life" (Proverbs 8:35).

28 APRIL

"I sought the Lord, and he heard me, and delivered me from all my fears" (Psalm 34:4).

With Him we have everything! This does not mean that the Lord will answer all your personal questions, but He will answer you in that you suddenly see everything in a different light. We torment ourselves with impossible questions, have sleepless nights maybe, and toss and turn over problems we cannot solve. Now and again we sigh, here and there we utter a prayer, but we find no peace and continue to worry. Then, perhaps after a long or short time, we begin to seek the Lord with all our hearts, with all our souls and with all our might. We call upon Him and do not hasten from His presence—and suddenly He answers us. How does He answer? He answers in our souls and says that He is with us, and in receiving the assurance that He is with us, our burden falls from our shoulders. What a wonderful experience! People who seek God are surrounded by an invisible wall of protection, and this is immediately perceptible. The Bible describes them as follows, "The hand of our God is upon all them for good that seek him" (Ezra 8:22).

29 APRIL

"For the grace of God that bringeth salvation hath appeared to all men,
teaching us that, denying ungodliness and worldly lusts,
we should live soberly, righteously, and godly, in this present world"
(Titus 2:11-12).

The Lord Jesus cannot grow in us and His glory is not increased through us, if we are not willing to decrease in our person. What does this mean? John the Baptist recognized this and said concerning the Lord Jesus, "He must increase, but I must decrease" (John 3:30). How can we decrease? Here we automatically come to speak of the goodness of the Lord and His grace. What does grace do? It disciplines us. Does this sound contradictory? How can grace discipline us if grace is in itself something lovely and pleasant? This is a great mystery. We can only receive grace if we recognize and admit: it is undeserved favor. By accepting this undeserved favor out of the hand of the Lord, I am already under His discipline, so that I deny my ungodly nature and worldly lusts. Live today out of this grace. The time will come when we who are born again out of sheer grace and goodness, will be transformed and raptured to meet the Lord. If our life's end should come before, we can look to the open gate of heaven and say, "It was grace alone, saved by grace!"

30 APRIL

"Come unto me, all ye that labour and are heavy laden, and I will give you rest. Take my yoke upon you, and learn of me; for I am meek and lowly in heart: and ye shall find rest unto your souls. For my yoke is easy, and my burden is light" (Matthew 11:28-30).

The Lord gives a twofold promise to those who accept this invitation. They experience this grace, the goodness of the Lord anew every day of their lives! This twofold promise is for all those who come to Him now, "I will give you rest," and, "ye shall find rest unto your souls." With these proclamations, the Lord is promising to give you new courage, to open up new perspectives to you, and to give you a new vision. He knows our frame, our very being. He knows our hearts' restlessness and the undefinable haste in us. Therefore, for today and every coming day the answer is, come to Jesus with all your cares and worries. Do not confer with flesh and blood, but with Him and Him alone, "Come unto me."

Spiritual
Strength
FOR EACH DAY

MAY

1 MAY

"And ye shall seek me, and find me, when ye shall search for me with all your heart. And I will be found of you, saith the Lord"
(Jeremiah 29:13-14).

*D*oes God want to send revival today? This is a question that concerns many Christians, and there are many opinions on this subject. There are some serious believers who think the Lord will not send any more revivals. I believe with all my heart, however, that revival is the only true preparation of the Church for the return of the Lord. Do we really have reason to believe that it is the will of God to send revival, however? Yes, for the Bible promises revival.

It is always imperative to search the will of God, even for our own lives, for a person can only function spiritually when he is in the center of the will of God. We can miss God's best for us if we withdraw from His will through disobedience. How does God reveal His will to us? Through the leading of the Holy Spirit. The Lord Jesus Himself said that the Holy Spirit will lead us into all truth. All those who really want to be led will be led by Him. The condition for this is that you want to do the will of the Lord at all costs. Then you cannot go wrong, for the Spirit of God will lead you into all truth.

2 MAY

"Who will have all men to be saved, and to come unto the knowledge of the truth" (1 Timothy 2:4).

*H*ere we have insight into the will of God. God wants everyone to be saved. If you confess your sins before the Lord, then know this, that the blood of Jesus Christ cleanses you from all sin and brings you into the sphere of the will of God. We know the will of God with regard to our sanctification, "For this is the will of God, even your sanctification" (1 Thessalonians 4:3). Sanctification is going a step further than having our sins forgiven. Forgiveness of sins is turning away from sin; sanctification is turning to Jesus. Whoever does not live in sanctification is already withdrawing from the will of God. It is an inevitable fact that in our lives as believers, there is always an either/or. Either we live within the sphere of the will of God and are happy, blessed and comforted, or we are within the sphere of the will of Satan and have to do things we do not want to do. You have to give way to your lust although you do not want to; you have to lie although you want to speak the truth; you have to be impure although you would rather be pure. The reason for your disobedience is that you have never determinedly come within the sphere of the will of God. Today, decide to do His will.

137

3 MAY

"Awake, thou that sleepest, and arise from the dead, and Christ shall give thee light" (Ephesians 5:14).

*H*ave you fallen prey to this deadly sleep? This is shown by whether you see the plight of the Church and of the world or not. Many believers have fallen asleep and do not realize what is taking place around them; they are simultaneously blind and deaf. To put it in Biblical language, they are "rich and satisfied." The risen Lord puts it in these words, "Because thou sayest, I am rich, and increased with goods, and have need of nothing; and knowest not that thou art wretched, and miserable, and poor, and blind, and naked" (Revelation 3:17). Wake up! To be awake means to see your sins as God sees them—which is terrible! The result is inner brokenness and repentance, but then revival takes place. We must also know, however, what revival is not. Revival is not a divine miracle. If it were, we would have no responsibility, for then everything would depend on God. The responsibility for revival in the family, in the Church, lies with you and me, each one of us personally. The question is whether or not we want it. God wants to send revival!

4 MAY

"Unto him that is able to do exceeding abundantly above all that we ask or think, according to the power that worketh in us"
(Ephesians 3:20).

When the burden becomes too heavy for us and we look around questioningly, there is only one answer: God is able! The infinite power of God is only comprehended and believed in by the Christian to a limited extent, and this is due to unbelief. When we direct a living faith on the Almighty God, who is able to do anything, then there are no limits to achieving the greatest blessings, for God is able! His infinite ability cannot be sufficiently described in words. He is able, He is exceedingly able, He is abundantly able. Even more, namely, "...above all that we ask or think." He can accomplish that in your life which you are not able to comprehend in your present situation. Perhaps you are saying, I do not experience His help. Everything is so dark around me. Why is this? The answer is that the power of God works in and through us according to the measure of our faith, "...according to the power that worketh in us." This is why the Lord Jesus said, "If thou canst believe, all things are possible to him that believeth" (Mark 9:23).

5 MAY

"By faith he [Abraham] sojourned in the land of promise, as in a strange country" (Hebrews 11:9).

If you are determined to follow the Lamb, you need not be surprised if the way is lonely. As a born-again Christian, you are no longer a guest and a stranger in the Lord's eyes, but a citizen with the saints and members of God's household. Yes, your life is hidden with Christ in God. The other side of the coin is that you become more and more of a stranger here on earth. The more intimate your fellowship with the Lord is, the more rejection you will experience from a world that that is permeated by the antichristian spirit. The way following Jesus is very narrow. The spirit of compromise, all worldly baggage and your own self have no room in it. This narrow way often divides us inwardly from our relatives and friends, who do not want to go this way to the cross. But it is the only way that leads to a meeting with Jesus in the clouds of heaven. We are strangers like Abraham, and look forward to His day with joyful expectation. Jesus will come suddenly—perhaps today—and we who are alive and remain will be transformed and be raptured into His presence. Will you have part in this joyful event?

6 MAY

"Not forsaking the assembling of ourselves together, as the manner of some is; but exhorting one another: and so much the more, as ye see the day approaching" (Hebrews 10:25).

What day is meant here? The day of the return of Jesus, and we are to wait for Him. The egocentric nature in us says, "I want to be free; I do not want to give myself up!" "Let us break their bands asunder, and cast away their cords from us" (Psalm 2:3). Self tries to maintain its individuality. That, however, is not waiting for "the day approaching." I am deeply convinced that when the Lord comes, He expects to find His own united as on the day of Pentecost, when He came upon them through the Holy Spirit. "And when the day of Pentecost was fully come, they were all with one accord in one place" (Acts 2:1). Do you have fellowship with other believers? If there is no true fellowship of the saints where you live, why don't you open your house for such fellowship in the Word and prayer? "And they, continuing daily with one accord in the temple, and breaking bread from house to house, did eat their meat with gladness and singleness of heart" (Acts 2:46). True fellowship with the Lord and His saints prepares for the rapture. This is expressed visibly through persevering fellowship with other Christians.

7 MAY

"And every man that hath this hope in him purifieth himself,
even as he is pure" (1 John 3:3).

There is a fateful forgetting, "He...hath forgotten that he was purged from his old sins" (2 Peter 1:9). Do you feel that you cannot get nearer to Jesus? Are your prayers to no avail? Is there no blessing and no fruit in your spiritual life? This is the cause: you have gotten stuck, on the way following Jesus, in sins from which you have not been cleansed. The precious blood of Jesus cleanses even from sins committed long ago, if we confess them in true humility. Then you can draw nearer to Jesus every day, not only timewise but also spiritually. In your heart the longing for Him will grow, "Come soon, Lord Jesus."

Cleansing from our sins means becoming free. Purification is a continuous process. Through the cleansing of your former sins, you recognize Jesus even more. Through sanctification, you hasten towards Jesus. The person who is cleansed from his sins is willing to say, "My life belongs to Christ." But when he is led into the mystery of deeper purification, he will exclaim, "For me to live is Christ" (Philippians 1:21).

8 MAY

"By faith he [Abraham] sojourned in the land of promise, as in a strange country" (Hebrews 11:9).

*W*here the return of the Lord is concerned, two groups of believers will appear before Him. On the one hand there are those who trusted in religious experiences but did not do the will of the Father, and on the other hand there are those who served Him in faithful obedience until He returned. He turns away from the first group with the words, "I never knew you: depart from me, ye that work iniquity" (Matthew 7:23). To the second group He says, "Well done, thou good and faithful servant: thou hast been faithful over a few things, I will make thee ruler over many things: enter thou into the joy of thy lord" (Matthew 25:21). Please ask yourself the question: Are you living in a *strange country* spiritually? Are you walking towards Jesus on the straight and narrow path? If you are, the Lord gives you supports so that you can walk this path of sanctification perseveringly:

• Through watching and praying to Him, "Watch ye therefore, and pray always" (Luke 21:36).

• Through waiting for Him, "and ye yourselves like unto men that wait for their lord" (Luke 12:36).

• Through abiding in Him, "And now, little children, abide in him..." (1 John 2:28).

9 MAY

"...In lowliness of mind let each esteem other better than themselves"
(Philippians 2:3).

*W*hether we have the mind of Jesus is expressed by our relationship with our neighbor. Please examine this relationship according to the Biblical principles of the mind of Jesus:

• Humility is not a virtue but the actual foundation of the mind of Jesus. He says, "I am meek and lowly in heart" (Matthew 11:29). We only have true humility in the immediate presence of the holy God. Only in this way are we capable of esteeming our brother or sister higher than ourselves. Whoever sees himself in the light of the majesty of God always esteems the spiritual quality of the other higher than his own. This is why spiritual pride is the greatest self-deception.

• Brotherly love is another principle of the mind of Jesus and is closely connected to the first. "Be kindly affectioned one to another with brotherly love; in honor preferring one another" (Romans 12:10). Those who practice this love honor the Lord in their brother or sister. Such a person knows no man after the flesh; thus, he honors every brother and sister. He sees and honors the Lord in them. Such honoring is also seen by the fact that you do not speak too much of your own holiness and experiences.

10 MAY

"Let every one of us please his neighbor for his good to edification"
(Romans 15:2).

*H*ere we have a third principle of the mind of Jesus: see what is good, what is holy, what is eternal, in your neighbor, and behave towards him accordingly. In other words, to be self-effacing encourages others to do good; it edifies them.

From this comes the fourth principle: the willingness to bear. "Bear ye one another's burdens, and so fulfil the law of Christ" (Galatians 6:2). Where do your problems and the friction in your relationship with your neighbor come from? It comes from your wanting to receive instead of to give. You expect something of him or her, while they expect something of you. You want to receive their love, while they are seeking a revelation of the love of Jesus Christ in your life. Think for a moment how you could make your neighbor's life easier. "I have enough to carry myself," you may object. Then look at Jesus and let His mind be in you. Through this you will be able to bear the burdens of others, and you yourself will be blessed. Jesus gave. He always gave. He gave everything. He gave His love. He bore our burdens. He carried away our sins. And He will bear you even into your old age.

11 MAY

"Even as the Son of man came not to be ministered unto, but to minister, and to give his life a ransom for many" (Matthew 20:28).

The fifth principle of the mind of Jesus is holy service to our neighbor. "By love serve one another" (Galatians 5:13). Jesus Himself is the actual source. He loved you and me so much! The highest service for God is the surrender of our lives. To serve Him means to take the lower path and to expect no recognition, no reward, no thanks, but simply to serve because Jesus served you. This is victorious service!

The sixth principle is, "Be ye kind one to another, tender-hearted, forgiving one another, even as God for Christ's sake hath forgiven you" (Ephesians 4:32). Have you forgiven your brother or sister, as the Lord has forgiven you? I do not doubt that you have been hurt and ignored by them, but have you forgiven them? What a blessed atmosphere unfeigned kindness creates. It was there when Jesus was a guest of Martha and Mary, and Mary anointed Jesus' feet with precious ointment, "...and the house was filled with the odour of the ointment" (John 12:3). When someone enters your house, they notice immediately whether this glorious aroma of heartfelt kindness fills your house.

12 MAY

"And when he had spoken these things, while they beheld, he was taken up; and a cloud received him out of their sight" (Acts 1:9).

To prove how genuine His resurrection was, Jesus remained for forty days on the earth and showed Himself to many witnesses. These forty days were something like a school of faith for His disciples, so that they believed in the reality of His resurrection. Our blessed Lord was also in a "school of faith" in the wilderness for forty days, and proved Himself to be obedient. Now, however, He ascended to heaven from the Mount of Olives. We can never describe the further course of His ascension. Only faith sees in the spiritual realm. First, there was His triumphant passage through the spheres of darkness. We must realize what Paul says later on in Ephesians 6:12, that principalities, powers, rulers of the darkness of this world and spiritual wickedness in high places are a fact. When the Lord Jesus ascended through these regions to heaven, all these powers of darkness were paralyzed. It says in Psalm 68:18, "Thou hast ascended on high, thou hast led captivity captive." This means nothing less than that the Victor of Calvary took the whole of hell captive at His ascension. The triumphal conclusion of His ascension is that He then seated Himself at the right hand of the Majesty on High.

13 MAY

"And hath put all things under his feet, and gave him to be the head over all things to the church, which is his body, the fullness of him that filleth all in all" (Ephesians 1:22-23).

Notice the word "all" in this text: "all things" twice and "all in all." We see here that the triumph of our Lord was portrayed in His ascension. Yes, the ascension of the Lord was the concluding triumph over all the power of Satan. Let us look into the deep and glorious significance of this event. His descent came to an end when He ascended. The Lord's ascension fulfilled His Word, "Wherefore God also hath highly exalted him, and given him a name which is above every name" (Philippians 2:9). When we are crowned with glory, it will be because we humbled ourselves in the Lord Jesus Christ. The glorious significance of the ascension of the Lord Jesus is revealed to us in the epistle to the Ephesians, "He that descended is the same also that ascended up far above all heavens, that he might fill all things" (4:10). This means that the ascension of the Lord was the concluding fulfillment of the prophecies of His first coming in the Old Testament. In the same way, the prophecies concerning His second coming will also be fulfilled. What a wonderful promise. How can we be sad when the ascension of the Lord guarantees His return?!

14 MAY

"Behold, I come quickly: hold that fast which thou hast,
that no man take thy crown" (Revelation 3:11).

The Lord still has not come; He is still waiting. But we are looking out undeterred for the moment when we shall be changed and receive a body "like His glorious body," and be raptured to Him with inconceivable speed to meet Him in the air. Now, however, we find ourselves exactly in the period of time of which the Lord says, "While the bridegroom tarried, they all slumbered and slept" (Matthew 25:5). I emphasize, on this last stage of our journey we are all in danger of becoming tired and going to sleep. Paul writes to Timothy, "Now the Spirit speaketh expressly, that in the latter times some shall depart from the faith, giving heed to seducing spirits, and doctrines of devils" (1 Timothy 4:1). Those who do not walk before the Lord in all truth will become tired and open to the lying doctrines of demons. To walk in all truth means to put on the whole of Christ, "Put ye on the Lord Jesus Christ" (Romans 13:14). He alone is the truth. Whoever puts Him on remains awake and receives power to overcome, "And they overcame him by the blood of the Lamb, and by the word of their testimony" (Revelation 12:11). Stay awake! If you have already fallen asleep, the Lord is calling to you, "Awake thou that sleepest, and arise from the dead, and Christ shall give thee light" (Ephesians 5:14).

149

15 MAY

"Let us not sleep, as do others; but let us watch and be sober"
(1 Thessalonians 5:6).

The exalted Lord is speaking through His words to the Church at Sardis, and also to us with great earnest, "Be watchful" (Revelation 3:2). We are spiritually asleep where three things are concerned: prayer, the Word of God and our testimony.

• To be awake in our prayer lives means that we take the power of prayer seriously; that "above all things" we are on our knees and continually pray to God because we know that He hears prayer. The Lord is waiting for you now. Perhaps He has been waiting all day to see if you would seek Him. He is the source of blessing, but He says, "Ye have not, because ye ask not" (James 4:2).

• Sleep where the Word of God is concerned is just as deceptive. Are you holding fast to the promises that God has given you? God's will concerning our sanctification is clear from His Word, just as clear as the fact that He desires the salvation of all men.

• Only the victorious prayer warrior has power and authority in his witness; only those who take the Word of God seriously and do not let themselves be held up by mental tiredness, but persevere before the throne of God until they are heard. Only those who live in prayer and stand on the Word of God, have power in their testimony.

16 MAY

"Be watchful, and strengthen the things which remain, that are ready to die: for I have not found thy works perfect before God"
(Revelation 3:2).

What dies if we are not watchful? The vital connection with the Son of God! The call of a Gentile came to the sleeping man, Jonah, a preacher of the Word of God, "What meanest thou, O sleeper?" (Jonah 1:6). Or, as the NIV puts it, "How can you sleep?" Our blessed Lord said in one of the hardest hours of His life to His sleeping disciples, "What, could ye not watch with me one hour?" (Matthew 26:40). It seems to me that as this fatal, all-destroying spiritual sleep threatens to come over us more and more, the nearer the hour of the return of Jesus comes. "While the bridegroom tarried, they all slumbered and slept" (Matthew 25:5). Wake up! Why are you sleeping? What is the reason that you have gotten into this state of sleep? We have already read it, "For I have not found thy works perfect before God." This is not about your good works, but about the works of Christ, which have not been found perfect in you because your surrender is incomplete. Here we have the reason for all the trouble in your life: incomplete surrender. Will you wait longer to surrender yourself to Him completely?

17 MAY

"Whom have I in heaven but thee? And there is none upon earth that I desire beside thee" (Psalm 73:25).

The danger is great today that we hear the Word of God, read it, and yet do not live it out practically. What we need is knowledge of the Lord in our spirits, not in our minds or our understanding. Those who lack spiritual knowledge lack everything. Our outward actions may be in complete accordance with faith in Jesus Christ, and yet the Lord says through Hosea, "I desired mercy, and not sacrifice; and the knowledge of God more than burnt offerings" (Hosea 6:6). You may be asking, "How can I attain to greater knowledge of Him?" The answer is, "The fear of the Lord is the beginning of wisdom [or knowledge]" (Psalm 111:10). Those who do not know Him cannot love Him with all their hearts. Such a person has emotional feelings toward the Lord, but the all-controlling love in the spirit is lacking. This lack of love for the Lord is perceptible and visible in our self-love, which is expressed in vanity, self-esteem and bigotry. The Lord is seeking, however, those who love Him with all their hearts. In Deuteronomy 13:3, it even says, "The Lord your God proveth you, to know whether ye love the Lord your God with all your heart and with all your soul."

18 MAY

"Hearken diligently unto me, and eat ye that which is good, and let your soul delight itself in fatness. Incline your ear, and come unto me: hear, and your soul shall live" (Isaiah 55:2-3).

How can you joyfully obey Him if you do not know and love Him? "O that thou hadst hearkened to my commandments! then had thy peace been as a river, and thy righteousness as the waves of the sea" (Isaiah 48:18). When you do what pleases Him, He is always with you. To do His will is the only food that can satisfy your soul. But it is clear that if you do not know the Lord, you cannot love Him, obey Him or trust Him with all your heart. And yet this trust in Him is the only solution to all your problems, "Trust in the Lord with all thine heart; and lean not unto thine own understanding. In all thy ways acknowledge him, and he shall direct thy paths" (Proverbs 3:5). What do you have to do, then? Respond to His invitation, "Come now, and let us reason together, saith the Lord: though your sins be as scarlet, they shall be as white as snow; though they be red like crimson, they shall be as wool" (Isaiah 1:18). Often and urgently this invitation of the Lord is repeated in the Scriptures, "Turn ye unto me, saith the Lord of hosts, and I will turn unto you" (Zechariah 1:3).

19 MAY

"By faith Enoch was translated that he should not see death"
(Hebrews 11:5).

The name Enoch means "dedicated." Enoch was a man who was dedicated to God in a godless age. What is a person who is dedicated to God? Someone who lives undeterred in the center of the will of God. The Lord Jesus was a Man who was dedicated to God. "And he that sent me is with me: the Father hath not left me alone; for I do always those things that please him" (John 8:29).

In Enoch we see three results of a dedicated life, namely his walk with God (Genesis 5:24), his faith in God (Hebrews 11:5), and his testimony for God (Jude 14).

Enoch's faith in God led him to his rapture. From this we see that, like Moses, he endured "as seeing him who is invisible" (Hebrews 11:27), and he believed the invisible God more than visible things. Faith was the basis of his rapture. What was his testimony for God? Just this: "The Lord cometh with ten thousands of his saints" (Jude 14). Those who believe in God and walk with God recognize the Lord's intentions for the future; thus, they have to proclaim the coming of the Lord.

20 MAY

"Now the Spirit speaketh expressly, that in the latter times some shall depart from the faith, giving heed to seducing spirits, and doctrines of devils"
(1 Timothy 4:1).

Why was it so important for Enoch to walk with God? Because he was an end-times figure. According to Genesis 6, a mixing of men and spirits took place. Our time corresponds to this time. The increasing occultism, spiritualism, clairvoyance, etc., reveal a Christianity with a divided heart: people who say yes to the Lord and yes to Satan. Then as now, an invasion of spirits is taking place. Enoch walked with God; therefore, he was not drawn into occultism. I say this with great earnest: we must walk with God more than ever today; otherwise, we will fall prey to the Antichrist, the devil in Christian camouflage. But there is also a positive reason that Enoch had to walk with God. He was destined for the rapture before the judgment. Only after his rapture did the flood occur. It has become very clear to me that all true "Enochs" are destined for the rapture before the judgment that will come upon this whole world.

21 MAY

"But as he which hath called you is holy, so be ye holy in all manner of conversation" (1 Peter 1:15).

*C*onversation could here be translated "conduct" or "way of living" (see Amplified Bible). What does it mean to walk with God as Enoch did? In his life I see two things:

• **A holy conversation.** Enoch spoke with God, and God spoke with Enoch. They talked about everything together. We can only walk with God when we have this continual, holy conversation with God, and only in this way will our conversation be a conversation in heaven. Are we examples in our conversation or conduct? The holy conversation with the Lord takes place through Bible reading and prayer.

• **His sanctified pace.** How must we walk with the Lord? "He that saith he abideth in him, ought himself also so to walk, even as he walked" (1 John 2:6). This means, not too fast and not too slow. Tired Christians are those who have run ahead of the Lord, made plans, and suddenly noticed the Lord has not blessed their plans in spite of their prayers. God does not want you to make plans, but He wants to reveal His plans to you. Keep in step with God! Christians who lag behind are those who walk too slowly, who are too lethargic to obey. Are you walking with God?

22 MAY

*"According as his divine power hath given unto us all things that pertain
unto life and godliness, through the knowledge of him that hath called us to
glory and virtue" (2 Peter 1:3).*

Through his persevering walk with God, Enoch learned
to know Him better and better, and therefore he became
more and more stable in his walk. Enoch walked with God
everywhere. The Lord was with him in the fields. The Lord
was with him in his house. When he visited someone, the
Lord was beside him. The more perseveringly we walk with
the Lord, the more we will come to know Him, and through
this we are able to walk with God even more closely. Enoch
had never seen God, and yet he clung to Him as though he
saw Him. One day it was as though a hand suddenly
stretched out to him from heaven and a voice said, "Come,
Enoch, the time has come...." Then he was with the Lord
and saw with unspeakable joy the One with whom he had
walked. The Bible simply says, "...and was not found, because God had translated him" ("taken him away," NIV)
(Hebrews 11:5). This sentence shows that apparently a search
was made for Enoch, but Enoch had disappeared. How was
Enoch's rapture possible? Genesis 5:24 tells us, "And Enoch
walked with God: and he was not; for God took him." For
three hundred and sixty-five years, he lived a life of holiness,
in love and in prayer. His life was a testimony.

23 MAY

"Be thou faithful unto death, and I will give thee a crown of life"
(Revelation 2:10).

Tribulation has blessed results. God's Word teaches us that "...we must through much tribulation enter into the kingdom of God" (Acts 14:22). Why is this? It is because, "Our light affliction [or tribulation], which is but for a moment, worketh for us a far more exceeding and eternal weight of glory" (2 Corinthians 4:17). What are the blessed results of tribulation?

• Tribulation moves us to pray more fervently, so that we begin to attach more value to the working of God than our own working, "Let him [the Lord] deliver me out of all tribulation" (1 Samuel 26:24).

• Tribulation helps us experience the joy of the Lord in a special way, "I am exceeding joyful in all our tribulation," wrote Paul in 2 Corinthians 7:4.

• In tribulation, we experience the comfort of the Lord in a special way, "Blessed be God...who comforteth us in all our tribulation" (2 Corinthians 1:3-4).

• Tribulation teaches us that which we normally seldom possess, namely patience, "Tribulation worketh patience" (Romans 5:3).

Paul also asks in Romans 8:35, "Who shall separate us from the love of Christ? Shall tribulation...?" And he answers his own question in verse 37, "Nay, in all these things we are more than conquerors through him that loved us."

158

24 MAY

"But he held his peace, and answered nothing" (Mark 14:61).

I have been deeply moved by this silence of Jesus during His sufferings. This silence is a part of His accomplished victory. The mocking challenge of the enemies, "Save thyself, and come down from the cross" (Mark 15:30) was silenced by His silence. His triumphal cry, "It is finished!" (John 19:30) was made all the mightier through His preceding silence, and caused the centurion to exclaim, "Truly this man was the Son of God!" (Mark 15:39). How little of this nature of Jesus we have! Why do you defend your doings so vehemently? Why do you continually justify yourself? Remember what your Savior did, "Who, when he was reviled, reviled not again; when he suffered, he threatened not; but committed himself to him that judgeth righteously" (1 Peter 2:23). The Lord Jesus was determined to go the way of dying, that we might live. This is why He was silent. We can go no other way than that which He went, and this is the way of dying. The flesh seeks its rights, but the spirit is silent. Those who belong to Christ can be silent, even in the face of gross injustice. Those who love their flesh, however, become indignant and talk a lot. Do you know this silence before God? Our speaking to God in prayer is important, but it is even more important that God can speak to us. Do you listen to Him? He tells us, "Hear, and your soul shall live" (Isaiah 55:3).

25 MAY

"But Jesus held his peace" (Matthew 26:63).

*T*he high priests and elders sought false witness against Jesus. But Jesus held His peace. When Christians are together, it is often the case that they go home troubled because, "In the multitude of words there wanteth not sin" (Proverbs 10:19). God takes the sins of the tongue seriously, not only "loose talking" but also "holy" slander. How unmerciful the tongue is! Whole churches are ruined by it and hearts are broken. God hears what we say. One of the most devastating results of slander is that the Lord no longer hears our prayers. Then it is written over our lives, "But Jesus held his peace." Regular reading of the Bible makes us put our hands on our mouths and keeps us from touching other or the Lord's anointed servants. "But Jesus held his peace." This silence annoyed Caiaphas and made Pilate afraid. In this way, Jesus' silence was a mighty answer to Pilate's question. Perhaps you speak a lot with the Lord, but He is silent. Why is He silent? Is it not because He is silently waiting for you to do something? Perhaps you are praying, for instance, "Lord, take this sin from me." But that is vain. You must lay aside sin. Say a wholehearted "no" to everything that is sinful, and then a victorious rejoicing will break out in your heart.

26 MAY

"...whom he hath appointed heir of all things" (Hebrews 1:2).

Jesus Christ is the heir of all things. What has He inherited, then? All that which Adam lost through his sin. In Biblical terms this means, that which the first Adam lost through his disobedience, the last Adam, Jesus Christ, won back through His obedience. He is the heir of all things. You may have an earthly inheritance, but when you die you will have to leave it all behind. If you are a child of God, however, then you can become a joint-heir with Christ, "And if children, then heirs; heirs of God, and joint-heirs with Christ" (Romans 8:17). The same verse continues, however, "...if so be that we suffer with him, that we may be also glorified together." To receive the inheritance is not the same as having eternal life. The Bible promises, "Every one which seeth the Son, and believeth on him, may have everlasting life" (John 6:40). We received eternal life through faith in Jesus Christ. Now we must be willing not only to believe on the Lord Jesus Christ, but also to follow Him, even suffer as He suffered. That is simply part of being a Christian. Why do you have to suffer? Through suffering the Lord separates you from the things of this earth and binds you to His heart. Through suffering you are made ready for glory.

27 MAY

"Jesus saith unto him, Have I been so long time with you, and yet hast thou not known me, Philip?" (John 14:9).

It is of vital importance for Christians to grow in the knowledge of the Lord Jesus. When the Bible speaks of this knowledge, however, it does not mean an intellectual knowledge of Him, but a spiritual one. The spiritual knowledge of the Lord Jesus is transformed in and through us into streams of living water. The glorious fruit of the knowledge of Jesus Christ is that you will become conformed to His death. Paul spoke of this in Philippians 3:10 when he said, "That I may know him, and the power of his resurrection, and the fellowship of his sufferings, being made conformable unto his death." What tremendous words! Those who know Him are willing to be conformed to his death on the cross. This means the end of our own works, the end of the lust of the flesh. The acceptance of the cross for our flesh has always been our greatest battle. We fight and wrestle, but often do not know the crucified Savior and therefore the mystery of His cross, His victory, "It is finished!" (John 19:30). The victory over our sinful flesh has long since been won. You only need to be willing to be conformed to His death. You must acknowledge, "I know that in me (that is, in my flesh,) dwelleth no good thing" (Romans 7:18), and then remain united with Jesus on the cross.

28 MAY

"Behold, I lay in Sion a chief corner stone, elect, precious: and he that believeth on him shall not be confounded"
(1 Peter 2:6).

The Holy Spirit reveals the glory of the Lord Jesus through the simplest pictures; in this case, a stone. It is extremely precious to God. What an unspeakably tender relationship it is between the Father and the Son! We sense something of this when we hear the many statements of Jesus concerning His Father, particularly when He cried in greatest desperation, "Abba, Father..." (Mark 14:36). Or the other way round, when the Father could not restrain Himself any longer and called from heaven, "This is my beloved Son, in whom I am well pleased" (Matthew 3:17). In light of this, we are all the more amazed and worship Him for those mighty words, "For God so loved the world, that he gave his only begotten Son..." (John 3:16).

Jesus is the elect Cornerstone of the Church, the foundation of salvation determined by God. No man can lay any other foundation. Because He is the Cornerstone chosen by God, we sense something of the mystery of the election of His own, for all who come to Him are chosen in Him, "According as he hath chosen us in him before the foundation of the world" (Ephesians 1:4).

29 MAY

"Unto you therefore which believe he is precious: but unto them which be disobedient, the stone which the builders disallowed, the same is made the head of the corner" (1 Peter 2:7).

Jesus is the rejected stone. He was rejected by the builders, that is, the religious leaders. This was the case then, and it is the case today. God chooses and uses, however, the rejected and despised ones. For instance, in the case of Bethlehem, "But thou, Bethlehem Ephratah, though thou be little among the thousands of Judah..." (Micah 5:2), or Nazareth, "Can there any good thing come out of Nazareth?" (John 1:46). And of Jesus Himself it says, "He is despised and rejected of men" (Isaiah 53:3).

Jesus is not only the rejected stone, but also the tried stone, "Therefore thus saith the Lord God, Behold, I lay in Zion for a foundation a stone, a tried stone" (Isaiah 28:16). He was tried and tempted, and proved steadfast. Adam lived in a sinless world with only one tree which he had to avoid, but he failed. The last Adam, Jesus, came into a dark world that was contaminated by sin. He was tried, just as we are, but He triumphed. Who can fathom the depths of these words? Jesus overcame with two weapons: 1. the Word of God—"It is written," and 2. His continual fellowship with His Father.

30 MAY

"And they thirsted not when he led them through the deserts: he caused the waters to flow out of the rock for them: he clave the rock also, and the waters gushed out" (Isaiah 48:21).

O h, that you could grasp this anew! All that you lean on now will disappoint you; it will leave you in the lurch. Those who lean on Jesus Christ, however, will not be put to shame and will remain in eternity, because Jesus is eternal. He is the Rock of Ages from which the water of life flows. Who was this rock in the desert that was struck by Moses until the streams of water flowed out of it? It was Christ Himself! What a wonderful picture! The rock, struck by Moses, the giver of the Law, quenched the thirst of the people by providing them with clear water. Jesus Christ, who was struck for our failing to keep the Law, is the eternal Rock from which the water of life flows. He calls, "Let him that is athirst come. And whosoever will, let him take the water of life freely" (Revelation 22:17). This river of life flows throughout the Bible. Ezekiel saw it and exclaimed, "Every thing shall live whither the river cometh" (Ezekiel 47:9). We know what this river of life is, namely the poured out life of Jesus, His precious blood. He is the river of life of Calvary.

31 MAY

"Thine eyes shall see the king in his beauty" (Isaiah 33:17).

*W*hen we ask, "How long will it be, Lord, till You return?" do we not hear the answer in our hearts, "Until you are truly ready." I am reminded here of Revelation 19:7, where it says, "...his wife hath made herself ready." The Holy Spirit is making the last preparations so that the Bride of the Lamb is ready to meet her heavenly Bridegroom. The question is, will we allow the Holy Spirit to prepare us through the living Word of God, to be able to see Him as He is? The Lord is not as you imagine Him or as you have experienced Him. His glory, His mercy, even His beauty, are far greater and overwhelming. When we see Him, we will fall down before Him and exclaim, like the Queen of Sheba did, "Behold, the half was not told me" (1 Kings 10:7). Here His ever-louder command meets our ear, "Follow peace with all men, and holiness, without which no man shall see the Lord" (Hebrews 12:14). Stop for a moment and ask yourself, will I be able to see Jesus as He is? Am I following peace and holiness?

Spiritual
Strength
FOR EACH DAY

JUNE

1 JUNE

"How long wilt thou forget me, O Lord? For ever? How long wilt thou hide thy face from me?" (Psalm 13:1).

It is the Holy Spirit here who expresses, through the mouth of David, the longing, the desire of the true Church of Jesus Christ on earth. This is the reason for this question, this cry of the soul who is waiting for the Lord, "How long wilt thou forget me, O Lord?" We have been waiting for the Rapture for so long, and in many believers the question arises, has the Lord forgotten us? Has He passed us by? When Israel was in trouble in olden days and spoke like this, the Lord said, "Can a woman forget her suckling child, that she should not have compassion on the son of her womb? Yea, they may forget, yet will I not forget thee" (Isaiah 49:15).

Then the second question, "How long wilt thou hide thy face from me?" When will I see Your face, as You have promised, "...when he shall appear, we shall be like him; for we shall see him as he is" (1 John 3:2). When will this take place? At the Rapture, and this is imminent. "Cast not away therefore your confidence, which hath great recompense of reward" (Hebrews 10:35). I can assure you, His desire to come and fetch you is far greater.

2 JUNE

"Wherefore comfort one another with these words"
(1 Thessalonians 4:18).

It is a part of our discipleship to comfort one another. It is my heartfelt desire that you should truly understand the expression "the God of all comfort," which we read of in 2 Corinthians 1:3. Because the nature of God is love, He is the "God of all comfort." Whatever trials and temptations, disappointments, sadness and sickness you may have, He is prepared to comfort you in such a way that you are simultaneously helped. The wonderful comfort that we can give one another through true fellowship with the Father and the Son is that we testify, "Our Lord is coming soon!" Our comfort and our hope is the return of our Lord Jesus Christ, which will take place very soon! Because God is love and therewith "the God of all comfort," we love Him and we "love his appearing" (2 Timothy 4:8). We are willing, through His indwelling love, to give up all worldly things and to concentrate all our love on the coming Lord. "The love of God is shed abroad in our hearts" (Romans 5:5). Only in this reality are we able to pass on the comfort of the love of God to a world full of trouble and tears. Soon Jesus Christ will return and "God shall wipe away all tears" (Revelation 21:4), from our eyes too!

3 JUNE

"Now the God of patience and consolation grant you to be likeminded one toward another according to Christ Jesus" (Romans 15:5).

If we put on the patience of the Lord, the written Word of God will give us the comfort of the Scriptures so that we have a living hope. If we let the Word of God work in our hearts, we will experience, as a miracle of His grace, the Word, as God Himself gives us the wonderful gift of true unity among ourselves. When we read the above verse carefully, we see that it is God who gives us this comfort through Jesus Christ. It is very moving how the Lord Jesus assures His disciples before leaving them that His Father will give them another Comforter after He leaves. This other Comforter is the Holy Spirit. In connection with this wonderful promise, the Lord Jesus points indirectly to the time when He will return to rapture us. As long as the other Comforter, the Holy Spirit is on earth, the Lord cannot return. But as soon as this Comforter ascends into heaven, in and with the Church, Jesus will come to meet us in the air.

4 JUNE

"The Lord hath anointed me to preach good tidings unto the meek; he hath sent me to bind up the broken-hearted. . .to comfort all that mourn" (Isaiah 61:1-2).

These words, "to comfort all that mourn," show us Jesus' ultimate goal. I want to illustrate the quality of comfort that only Jesus can give. Let us suppose you lose the person who is most dear to you on earth. And many among my readers are in mourning for someone, but what did the comfort of you friends, neighbors and relatives bring you? Let us stick to the reality here. Neither flowers nor wreaths can do away with the relentlessness of loss and death. They cannot undo the finality of the parting. The heartfelt, most fervent expressions of sympathy cannot remove the painful emptiness and loneliness. However great their participation in your suffering is, you may think of the words of Job, "Miserable comforters are ye all" (Job 16:2).

But then Jesus Christ comes, who calls to us in the midst of the relentlessness of death, "I am the resurrection, and the life: he that believeth in me, though he were dead, yet shall he live" (John 11:25). When He comforts, He also acts mightily and regally. He is the Resurrection and the Life in person, which is why death cannot withstand Him. That is our comfort.

5 JUNE

"Young man, I say unto thee, Arise" (Luke 7:14).

Two entirely different groups of people met one another by the gate of the city of Nain. The one had come about through death, the king of terror. The other was led by the Prince and King of life, Jesus the Christ. The sorrowing widow walked before the bier, and friends and acquaintances followed it. When the Lord met the mourning widow and mother, He had compassion on her and tenderly spoke the words, "Weep not" (verse 13). Only Jesus can give comfort like this. He who heard the heart-rending weeping of the lonely mother, He who understands her desperation, stoops down to the woman. It is a gentle, yet strong and comforting, very simple thing that we hear from the mouth of the Savior. The words, "Weep not" reveal the strongest power of divine comfort. That which He said to the widow in her plight is a testimony to His compassionate love for those who weep. Perhaps you are for some reason without comfort and without perspective at this moment. Or perhaps you are weeping in your heart over an irreplaceable loss. Then He is saying to you, "Weep not"! Only Jesus can comfort like this. These two simple words are enough.

6 JUNE

"And Jesus stood still, and commanded him to be called. And they call the blind man, saying unto him, Be of good comfort, rise; he calleth thee" (Mark 10:49).

There are innumerable "blind" people in our day who hear Jesus' voice but cannot see Him. Among these are the depressed. Perhaps your vision of Him is obscured because there is darkest night inside you. The Bible does not speak to you as it used to do. Your heart is so heavy that you cannot even pray properly. Then listen, I have a comforting message for you: Jesus of Nazareth is passing by right now! He knows everything! Take advantage of this unique opportunity. Call on Him, just as this blind man did. If you cannot pray aloud, then cry to Him in your heart, "Jesus, thou son of David, have mercy on me" (verse 47). He hears you, even if you are in the midst of a crowd. Blind Bartimaeus did not let himself be deterred, and Jesus stood still on account of him, just as He is standing still if you call upon Him. Did the Lord Jesus heal the blind man immediately? No, Bartimaeus had to go right up to Him first. Did He then open His eyes so that he could see? No, first He demanded proof of his faith. Bartimaeus understood this and said, "Lord, that I might receive my sight" (verse 51). And Jesus said to him, "Go thy way; thy faith hath made thee whole." He also wants to hear from you just what you desire of Him.

7 JUNE

*"We know that, when he shall appear, we shall be like him; for we shall
see him as he is" (1 John 3:2).*

any believers are perplexed when they come across
events in the Bible where the Lord reveals Himself visibly to people. We have the announcing of the birth of Samson, for instance, through an angel of the Lord, or that of the
birth of Jesus to Mary through the angel Gabriel. Have you
ever thought how wonderful it would be if something ex-
traordinary would happen to you, if a messenger from
heaven would stand before you and announce something to
you or give you a commission? Would it be easier for you to
believe if that would happen? No, be thankful that you do
not experience such things, for the more you see, the harder
it is for you to believe. Even Zacharias doubted after the appearing of the angel and his promise. Peter says to the many
believers who love the Lord although they have never seen
Him, that this will take place and then their joy will be all
the greater. When will this be? At the moment when our eyes
are opened at the Rapture. Then we shall see Him as He is
with unspeakable joy.

8 JUNE

"That we should be to the praise of his glory, who first trusted in Christ"
(Ephesians 1:12).

When we speak of the fact that we should be "to the praise of His glory," we are treading on very neglected territory in the Church. When I put it in these words, I am thinking of what the Lord said at the end of His life, "And the glory which thou gavest me I have given them; that they may be one, even as we are one" (John 17:22). God the Lord has ordained that we should be to the praise of His glory through Jesus Christ. Through the prophet Isaiah, He says it even more directly to each one of us personally, "Thou shalt also be a crown of glory in the hand of the Lord" (Isaiah 62:3). If we are truly crucified with Christ, we are able to enter into the infinite depth and breadth of the exalted person of the Eternal God. In this position we are transported into the eternal spheres of rejoicing, and this praise and worship draws us out of all depression and unhappiness, strengthens our weak knees, and causes the Lord to place our feet on the Rock which neither moves nor trembles. In this way we are to the praise of His glory, for praise and worship are the highest expression of faith.

9 JUNE

"I will praise thee; for I am fearfully and wonderfully made: marvellous are thy works; and that my soul knoweth right well"
(Psalm 139:14).

We are God's work! God only creates originals. There are no two people on this earth who are completely alike. He made you wonderfully, just as you are, with all your diverse characteristics, gifts and limitations. Have you ever thanked Him for this? You are no product of chance, no creature marred in His hand. On the contrary, it says in Ephesians 2:10, "For we are his workmanship, created in Christ Jesus unto good works, which God hath before ordained that we should walk in them." It is wonderful and a reason to praise and give thanks that we are not victims of chance, misfortune or fate. God has planned your life and mine from beginning to end. Will you not thank Him that He made you as you are, and praise Him for the plan that He has with you? Your own personal way is planned by God! Don't compare it, therefore, with anyone else's. God only creates originals; He never repeats Himself. But through your praise and thanks you give Him the room to transform you through His Word and through His Spirit.

10 JUNE

*"And we know that all things work together for good to them that love
God, to them who are the called according to his purpose"
(Romans 8:28).*

*Y*ou can only thank God at all times and for everything
if you really believe that the Lord means well with you.
The Lord God leads you personally, because He never repeats
Himself in the way He leads the individual. The Lord rejects
your comparison with the way in which He leads another as
resistance to His personal leading. This comparison expressed
in your question, "Lord, why me?" reveals your rebellion
against the way in which He wants to lead you personally.
Through such questions, your character is not transformed
for good, but it becomes characterized by spiritual decline revealed as self-pity and envy. From envy comes mistrust, and
from mistrust estrangement, and from estrangement hatred—
and the devil rejoices. Begin now to thank the Lord for the
way in which He leads you, for it is the best way for you.
Then you will rise above your circumstances and be able to
rejoice.

11 JUNE

"For we wrestle not against flesh and blood, but against principalities, against powers, against the rulers of the darkness of this world, against spiritual wickedness in high places" (Ephesians 6:12).

The highest expression of faith is that we learn to thank God at all times in the face of spiritual hostility. If we do this, the Lord Himself will intervene immediately and mightily on our behalf. Praise glorifies Him, for it leads to the worship of His exalted person. Praise and worship are the way to the effective prayer that the Lord Jesus taught us, "After this manner therefore pray ye: Our Father which art in heaven, Hallowed be thy name" (Matthew 6:9). But it is more than this. Praise is the door into the presence of God, "...Thou shalt call...thy gates Praise" (Isaiah 60:18). Praise assures us the royal permission to enter into the courts of God, "Enter into his gates with thanksgiving, and into his courts with praise: be thankful unto him and bless his name" (Psalm 100:4).

Thank Him and praise Him—for what? Thank Him for His unspeakable gift, Jesus Christ, and praise and worship Him for His precious blood that He shed for you.

12 JUNE

"Bless the Lord, O my soul: and all that is within me, bless his holy name. Bless the Lord, O my soul, and forget not all his benefits"
(Psalm 103:1-2).

Thanksgiving and praise produce miracles, especially when you are in an inner prison and everything seems locked up and bolted, when the Bible no longer speaks to you and you can hardly utter the name of Jesus. Praise was offered by Paul and Silas when they lay in prison with bleeding backs. When they prayed, sang and praised God, He opened the doors of the prison and broke their chains.

Begin to give thanks and to praise God, whatever the "prison" may be in which you find yourself. When we sing to the Lord and praise Him, He opens the doors of our circumstances and difficulties. He does not solve the problem, maybe, but He makes us free of it. And if the answer to your prayer takes time, then praise the Lord all the more! When we go through trials, praising the Lord will strengthen our faith. The praise on our lips shows that there really is faith in our hearts. When you see that, you will be led through praise and thanksgiving into the secret of a continual supply of strength.

13 JUNE

"I will offer to thee the sacrifice of thanksgiving, and will call upon the name of the Lord. I will pay my vows unto the Lord now in the presence of all his people" (Psalm 116:17-18).

We can see and experience the meaning of the words "sacrifice of thanksgiving," when we make our way into the innermost sanctuary. The door of the sanctuary opens up to us when we give God thanks for His unspeakable gift, Jesus Christ; when we praise Him for His precious blood that He shed for us, and for His body that He gave for us. To go through the door of the sanctuary with praise and thanks, into the presence of the holy God, means to surrender yourself to Him who surrendered Himself for us through His blood and His body. Then we suddenly grasp the meaning of the words, "sacrifice of thanksgiving." We have the tendency to separate things that in the sight of God are inseparable, because He joined them. But this is not possible. We cannot, for instance, be one with Jesus Christ and simultaneously live for ourselves. We cannot thank God without simultaneously sacrificing to Him. Whoever separates thanksgiving and sacrifice loses his joy in the Lord. "Offer unto God thanksgiving; and pay thy vows unto the most High" (Psalm 50:14).

14 JUNE

"And I heard as it were the voice of a great multitude, and as the voice of many waters, and as the voice of mighty thunderings, saying, Alleluia: for the Lord God omnipotent reigneth" (Revelation 19:6).

Should we, as children of God who are on our way to this eternal glory, not take as an example that which takes up so much time and energy in heaven? We have completely neglected praise and thanksgiving toward our Lord. If the most significant task of the angels is to praise God, there must be a good reason for this. If it is so important for God in heaven to be praised day and night by the cherubim, then this must have tremendous results (cf. Revelation 4:8-11). Let us consider it from this aspect: if the most important function of the heavenly hosts is to praise God, then it is logical that this must also apply to man. In praise and in worship, we are gradually transformed from one glory to another into the image of the eternal God. Therefore, our true worship is the most meaningful activity; it puts God in the position to attain His highest goal with the universe, namely, to bring many sons and daughters to glory.

15 JUNE

"Rejoice in the Lord always; and again I say, Rejoice"
(Philippians 4:4).

The Lord Jesus said, "Ye are the light of the world" (Matthew 5:14). Light is seen. It does not speak; it shines. And true joy, not synthetic joy, is infectious. Ephesians 3:16 says, "That he would grant you, according to the riches of his glory, to be strengthened with might by his Spirit in the inner man." Divine strength will be perceptible to our surroundings. People who live in spiritual powerlessness are overcome with a great desire to have this strength. Does His strength shine through your weakness, or do you have to compensate the strength you lack with many words? The Lord Jesus says that He wants to give us rest, "...learn of me; for I am meek and lowly in heart: and ye shall find rest unto your souls" (Matthew 11:29). This presupposes that we go to Him! How wonderful it is when a child of God radiates this serenity in the midst of the hectic of daily life! This touches the hearts of the people of today, and they begin to desire what that child of God has. They begin to want Jesus and to pray, "Give me peace in the strife of this world."

16 JUNE

"Forasmuch then as the children are partakers of flesh and blood, he also himself likewise took part of the same; that through death he might destroy him that had the power of death. . . " (Hebrews 2:14).

*T*his means nothing other than that Jesus Christ, the eternal Son of God, made Himself one with death. He Himself wrestled with death—not the death that wanted to kill Him, but that dark, cruel power of death in itself. He eliminated it, overpowered it and extinguished it. Paul said, "The sting of death is sin; and the strength of sin is the law" (1 Corinthians 15:56). The law of God makes sin so terrible and accuses us, and the sting of death is the sin which separates us from God. And yet the apostle exclaims triumphantly, "O death, where is thy sting? O grave, where is thy victory?" (1 Corinthians 15:55). This is why Paul could also testify that death no longer meant death for him, "I am in a strait betwixt two, having a desire to depart, and to be with Christ; which is far better" (Philippians 1:23). I am sure many of my readers will feel the same way, and yet there is this innate doubt, suppose it is not true after all? If you have such doubts in your heart, you should be ashamed of yourself, for the Lord Jesus has promised eternal life to all those who have genuinely repented, "Today shalt thou be with me in paradise" (Luke 23:43).

17 JUNE

"Let not your heart be troubled: ye believe in God, believe also in me. In my Father's house are many mansions" (John 14:1-2).

How wonderful the first day in the Father's house will be! We all know of "first days" in our lives, the first day at school, the first day at work. They are all unforgettable days, especially the first day of our spiritual lives, the day of our conversion. The memory of this should always remain alive in our minds. It should not be the case, however, that you say, "The first day after my conversion was the most glorious." You also need this glory, this fervent love that you had then, today. You have the same Savior today as you had then. The Scriptures say He is, "Jesus Christ the same yesterday, and to day, and for ever" (Hebrews 13:8). The first day you experience in eternity will also be the last day for you on earth. We must not ignore this tremendous fact. The Psalmist does not say for nothing, "Teach us to number our days, that we may apply our hearts unto wisdom" (Psalm 90:12). The fools who behave here on earth as though they would live forever are shortsighted, for the moment will come for us all when we have to cross the threshold into eternity, often suddenly and inevitably. On this day we will spend our last day here on earth and the first in eternity.

18 JUNE

"And as we have borne the image of the earthy, we shall also bear the image of the heavenly" (1 Corinthians 15:49).

Where will you spend the first day of eternity? This depends on your relationship with Jesus. Those who love Jesus and follow Him, the Lamb of God, will reach the goal. Your last day here on earth will also be the first day of eternity with Jesus. What will take place on this day? First, the great journey. Either at your death or at the return of the Lord, you will leave your earthly house here and go to the Father's house with its many "mansions." Let us not forget that we are living here "on call," and this call could take place very suddenly. There is rarely notice given of it. If you suddenly have to leave your earthly house, you will not be "out on the street," for Jesus Himself has a place prepared for you, if you are following Him with all your heart. He has gone ahead of you and has assured you in His Word, "In my Father's house are many mansions: if it were not so, I would have told you" (John 14:2). How wonderful that every child of God knows, "There is a place prepared which Jesus Himself has guaranteed me!"

19 JUNE

"And ye now therefore have sorrow: but I will see you again, and your heart shall rejoice, and your joy no man taketh from you"
(John 16:22).

The first day in eternity will bring us the ultimate answer to all our unanswered questions here on earth. Jesus said in this connection, "In that day ye shall ask me nothing" (verse 23). Why not? Because Jesus Himself, the crucified and risen Lord, is the answer to all our questions. We cannot explain this logically, for the mystery is hidden at Calvary. Calvary is the great, wonderful and marvelous answer of God to all injustices, perplexities and difficulties you experience here on earth. On our last day on earth, when our eyes close, on the same day they will be opened in eternity and see what they could not see here. This first day in eternity will bring you much more, however, namely the end of all your physical complaints, for we have the promise, "...who shall change our vile body, that it may be fashioned like unto his glorious body, according to the working whereby he is able even to subdue all things unto himself" (Philippians 3:21).

20 JUNE

"Eye hath not seen, nor ear heard, neither have entered into the heart of man, the things which God hath prepared for them that love him"
(1 Corinthians 2:9).

What will this first day in heaven bring? I am aware that when we consider this question, we can only do it from the periphery. But the Bible does say something quite concrete about it, "We shall see him as he is" (1 John 3:2). We can experience and sense something of the presence of the Lord here on earth; we know His help and taste that He is good, but we have never seen Him as He really is. That will be glory when we see Him! Never think that Jesus is as you have experienced, for He is infinitely more glorious, greater, mightier and more exalted. Our greatest battle on earth is to enter into this glorious rest through faith. Never forget that the first day of man on this earth was a day of rest. Then the trouble of sin came into the world, but behold, God created a new rest through Jesus Christ. The first day in eternity will be glorious rest in God through the Lord Jesus Christ for all those who were saved through the finished work of Jesus on Calvary's cross.

21 JUNE

"They that wait upon the Lord shall renew their strength; they shall mount up with wings as eagles; they shall run, and not be weary; and they shall walk, and not faint" (Isaiah 40:31).

*A*re you waiting for Jesus, or are you waiting for better times to come? There will not be better times. It will only become darker. Do not behave as though you will live on this earth forever. Be honest! The years are passing by, and suddenly we will have to leave this world. If you are waiting for Jesus, however, you will continually receive new strength and your chronic tiredness will disappear. The Scriptures tell us, "And ye yourselves like unto men that wait for their lord..." (Luke 12:36). The terrible thing in our day is that we see many around us falling because they did not remain in their first love, because this bridal love, this devotion to Jesus Christ, is lacking. They have no spirit of prayer and would not give their lives for the lost. They have become indifferent. If you know that you have you lost this first bridal love for Jesus and are no longer waiting for Him with fervent desire, then make a new beginning now. Let the precious blood of Jesus cleanse you from the loss of your first love, from all impurity and all sin. Who knows whether today will be your last day here on earth and your first in eternity.

22 JUNE

*"If a man abide not in me, he is cast forth as a branch, and is withered;
and men gather them, and cast them into the fire,
and they are burned" (John 15:6).*

When we ask ourselves, does God want to send revival today, we know what we have to do and what time it is. The opposite of revival is the hardening of our hearts, gradual spiritual rigidity, and ultimately, death. Believers become unusable branches that are not good for anything but burning. The quintessence of Jesus' words is more than clear. We are always witnesses of Jesus, either for Him or against Him. A branch on a vine is a branch that is destined to bring forth fruit. When I put my ear to the Bible I hear, through the Spirit of God, the call for revival to every child of God that is vegetating away and dozing on without spiritual power or fruit. Why do you think the fatal, Satanic, false doctrines are experiencing such a tremendous increase? It is because the counter-movement from above, through the Spirit of God in fervent believers, is lacking. This is why the Holy Spirit is shaking you in order that you awaken. "Break up your fallow ground: for it is time to seek the Lord" (Hosea 10:12).

23 JUNE

"In whom we have redemption through his blood, the forgiveness of sins, according to the riches of his grace" (Ephesians 1:7).

*T*he Lord has finished everything. He has overcome the whole hierarchy of hell together with its head, Satan. And yet, countless believers hesitate to set their feet on the ground of Calvary to claim for themselves, step by step, the unlimited victorious power of the redemption accomplished by Jesus Christ in all spheres of their lives. You do not have the power to liberate yourself from all bondage and wrong conduct, but you can set your feet in faith on the ground of Calvary and, like Israel in olden times, take possession of the land little by little. Through this you are claiming a power that is outside of your personality: the wonderful, unfathomable, infinite power of the precious blood of Jesus. It is high time that you begin to claim for yourself the domain that was won for you through Jesus Christ on Calvary's cross. Remember the words, "…there remaineth yet very much land to be possessed" (Joshua 13:1).

24 JUNE

"But the path of the just is as the shining light, that shineth more and more unto the perfect day" (Proverbs 4:18).

We would all like nothing more than for it to be sunshine all the way. Fog is unpleasant, and can even be dangerous for those who are driving. Once when we were surrounded by thick fog in the lower hill country where we lived, I said to my family, "Let's go and find some sun!" We only had to drive a few hundred meters higher up, and we were suddenly in bright sunshine.

This is how it is in the lives of Christians. Do you often have to go through foggy periods where your vision is clouded, and the danger of colliding with your neighbor is far greater because you no longer see things clearly? Does it often appear to be dismal inside you because the sun of grace is veiled? What do you do in such a situation, when you feel depressed? Do the only right thing! Go up higher! "Nearer my God to Thee!" By resisting the enemy and drawing near to God, the dangerous fog in your soul will disappear. The darkness will leave you, and you will regain your clear vision of Jesus, the Author and Finisher of your faith.

25 JUNE

"Blessed is the man whose strength is in thee; in whose heart are the ways of them. Who passing through the valley of Baca make it a well; the rain also filleth the pools" (Psalm 84:5-6).

When you are led through the thick fog of tribulation, cling to the invisible One, for whether you feel the presence of the Lord or not, He is there! He says, "Who is among you...that walketh in darkness, and hath no light? Let him trust in the name of the Lord, and stay upon his God" (Isaiah 50:10). In other words, never let yourself be influenced by the fog of unbelief, for then you will turn everything upside down. You have eternal life in you because God in His great mercy has given you a living hope through the new birth. This life is indestructible. If you have to go through patches of fog in your walk on earth, then let me tell you again, go up higher, go into the presence of God. There is no fog where the Lord is, nothing unclear, only light and joy. Thank God for the fog in your life that teaches you to cling all the more to the reality of life in Jesus Christ.

26 JUNE

"Submit yourselves therefore to God. Resist the devil, and he will flee from you" (James 4:7).

According to Scripture, every promise contained in the Bible has a key we must use before we can claim it. This key is called "obedience in faith." We must use this key before we do anything else. Notice that this key is not only faith, but also obedience in faith.

We read in verse 3, "Ye ask, and receive not." What is the reason for this powerlessness and inability to receive? In his first letter, the Apostle John wrote: "Whatsoever we ask, we receive of him" (1 John 3:22a). Therefore, we have the power to receive answers to our prayers in faith.

However, something else is written in James 4:3: "Ye ask, and receive not." Why? Because the motives in our hearts are not pure and clear: "...because ye ask amiss, they ye may consume it upon your lusts." In other words, we don't receive answers to our prayers when our motives for prayer don't focus on Jesus and Jesus alone.

27 JUNE

"Blessed is the man that endureth temptation: for when he is tried, he shall receive the crown of life, which the Lord hath promised to them that love him" (James 1:12).

We see here two conditions for receiving the crown of life. First, we have to endure temptation. We are not free from temptation when we follow Jesus. On the contrary, there are spiritual temptations when we as children of God have to go through a dark tunnel. It seems to us then that the Lord is far away, but it is then that He is nearest. It is then that the pierced hand of Jesus is holding you tight. There are also mental temptations. We may be cornered and burdened, but it says that Christ dwells in our hearts "by faith" and not by feelings! Then there are physical temptations when we are plagued by sickness. The Lord Jesus is our Great Physician, however.

The second condition for receiving the crown of life is that we love Him. We can believe in Jesus, we can speak of Him with great conviction, and we can strive to follow in His footsteps, but the Lord is primarily interested in whether or not we really love Him. Do you love Jesus? Does your heart beater faster when you think of Him? The Word of God promises, "The Lord preserveth all them that love him" (Psalm 145:20).

28 JUNE

"I have fought a good fight, I have finished my course, I have kept the faith: henceforth there is laid up for me a crown of righteousness, which the Lord, the righteous judge, shall give me at that day: and not to me only, but unto all them also that love his appearing" (2 Timothy 4:7-8).

*H*ere the condition for receiving the crown of righteousness is named: keeping the faith. We do not have to hold on to our faith, however, but to the object of our faith, and that is Jesus Christ Himself. When everything visible collapses, He remains. Cling to Him under all circumstances, even when the storm rages, so that you can say at the end of your life, "I have kept the faith."

The second condition for receiving the crown of righteousness is to love His appearing; this means to watch for the return of Jesus with great longing and increasing desire. Do you desire Him? This is the best proof that you belong to Him and are living in sanctification. Would you be glad if Jesus came today? Say "Amen" with all your heart if you love His appearing. He will come soon.

29 JUNE

"Feed the flock of God which is among you, taking the oversight thereof,
not by constraint, but willingly; not for filthy lucre, but of a ready mind;
neither as being lords over God's heritage, but being examples to the flock.
And when the chief Shepherd shall appear,
ye shall receive a crown of glory that fadeth not away"
(1 Peter 5:2-4).

The crown of glory is firstly for the shepherds of the Church, for the pastors. These have a great responsibility. They are also a special target of the enemy. Do not criticize your pastor but pray for him rather, so that he preaches the Word in the power of the Spirit and is able to do his job and one day receive the crown of glory.

It is my opinion, however, that this crown is also intended for fathers and mothers in Christ, who are examples for the flock. Are you an example? Can they see Jesus in you? Are you a pillar in your church? It is of utmost importance that Jesus Christ can grow in us and that we become examples. We should not remain spiritual babies, but grow to reach full stature in Christ. The crown of glory is prepared for you too!

30 JUNE

"Know ye not that they which run in a race run all, but one receiveth the prize? So run, that ye may obtain. And every man that striveth for the mastery is temperate in all things. Now they do it to obtain a corruptible crown; but we an incorruptible" (1 Corinthians 9:24-25).

How do we get this incorruptible crown? Through doing without things. Paul uses the picture of the Olympic games. The athletes give up all that could hinder their running and do everything that helps it, in order to receive a corruptible crown. My dear reader, ask yourself in everything you do, can I serve Jesus better by doing it? Then you will know what you have to do and what not to do. The measure for our spiritual lives can be found in Colossians 3:17, "Whatsoever ye do in word or deed, do all in the name of the Lord Jesus, giving thanks to God and the Father by him." Can you complain in the name of Jesus? No. How easy and glorious a life is that is completely centered on Jesus. Keep that which you have, for "If a man also strive for masteries, yet is he not crowned, except he strive lawfully" (2 Timothy 2:5). Follow the Lord determinedly. Dedicate your life, your heart, your gifts, your time and your strength to Him. Then your eyes will one day see the King in His beauty.

Spiritual
Strength
FOR EACH DAY

JULY

1 JULY

"For what is our hope, or joy, or crown of rejoicing? Are not even ye in
the presence of our Lord Jesus Christ at his coming?
For ye are our glory and joy"
(1 Thessalonians 2:19-20).

The crown of rejoicing is made up of the souls we have won for Christ. Are you a soul-winner? Jesus once said to "fishermen," "Follow me, and I will make you fishers of men" (Matthew 4:19). You can "fish" when you talk with people. You can win souls in prayer. Does your heart burn for the lost? Are souls won for Jesus in your church? If you ask the Lord, He will give you souls. How wonderful it will be for those who receive a crown of rejoicing!

In the New Testament, the Lord promises us five different crowns. These crowns are for those who overcome, those who have dedicated their lives completely to Jesus. Do you have to pursue five different goals? No, for in Revelation 19:11-12 it says, "And I saw heaven opened, and behold a white horse; and he that sat upon him was called Faithful and True, and in righteousness he doth judge and make war. His eyes were as a flame of fire, and on his head were many crowns." All these wonderful crowns are united in one person: Jesus Christ!

2 JULY

"But as many as received him, to them gave he power to become the sons of God, even to them that believe on his name" (John 1:12).

In the name of Jesus lies a unique and unlimited, redeeming power. Only faith can grasp and experience this power. How would it otherwise be possible that everyone who calls on this name in faith is saved from eternal death? This is exactly what the prophet Joel says, "And it shall come to pass, that whosoever shall call on the name of the Lord shall be delivered" (Joel 2:32). Such a person is also saved from the power of darkness, "Who hath delivered us from the power of darkness" (Colossians 1:13). All men are under the power of Satan on account of their sins, "He that committeth sin is of the devil" (1 John 3:8). As soon as a person calls upon the name of Jesus in faith, realizing the redeeming power of this name, his chains of sin are broken. Satan loses his hold on him; he may no longer touch such a person, "He that is begotten of God keepeth himself, and that wicked one toucheth him not" (1 John 5:18). When Satan touches a born-again person, he is touching the Lord Himself, "He that toucheth you toucheth the apple of his eye" (Zechariah 2:8). Whoever calls in faith upon the name of the Lord, takes claim to the whole of the victory of Jesus.

3 JULY

"To him give all the prophets witness, that through his name whosoever believeth in him shall receive remission of sins" (Acts 10:43).

What mighty words! There is forgiving power in this name, for behind the name of Jesus is His shed blood. Whoever calls upon Jesus, calls upon His precious blood and becomes white as snow, for "the blood of Jesus Christ his Son cleanseth us from all sin" (1 John 1:7).

His name is also a life-giving power, however. If you believe on His name, you believe on His person. And He, Jesus Christ, not only died but also rose again from the dead. He is "...the resurrection, and the life" (John 11:25).

But His name is even more. It is an ointment poured forth. Jeremiah cried at the sight of the immeasurable damage that had come upon the people of God through their idolatry, "Is there no balm in Gilead; is there no physician there?" (Jeremiah 8:22). And the Song of Solomon answers, "Thy name is as ointment poured forth" (Song of Solomon 1:3). Perhaps your sins have done grievous harm, and the wounds in your soul are deep. Do you think nobody can help you? The precious name of Jesus can! Only Jesus understands you. His name can heal you in body and soul.

4 JULY

"...How ye turned to God from idols to serve the living and true God"
(1 Thessalonians 1:9).

What was the service of the Lord Jesus here on earth? It was complete surrender to His Father, unconditional acceptance of His Father's will. The life of Jesus was continual, holy service. This highest service culminated in the giving of His eternal life in His blood on a mortal earth. "I give unto them eternal life" (John 10:28). How should the service be of those who love Him and follow Him—your service? Just as that of your Master. Only in the same service can we become like Him. Turn your eyes on the servant Jesus, consider Him and you will know how you should serve, "Whosoever will be chief among you, let him be your servant: even as the Son of man came not to be ministered unto, but to minister..." (Matthew 20:27-28). The truly converted can be recognized by their continual service for others. The religious activity of so many is a sad caricature of this selfless service. Are you a servant of Jesus Christ or a servant of your flesh, and therewith of Satan? I fear that many Christians have departed from Christ because they departed from the path of service.

5 JULY

"I beseech you therefore, brethren, by the mercies of God, that ye present your bodies a living sacrifice, holy, acceptable unto God, which is your reasonable service" (Romans 12:1).

Where does true service lead? It leads in the footsteps of Jesus. "If any man serve me, let him follow me" (John 12:26). This way is the least problematic. Those who tread it belong to those who "follow the Lamb whithersoever he goeth" (Revelation 14:4). Problems come from conflicts, and conflicts come from our self. Our self does not want to serve but to rule. So those who want to serve must first tread the path with Jesus. There he will be delivered from his proud, defiant self. Where does this path begin? The Scriptures tell us this too, for Jesus continues, "And where I am, there shall also my servant be" (John 12:26). Where did He go? He went to the cross! Just as He gave Himself to God as a living sacrifice on the Cross, so the path of a servant of Jesus also begins with the giving of himself, the sacrificing of self on the altar, that is, on the cross. All service that is not done from the cross is empty and fruitless, but all service from the position of being crucified with Him contains infinite opportunities for blessing.

6 JULY

"For the eyes of the Lord run to and fro throughout the whole earth, to shew himself strong in the behalf of them whose heart is perfect toward him" (2 Chronicles 16:9).

How should we serve the Lord? I am convinced of the fact that the Lord is looking for people who want to be a whole sacrifice. To these and through these He reveals Himself completely. Are you the man or the woman who is willing to give yourself to Him unconditionally? I ask pastors, counselors, deacons and church members, do you know that the blessing of the Lord departs from those who want to sit on the fence, so to speak? Only a total surrender to his claim brings total victory. Our commission is priestly, because we stand before God praying and wrestling for the souls of men. It is also prophetic, though, because our fervent testimony of redemption through the Lord Jesus carries an important message, "Be ye clean, that bear the vessels of the Lord" (Isaiah 52:11).

Let us serve the Lord fervently, for "The king's business require[s] haste"(1 Samuel 21:8). It is midnight—we must make haste because we do not have much time left. The Lord is coming soon, and then we shall be called upon to give account for our endeavors. He is calling to us to "Occupy till I come" (Luke 19:13).

7 JULY

"Behold, he cometh with clouds; and every eye shall see him, and they also which pierced him: and all kindreds of the earth shall wail because of him. Even so, Amen" (Revelation 1:7).

We must see one thing clearly. The rule of the Lord Jesus at the present time is a reality. If Jesus really is in charge, if everything really is subject to Him, then Satan's power is a lie. Satan himself, according to the words of the Lord Jesus, is the father of lies. If you are still bound in Satan's power, to spirits of depression or unclean passions, then do what the Bible says, "Resist the devil, and he will flee from you. Draw nigh to God, and he will draw nigh to you" (James 4:7-8). I am so grateful to be able to proclaim to you the absolute truth of the victory of Jesus. The conclusion is, if Jesus Christ, through His tears, His blood and His death on the cross, truly has won the whole victory, then Satan's power is not legitimate. If you say that you believe on Jesus Christ but are still in bondage, then you are illegitimately bound. I say to you, Jesus Christ has completely annulled the right Satan had to you through sin.

8 JULY

"Now Moses kept the flock. . .and came to the mountain of God, even to Horeb" (Exodus 3:1).

A meeting with the Lord always has overwhelming consequences. Regarding the decisive meeting that Moses had with the Lord, let us ask ourselves, whom did the Lord meet here?

• A man who had come to rest. Moses had become a shepherd. Is there a more restful occupation than that? Everything had come to rest in and around him. It had taken him forty long years to attain to this. Now he was ready to meet God.

• A truthful man. Moses and the sheep belonged together; they understood one another, or he would not have stood it for so long. In this we see his truthfulness. Jesus said later on, "Every one that is of the truth heareth my voice" (John 18:37), and, "My sheep hear my voice" (John 10:27). Moses had become truthful. This is the condition for a meeting with the Lord.

• A disappointed man. Moses was a man who was disappointed in life. His efforts to deliver his people from slavery had failed. On the contrary, he had to flee for his life and was considered lost in the desert. Here God met with him. Here Moses received a new commission.

9 JULY

"And the angel of the Lord appeared unto him in a flame of fire out of the midst of a bush" (Exodus 3:2).

Where does the Lord meet us?

• In the desert, in solitude. Moses had been cut off from his nation's relationship.

• On the mountain of God, on Horeb. Horeb means desert. If you feel as though there is a comfortless, empty desert in your heart, then the Lord is closest to you.

How does the Lord meet us?

• As the eternal, righteous God. "And he looked, and, behold, the bush was burned with fire, and the bush was not consumed" (Exodus 3:2). The flame of His righteousness never burns out, but He reveals Himself also as the God of eternal love. His love never ends.

• In His Word. Moses' ignorance reveals a great tragedy. Although the Lord was so near to him, he did not recognize Him. He even said, "I will now turn aside, and see this great sight, why the bush is not burned" (Exodus 3:3). There was only one way to wake Moses out of his ignorance: His Word! God called out of the bush and said, "Moses, Moses" (verse 4). And he answered, "Here am I." It was God's speaking to him directly that convinced him of the reality of the presence of God.

10 JULY

*"And he said, Draw not nigh hither: put off thy shoes from off thy feet,
for the place whereon thou standest is holy ground"
(Exodus 3:5).*

What did the Lord reveal to His servant, Moses?

• His holiness. This is always the first thing the Lord reveals to His children. His holiness! We are forced to take off our "shoes" in His presence; that is, to separate ourselves from all that is secular.

• His faithfulness. "I am the God of thy father, the God of Abraham, the God of Isaac, and the God of Jacob" (verse 6). In other words, I am the eternally faithful One who bore your father, and I will also bear you. I am He! By destroying Moses' faith in himself through the revelation of His holiness, he received faith in God through the revelation of His faithfulness.

How did Moses react to the meeting with the Lord? "And Moses hid his face; for he was afraid to look upon God" (verse 6). This was pure victory. This was what God was waiting for. Now He could call him. Only then when we are grasped by the fear of God through a meeting with the Lord, can He employ us effectively in His service.

11 JULY

"The Lord your God which goeth before you, he shall fight for you . . ."
(Deuteronomy 1:30).

*Y*ou may be tired of fighting and being exhausted. Great difficulties are continually mounting up before you. In your innermost being, you hear threatening sounds of unsolvable conflicts. You simply cannot rest. Unjust situations, unjust treatment, unjust punishment, threatening illnesses, distressing worries, exams—what is it that keeps you in a continual state of battle so that you find no rest? Listen to what the Bible says, "Ye shall not need to fight in this battle: set yourselves, stand ye still, and see the salvation of the Lord with you" (2 Chronicles 20:17). He can do it much better than you can! No enemy can withstand Him. Why are you still fighting the battle yourself, then? Because subconsciously you think you have enough strength to do it alone. But you will fail, for it is written, "He weakened my strength in the way" (Psalm 102:23). Why? So that you cease to fight, for Jesus has already fought the battle for you victoriously. Your futile battle has its origin in your supposing you can do it yourself. Our greatest battle is not to fight the battle ourselves. Let the Lord fight it for you!

12 JULY

"Why art thou cast down, O my soul? And why art thou disquieted within me? Hope in God: for I shall yet praise him, who is the health of my countenance, and my God" (Psalm 43:5).

*A*re you restless and stressed? The two words "no time" are like lashes from the whip of the devil. Stress digs an early grave for many. "No time"—in spite of all the technological advantages in our times. Many people are captives in the iron grip of this spirit of stress. But Jesus has overcome this spirit! How can you become free of it? Not through more effort on your part, but through more prayer. When you are on your knees, the Lord will show you the way to freedom from this spirit of stress in His Word. Anxiety is a product of stress. Proverbs 14:30 says, "A calm and undisturbed mind and heart are the life and health of the body" (Amplified Bible). Why is your heart so restless and anxious? Not on account of the amount of work you have to do, and not because your problems are so great, but because you are not trusting the Lord. Inner restlessness is lack of faith. But you can have an undisturbed mind and heart in the midst of a stressful world if your heart is resting in Jesus.

13 JULY

"For other foundation can no man lay than that is laid, which is Jesus Christ" (1 Corinthians 3:11).

Who can fathom the depths of the humiliation of Jesus? No matter how deeply you have been humbled or how profound your humiliation, when you reach rock bottom, you will realize that Jesus sank far deeper. In Bethlehem and on Calvary we see the stripping of His power, "God was manifest in the flesh" (1 Timothy 3:16).

Jesus Christ was not created; He is the Creator. He was not a man, but God. Only when we grasp the stripping of the power of Jesus in our spirit do we begin to grasp the mystery of His victory. Calvary, where He was completely stripped of His power and crucified in weakness, was the place where His power was revealed most gloriously. On Calvary, in greatest helplessness, He brought us the greatest help. There, completely overcome by His enemies, He won the greatest victory. Behold, the Lamb, stripped of His power! Jesus alone is now the source of our power.

14 JULY

"He humbled himself, and became obedient unto death, even the death of the cross. Wherefore God also hath highly exalted him, and given him a name which is above every name" (Philippians 2:8-9).

At Bethlehem and at Calvary we see Jesus stripped of His glory. There is no majesty and no radiance visible in the child in the manger in that stable. He, at whose Word the universe trembles; He, who from eternity was worshiped and adored by innumerable heavenly beings, "humbled himself." But it is here that the Lord causes us to bow our knees before Him in the dust. How great is He who was stripped of His outer majesty! We can only worship Him with all our hearts, because we recognize in the stripping off of His glory and majesty His innermost, hitherto veiled, nature. When Jesus says, "I am," He is revealing to us His inner majesty, "...despising the shame" (Hebrews 12:2). Do you see this casting off of His glory? He hangs there on the bloodstained cross, not only in inconceivable pain, but openly put to shame—a terrible shame! But see how, in the willing surrender of His glory, an indescribable radiance emanates from Him, the crucified One. He did it for you. He descended from utmost splendor to the depths of shame so that you and I could attain to eternal glory.

15 JULY

"Who did not sin, neither was guile found in his mouth: who, when he was reviled, reviled not again; when he suffered, he threatened not; but committed himself to him that judgeth righteously" (1 Peter 2:22-23).

On Calvary's cross the most inconceivable and complete humbling took place—the depths of which we may never fathom—when the sins of all men and women of all time were laid upon Him. This did not take place theoretically or symbolically, but was a terrible, shocking reality. The punishment for all our sins was laid upon Him, the sinless One. Here we see the One with no rights as the perfect righteousness of God for us. What a wonderful mystery! But ever more glorious perspectives open up to us. By seeing the world-embracing and eternal consequences of blessing by His humbling, the Holy Spirit moves us to follow the Lamb. Grasp it, child of God. When the Lord says to you, "Thou shalt be a blessing" (Genesis 12:2), this means, accept the humbling as Jesus did, so you too can testify, "As unknown, and yet well known; as dying, and, behold, we live; as chastened, and not killed; as sorrowful, yet always rejoicing; as poor, yet making many rich; as having nothing, and yet possessing all things" (2 Corinthians 6:9-10).

16 JULY

"Turn ye unto me, saith the Lord of hosts, and I will turn unto you, saith the Lord of hosts" (Zechariah 1:3).

There is a tragic, fateful turning point in the lives of many Christians when they turn away from the best that God wants to give them. Solomon turned around on the path of obedience to the Lord, and the Lord took the kingdom from him. Hymenaeus and Alexander turned away from the path of living faith, became blasphemers and were delivered unto Satan. The Church of Jesus Christ is in great danger of turning away from the way of the Lamb, for she is leaving her first love; if she does not repent, her candlestick will be removed. The Lord calls urgently and continuously to us to turn around. He does it gently and fervently, "Turn ye unto him from whom the children of Israel have deeply revolted" (Isaiah 31:6). He does it lamenting, "My people are bent to backsliding [turning] from me: though they called them to the most High, none at all would exalt him" (Hosea 11:7). He calls forgivingly, "I have blotted out, as a thick cloud, thy transgressions, and, as a cloud, thy sins: return unto me; for I have redeemed thee" (Isaiah 44:22). He also calls promisingly, "Turn ye unto me...and I will turn unto you" (Zechariah 1:3). Remember, your prayers asking Him to turn to you only make sense if you are willing to turn to Him.

17 JULY

"And it came to pass, when Moses came down from mount Sinai with the two tables of testimony in Moses' hand, when he came down from the mount, that Moses wist not that the skin of his face shone while he talked with him" (Exodus 34:29).

Unconscious holiness is something wonderful. It is the breakthrough of the shining of the glory of God in the life of a person. It is radiated unconsciously, because it is a work of the Holy Spirit and not the product of religious camouflage of the ego. What is the goal of your sanctification? Moses' goal was the Lord. Living in His presence, he reflected the glory of God. His face shone because he remained consistently in the presence of God, "And he was there with the Lord forty days and forty nights" (Exodus 34:28). We could praise Moses and say, that man really took the time to have fellowship with the Lord! But I am much more amazed at how much time the Lord takes to reveal His glory and His thoughts to the individual, as He did to Moses. Moses surely had reason to be tense and say, "I don't have time; thousands of people are waiting for me." But he persevered in the presence of the Lord. Do likewise.

18 JULY

"Yet now, if thou wilt forgive their sin——; and if not, blot me, I pray thee, out of thy book which thou hast written" (Exodus 32:32).

Moses' face shone because, among other things, he had spoken with the Lord. What did Moses say to the Lord? He had reason enough to lament how weak he was and how much he needed the power and help of the Lord for his task. But we do not hear anything of this. His prayer was not about himself. On the contrary, he was prepared to be blotted out of the Lord's book. As the mediator of the people, he is a pointer to our great Mediator, Jesus Christ. Moses had been redeemed from the circle of influence of his own interests and his own life. He was only zealous where the glory of the Lord was concerned, which was infinitely more important than anything else. But much more than this, Moses reflected the glory of God because the Lord had spoken to him. He showed him the way through the blood of the substitute, the way that leads the sinner to the heart of God. God revealed to him the sacrifice and the priest. Not in vain does the Lord speak so much of this, for from eternity God the Father planned in His immeasurably great love salvation through His Son, Jesus Christ. He was sacrifice and priest simultaneously. We perceive here something of the longing of the Lord to impart to man this wonderful mystery of redemption, which the angels longed to see (1 Peter 1:12).

19 JULY

"For by him were all things created, that are in heaven, and that are in earth, visible and invisible, whether they be thrones, or dominions, or principalities, or powers: all thing were created by him, and for him"
(Colossians 1:16).

Throughout the Old Testament, the will of God to reveal His Son as Redeemer breaks through. But Moses was surely the first man to whom the Lord could reveal His highest aim down to the last detail, namely the sacrifice of His beloved Son. It is deeply moving when the Lord speaks of the "blood of my sacrifice" in Exodus 34:25. Oh, that we might grasp what God's highest interest in us is! It is exactly the same as it was with Moses at that time. God wants to reveal the Lamb in and through us. This was the glory that Moses reflected. Jesus was the Lamb, the temple, the way, the sacrifice and the priest simultaneously. "The glory of God did lighten it, and the Lamb is the light thereof" (Revelation 21:23). God's highest interest is the revelation of the Lord Jesus Christ. Christ is all in all, in creation as also in the individual person. God created man in His own image, "...to be conformed to the image of his Son" (Romans 8:29).

20 JULY

"I press toward the mark for the prize of the high calling of God in Christ Jesus" (Philippians 3:14).

*C*onsistent faithfulness in pursuing the goal is what is needed. Have you let yourself be distracted from the goal the Lord has set for you? How urgently the letter to the Hebrews warns us, not to lose sight of the goal, "We must pay more careful attention, therefore, to what we have heard, so that we do not drift away" (Hebrews 2:1, NIV). Our goal is always Jesus! We should become more like Him, more and more united with Him, and more and more filled with Him. How can this take place? Through prayer, sanctification...treading the path of the Lamb. Especially now in our day this applies to us: keep the goal in sight! Let Him cleanse you of all material and selfish goals. Have you gotten lost in a side street of sin? Then you cannot see the goal clearly. If you have somehow become distracted from the goal, go back to where you left the straight and narrow way. Go to the cross, to the crucified One. The night of judgment is coming over our generation. A paralyzing darkness of futility and purposelessness has come over man. Blessed are those who have chosen Jesus as their goal! The Lord is coming again!

21 JULY

"And the same day, when the even was come, he saith unto them, Let us pass over unto the other side" (Mark 4:35).

While other ships were around them at first, ultimately the disciples were alone—alone with Jesus. There arose a great storm. Prophetically speaking, this storm is a picture of the storms of the end times in which children of God find themselves today. The disciples experienced these dangerous hours between the proclamation and the revelation of the kingdom of God. Only in Mark 5, on "the other side of the sea," do we see the revelation of this kingdom, when legions of spirits had to disappear like lightning at the approach of Jesus. What a wonderful picture! We still have the commission of proclaiming the kingdom of God and the return of Jesus. He will set up His kingdom of peace: soon it will be revealed. The powers of darkness to which millions of people are chained will disappear like lightning when He comes. I believe we are in an intermediate period between these times today. We are still calling, "Jesus is coming!"— but He has not yet come. Instead, the waves are growing higher, and the ship of the Church is in trouble. Blessed are those who know the presence of Jesus Christ in all the storms.

22 JULY

"And he was in the hinder part of the ship, asleep on a pillow; and they awake him, and say unto him, Master, carest thou not that we perish?"
(Mark 4:38).

This storm is a clear picture of the storm that rages in the life of each and every believer, between what we hear and what we believe. The way from theory of victory to practical experience of it is called faith, even during a stormy journey. But remember, child of God, that the storm only arises once Jesus is on board. It is because He is on board that this terrifying storm occurs! On the other hand, however, He is the guarantee that we will not perish.

There are negative and positive storms. Often it is the wrath of Satan which shakes us inwardly and outwardly, but it can also come from God, who is testing us to see if we cling to Him in faith. The storm that the disciples experienced here brought them into a desperate situation, because the waves not only beat against the ship but entered it, "...and the waves beat into the ship." It is a great trial when the waves begin to beat around us, but when the "ship," our innermost being, is affected, it becomes dark. Jesus is especially near to you in such situations. It says, "He was in the hinder part of the ship, asleep on a pillow."

23 JULY

*"He is despised and rejected of men; a man of sorrows, and acquainted
with grief: and we hid as it were our faces from him"
(Isaiah 53:3).*

When we consider the life of Jesus, we see how He decisively rejected the path of success. His miracles were blessings, but He warned some of the blessed not to tell anyone, so that the blessing did not turn into success. Blessing is divine; success is human. Blessing remains, success passes. Have you had success in your business life? Have you been able to accumulate riches, have you built houses, and yet you found that your heart was still empty? That is because you had success but not blessing. Were you successful in your moral endeavors? Are you a "good person" who would not harm anyone? Then you are certainly esteemed of men, but not necessarily of God. His Word says that, "All our righteousnesses are as filthy rags." Your righteousness will disappear like snow in the sun, but His righteousness will remain forever. Are you successful or blessed? Is your own righteousness your justification before God, or is Jesus, who shed His blood for you, your righteousness?

24 JULY

God hath chosen the foolish things of the world to confound the wise; and God hath chosen the weak things of the world to confound the things which are mighty"
(1 Corinthians 1:27).

Are you educated? Do you have a university degree? Did your children go to college? Are you proud of that fact? Have education and knowledge made you proud? Perhaps the children whose education you paid for do not want to know about the Gospel. Why not? Because you sought success for them and not blessing; you wanted human glory and not God's glory for them. Are you full of human wisdom but lacking the divine wisdom that transforms the hearts of men? Where can you find this wisdom? The Word of God gives the answer to this question, "The fear of the Lord is the beginning of wisdom: a good understanding have all they that do his commandments" (Psalm 111:10). You will not find this wisdom in books; you cannot study to attain it. No, you can only find this divine blessing instead of human success in the breaking of your old nature at the cross. Only there will you find the eternal wisdom of God in Jesus Christ our Lord.

25 JULY

"We then that are strong ought to bear the infirmities of the weak, and not to please ourselves" (Romans 15:1).

*A*re you spiritually strong, because you have experienced the Lord in a special way, so that your faith and your knowledge surpass that of your brethren? But can you become like Jesus? That must be your goal. Those who really increase in the knowledge of God decrease in their own selves. The genuine nature of your strong faith is proved in your ability to bear with the weak. Jesus said, "Learn of me: for I am meek and lowly in heart" (Matthew 11:29). Jesus was not proud of His humility. Humility and not self-pride was the essence of His being. How is it with you? Is your self-satisfied nature covered by a thin layer of false humility? How can you become like Jesus? Only through the Word of God. This eternally valid Word is written down for us so that we can learn from it. Here we learn about the patience and perseverance of the Lord Jesus. He lived in and from the Word. Are you seeking patience and consolation in your afflictions? Here is the source—the written Word of God.

26 JULY

"That ye may with one mind and one mouth glorify God, even the Father of our Lord Jesus Christ" (Romans 15:6).

This is the secret of victorious prayer. Praise is the highest expression of faith. If you cannot praise and give thanks victoriously, it is because you do not believe. Why can't you believe? Jesus gives us the answer, "How can ye believe, which receive honour one of another?" (John 5:44). Notice the words "with one mind," for praise and thanksgiving in unity with others culminates in the breakthrough to a mighty revival. How can this come about? By taking the earnest admonition to heart, "Receive ye one another, as Christ also received us to the glory of God" (Romans 15:7). We have the conclusion before us. You have nothing to be proud of: your strong faith and your blessed experiences are only by the grace of God. Never forget that you are corrupt by nature, but Jesus Christ has received you in this corrupt state. Therefore, receive one another! But don't do it out of politeness, but rather out of the attitude of heart with which Jesus met you. This standard contains all that God requires of us: to receive one another just as Christ received us, through the surrender of His own life!

27 JULY

"When Jesus then lifted up his eyes, and saw a great company come unto him, he saith unto Philip, 'Whence shall we buy bread, that these may eat?'" (John 6:5).

The feeding of the five thousand is simultaneously a demonstration, a portrayal of the worldwide task of the children of God. It is as though the Lord wanted to proclaim His holy will through this wonderful act, "Give ye them to eat" (Matthew 14:16). In the feeding of the five thousand we see three elements:

• The first element is the bread. Through the wonderful multiplication of the bread, we see how Jesus Christ as the Bread of Life is enough for billions of people, for innumerable people. He Himself said in John 10:10, "I am come that they might have life, and that they might have it more abundantly."

• The second element is the hungry, the five thousand. We are reminded of the world's five continents. The whole world is hungry today for the true message of the Gospel.

• The third element consists of the instruments, the disciples, who receive the bread out of Jesus' hands and pass it on, satisfying the hungry people. Only what Jesus has and what Jesus is can satisfy the deepest hunger in the soul of man.

28 JULY

*"Hear my prayer, O Lord, and give ear unto my cry;
hold not thy peace" (Psalm 39:12).*

God's silence in our lives can have various reasons; for instance when, in spite of our prayers, we do not want to accept the whole truth. "But Jesus held his peace" (Matthew 26:63). The high priest, who was questioning Jesus, wanted to believe a lie and not recognize Him as "the truth." They "… sought false witness against Jesus" (verse 59). The trouble with many believers is that they pray to the Lord for help and tell Him how they long to be sanctified, but they are not willing to be obedient to the light the Lord gives them concerning their inner nature. Then the Lord is silent, and His silence is the most profound answer.

Another reason for His silence is when He has nothing more to say. "Then he [Herod] questioned with him [Jesus] in many words; but he answered him nothing" (Luke 23:9). King Herod thought he could have an interesting discussion with Jesus, the King of all kings, but Jesus "…answered him nothing." Why not? Because Herod was not interested in a meeting with Jesus in his heart. Is this the reason that you do not receive an answer? Do you want His miracles or do you want Him? Do you want the help or the Helper?

29 JULY

"I have yet many things to say unto you, but ye cannot bear them now"
(John 16:12).

How the Lord longs to tell us more! How He longs to give us light concerning His intentions in our hearts! But often He has to wait—like here with His disciples. He had things to tell them that only those who had experienced Pentecost could understand with their hearts. He can only impart to us the deepest secrets of His heart according to the measure in which we are filled with the same Spirit. When He washed the feet of His disciples, Peter asked Him, "Lord, dost thou wash my feet?" Jesus answered him, "What I do thou knowest not now; but thou shalt know hereafter" (John 13:6-7). Here is the answer to the question of why there are many things in the Holy Scriptures that you do not understand and cannot grasp. Humble yourself even more! Be emptied of your own nature, so that you can be filled more with the Holy Spirit. Then He can reveal the depths of the Godhead to you, "God hath revealed them unto us by his Spirit: for the Spirit searcheth all things, yea, the deep things of God" (1 Corinthians 2:10).

30 JULY

"At midnight there was a cry made, Behold, the bridegroom cometh; go ye out to meet him" (Matthew 25:6).

We are standing directly before midnight in human history. The Bible is the eternally true Word of the living God. It is the history book of the future. This is why it reveals what has to happen before Jesus Christ comes to set up His kingdom of peace on this earth. Why can we say that it is midnight in human history? Because the signs of the end times are being fulfilled. The perplexity of the world's governments is compounding. Everywhere there is an increasing, paralyzing fear among the people. Millions are being diagnosed with various heart problems or nervous disorders. They are gripped by the spirit of our time and uncertainty where the future is concerned. This is black and menacing. Mankind can cause tremendous destruction with technology such as atomic bombs. Tension is increasing. What can we do? Where can we turn? There is one answer. Only Jesus can help! He will soon return in great power and glory. His kingdom will be a kingdom of peace and righteousness. God's plan of salvation is coming to its goal. But He is calling to you now, "Come unto me, all ye that labour and are heavy laden, and I will give you rest" (Matthew 11:28).

31 JULY

"Yea, let God be true, but every man a liar" (Romans 3:4).

*T*his is a hard saying! When a child is born, we say that it sees "the light of day." In reality, however, this child only sees the world's light. The light that comes from man is a false light. Only those who live in Jesus Christ have "the light" and are themselves lights of the world. Then deception is impossible. When we drive a car at night, we see the white pavement markers at the side of the road, but they are not lights; they are only the reflection. Those lights shine only so long as the car's headlights shine on them. It is strange but also shocking that many believers are only lights when they are illuminated by others. This is the cause of the shipwreck of so many who believe and yet continually fall and backslide. Where does this come from? It is because they do not have a real, vital relationship with the Lord Jesus Christ. If you have to live from the experiences of other believers, it will remain dark within you. Is this your trouble? Then look to Jesus: let His light shine through you when you have put your trust in Him personally.

Spiritual
Strength
FOR EACH DAY

AUGUST

1 AUGUST

"Likewise the Spirit also helpeth our infirmities: for we know not what we should pray for as we ought: but the Spirit itself maketh intercession for us with groanings which cannot be uttered" (Romans 8:26).

Just as a person is only alive if he is breathing, a person only has spiritual life if he is praying. Prayer is an expression of divine life. It is the indispensable connection with the living God. Do you pray? I do not mean the customary prayer before a meal or before you go to sleep. I do not mean the prayers that you utter when you are in trouble or danger, even if they really come from your heart. I mean prayer in fellowship with other believers. Whether a church is alive and has many born-again believers cannot be told from the number of people who attend the church service on Sunday, but by the number of those who pray in the prayer meeting. Dear reader, have you a spirit of prayer, or are you just religious? If you have been born again, it is not you who prays, but the Spirit of God prays in you. Many believers fail where the holy duty of prayer of the Church is concerned. The unanimous prayers of the Church have particular promises; therefore, Satan's intent for you is not to attend the prayer meetings. Repent over your failure and hasten to the prayer meeting in your church!

2 AUGUST

"Blessed is the man that endureth temptation: for when he is tried, he shall receive the crown of life, which the Lord hath promised to them that love him" (James 1:12).

The hardest battle of a born-again person is prayer. Notice how Satan attempts at all costs and by all means to keep you from praying, because through earnest, persevering prayer, souls are snatched away from him. Beware of the kind of enemies that Satan uses in order to resist you: people. What kind of people? Religious people! When Jesus Christ walked on this earth, it was not the sinners who were His greatest enemies. On the contrary, He was always surrounded by them. His bitterest enemies were the religious people. These were the people who ultimately nailed Him to the cross. It is the same today. You will encounter the most disapproval from "Christians without Christ." I would like to ask these so-called Christians, do you know where you are going? The devil does not mind your armchair Christianity at all. If you do not experience the new birth, that is, if your heart is not renewed, you will one day belong to Satan, the enemy of your souls, forever. Take the words of James in chapter 4:7 to heart, "Submit yourselves therefore to God. Resist the devil, and he will flee from you."

3 AUGUST

"Search the scriptures; for in them ye think ye have eternal life: and they are they which testify of me" (John 5:39).

There are people who say, "I go to church, and that is enough for me." What sort of people are these? Mostly those who are satisfied with a Sunday church service. With such Christians, I often find that their desires, apart from a certain religiosity, go in another direction. A person who has no hunger for the Word of God, even if he calls himself a Christian, should ask himself whether he is born again. All too often such people try to erase the border between the world and discipleship. You may be asking indignantly, "Can't I do anything anymore? Can't I go to the cinema, see a good film, dance?" I would answer, "Go as often as you feel the need for it." But this is the point. The direction in which your appetite leads you is an infallible measure of how much of Jesus you really have. Those who have experienced a true rebirth can no longer go with the world. They are in the world but not of the world. Jesus Christ has become the content and the goal of their whole lives. For this reason, they cast from them all that would hinder them in the pursuit of this goal.

4 AUGUST

"For we wrestle not against flesh and blood, but against principalities, against powers, against the rulers of the darkness of this world, against spiritual wickedness in high places" (Ephesians 6:12).

A child of God is exposed to many trials. The silence of a cemetery is a deathly silence. But where there is life, there will be battles. A person who knows that he is risen with Christ, who is born again, knows simultaneously that he will be severely attacked by Satan. Satan sends enemies to him who mock his faith, and also makes trouble for him through his own sinful desires. A nominal Christian does not need to fear these things. He is not dangerous to Satan's kingdom. The true child of God, however, is always on the offensive where the kingdom of darkness is concerned. Ephesians 6 is his suit of armor. He knows that the Lord has left him on this earth to proclaim the redeeming Gospel to other souls that are still bound. And he knows that because his "Yes" to Jesus is active, the "No" of the devil is active toward him. Have you shed tears on account of severe outward and inward trials? This is a good sign! The Lord Jesus said, "In the world ye shall have tribulation; but be of good cheer; I have overcome the world" (John 16:33).

5 AUGUST

"This is the victory that overcometh the world, even our faith"
(1 John 5:4).

The born-again Christian has victory over trials and sin. Victory is the glorious result of the sacrifice of Jesus Christ on the cross. When He cried out, "It is finished!" (John 19:30), He had become Victor over Satan, sin and death. All those who are in Christ, those who are born again, are also victors in Jesus. Even if a Christian is tempted and feels his own weakness and impotence, he does not stop there, but gives thanks for the victory of Jesus Christ that has been given him. Does a born-again Christian become such a stronger person? No, he is all the weaker, but Jesus lives in him. "Christ in me" is the guarantee of victory in our daily lives. The new birth is not a theoretical invention, something unreal, but a tremendous, overwhelming event in a person's heart! Jesus Christ, God Himself, takes up residence in our hearts through His Spirit. He Himself overcomes through the born-again person. Therefore, the person who has come to the cross may rejoice, "There is therefore now no condemnation to them which are in Christ Jesus, who walk not after the flesh, but after the Spirit" (Romans 8:1).

6 AUGUST

"And at midnight there was a cry made, Behold, the bridegroom cometh; go ye out to meet him" (Matthew 25:6).

The born-again Christian is waiting with joy and desire for the return of Jesus. We can summarize this glorious fruit of the new birth in three words: salvation, filling, expectation. Salvation from sin, Satan, death and judgment; being filled with the Holy Spirit; and a living expectation of the return of Jesus. We know that the return of Jesus is near. He can come at any moment, for He said, "When these things begin to come to pass, then look up, and lift up your heads; for your redemption draweth nigh" (Luke 21:28). With "these things" the Lord meant the present signs of the times, particularly Israel. We can actually see how born-again Christians all over the world are looking up expectantly and saying in spirit, "Amen. Even so, come, Lord Jesus!" (Revelation 22:20). We are living in a tremendous time. Biblical prophecies are being fulfilled before our very eyes. For this reason, we await the Lord at any moment. Are you waiting for Him with joy? Are you ready? "And the Spirit and the bride say, Come. And let him that heareth say, Come" (Revelation 22:17).

7 AUGUST

"Come unto me, all ye that labour and are heavy laden, and I will give you rest" (Matthew 11:28).

To whom shall we come? To Jesus! This means that we should accept His invitation, which is valid up to the present day, "Come unto me!" You may ask, "Does that apply to me?" Yes, for He also said, "Him that cometh to me I will in no wise cast out" (John 6:37). Jesus not only invites you to come to Him, but He also comes to you! When Jesus once walked by the pool of Bethesda, He saw a paralyzed man who had been lying there in despair for 38 years, and Jesus asked him, "Wilt thou be made whole?" (John 5:6). The man replied in his resignation, "Sir, I have no man..." (verse 7), whereupon Jesus gave him the wonderful answer that liberated him from his despair, "Rise, take up thy bed, and walk" (verse 8). Why did Jesus ask this man whether he wanted to be made well? Because He, the Son of God, never said a word too many or too few, this must have had a definite, profound reason. The body of this man had been paralyzed for so long because his spirit was contaminated by sin. How do I know that? I know it from Jesus' statement that He made afterwards in the temple to the man he had healed, "Behold, thou art made whole: sin no more, lest a worse thing come unto thee" (verse 14).

8 AUGUST

"Verily, verily, I say unto you,
He that believeth on me hath everlasting life" (John 6:47).

There have only been three people on earth who were perfectly healthy in body, soul and spirit: Adam and Eve before the fall of man, and Jesus. The first two people were perfect, without sin, until Satan deceived them. Jesus never sinned. He never hurt anyone through words or deeds. As He possessed a complete "No" to sin, He was not contaminated by the sins of the people around Him. Jesus was never a channel for sin but a terminus. He was apart from sin and did not participate in any doubtful things, yet He ate and drank with sinners, touched them with His blessed hands and healed many sick. Jesus, the Son of God, became a man like you and I. He was made like us in all things. He was tempted as we are, but in contrast to us, He never sinned. Jesus could say, "He that hath seen me hath seen the Father" (John 14:9). Whoever receives Jesus in faith is changed back into the image of God, because he is transformed into the image of Jesus. This is God's plan and goal with you!

9 AUGUST

"For he hath made him to be sin for us, who knew no sin;
that we might be made the righteousness of God in him"
(2 Corinthians 5:21).

I am sure that among my readers there are those whose hearts are filled with hopelessness and desperation, and they do not know where to go with it. Do you belong to these hopeless and desperate people? The Lord Jesus is standing before you and asking you, "Wilt thou be made whole?" (John 5:6). If you say "Yes" to Him, He will give you His life, and you can bring Him your sinful life in exchange for it. Then the corrupting pride in you, your self-admiration, will be cast out, and the good things to which you attached no value will be planted in you. How is such an exchange possible? Through the fact that Jesus carried away the sins of the world on Calvary's cross. I can well imagine that you are saying, "Yes, I want to be free of my desperation. I want to be like Jesus." Yet, I have to say to you, think it over! To be like Jesus requires a total surrender of yourself to Him. You can only attain to this high goal when you give Him your life completely.

10 AUGUST

"To this end was I born, and for this cause came I into the world, that I should bear witness unto the truth.
Every one that is of the truth heareth my voice" (John 18:37).

*Y*ou can be fully healed through the absolute love of the truth. Somewhere I read the statement, "Only God is objective." This is true. Only He is the truth. Many people, however, resist the real truth. Through their untruthful, sick nature, they are quick to misjudge others. Do you want to be healed of this illness? Are you willing from this moment on to speak nothing but the truth to God and your fellow men? The Lord Jesus could rightly say of Himself, "I am...the truth" (John 14:6). Many people would have little to say if they were only allowed to speak the truth! How many lies have you spread? If you cannot forget an insult, this is because your soul is sick. For the same reason, you hit back if someone dares to tell you the truth. As soon as you have become inwardly well, however, you will be able to forgive everyone who insults you, and will be filled with the love of God for that person. Do you want to be made whole? Then you will become a new person in Jesus Christ. He says, "Behold, I make all things new" (Revelation 21:5).

11 AUGUST

"Seek ye the Lord while he may be found, call ye upon him while he is near" (Isaiah 55:6).

*D*o you want to be healed of your anger, your impurity, your impatience? Do not boast of what you are! Do not be proud of your thriftiness; it is no more than avarice and greed. Do not boast of your career, if it only serves to increase your pride! The Bible says, "...Knowing the judgment of God, that they which commit such things are worthy of death, not only do the same, but have pleasure in them that do them" (Romans 1:32).

If Jesus is saying to you now, "Wilt thou be made whole?" (John 5:6), then answer in the affirmative, not only on account of your condition, but also because He wants you to be ready when He comes. You do not have much time left. Jesus wants to make all things new in you, but you must say "Yes" to Him. This great turning point can take place in your life today. Perhaps you have been disappointed by those around you. Maybe people have let you down. They are all seeking their own good. But Jesus never lets anyone down. He says to those who receive Him in faith, "I am with you always" (Matthew 28:20). Do you want to be healed inwardly? Then I would remind you of the Word of the Lord, "Seek ye the Lord while he may be found; call ye upon him while he is near" (Isaiah 55:6).

12 AUGUST

"Let not your heart be troubled: ye believe in God, believe also in me"
(John 14:1).

*M*illions of people today are subject to fear. There are fears which one person can inflict upon another through wrong words and deeds. Diseases and threatening dangers cause fear. The world political situation and what the future will bring, are also reasons for fear and anxiety. This fear is increased by the media. Most people suffer from indefinable fear. Is this true of you? Do you have fears that completely absorb and consume you? Fear in the morning, fear in the evening, and fear at night? Where does this come from? The definition of this fear is unforgiven sin. This is the fear that can only be described as unatoned for sin. The Zeitgeist, the spirit of our time, urges us to fear. But there is one Person who has overcome the world and therefore all fear— Jesus, who repeatedly said, "Fear not!" By this statement He is inviting you to come to Him now with all your fears. Come to the light, to Jesus! Confess your guilt to Him and His blood will cleanse you from all sin, so that you can rejoice with the Psalmist, "Thou art my hiding place; thou shalt preserve me from trouble; thou shalt compass me about with songs of deliverance" (Psalm 32:7).

13 AUGUST

"For God so loved the world, that he gave his only begotten Son, that whosoever believeth in him should not perish, but have everlasting life" (John 3:16).

We are living today on this earth as though it were a volcano that could eject its glowing lava masses at any moment. Jesus was referring to our time when He said, "Men's hearts failing them for fear, and for looking after those things which are coming on the earth: for the powers of heaven shall be shaken" (Luke 21:26). People today are ruled by a growing fear of the future. This is why there are so many depressed people. Psychiatrists are busier than ever. Man was created as an element of sinlessness, but has been transformed through "nuclear fission" into an element of sin. Truly, there is nothing new under the sun. There in the Garden of Eden, the first "nuclear fission" took place on a spiritual level. Sin is the dividing element between God and man. But the loving God did not merely leave man in Satan's hand. The sacrificial death of His Son released tremendous renewing energy, so that Paul could write triumphantly to the Christians in Rome, "Where sin abounded, grace did much more abound" (Romans 5:20).

14 AUGUST

"For the life of the flesh is in the blood: and I have given it to you upon the altar to make an atonement for your souls: for it is the blood that maketh an atonement for the soul" (Leviticus 17:11).

The blood of Jesus is the saving element! When He hung on the cross and carried away the sin of the world, the whole universe was affected. This second spiritual "nuclear fission" took place for your and my salvation, however. While the first "nuclear fission" separated mankind from God, at the second the way to reconciliation was paved. The evangelist Matthew tells us that a darkness came over the whole land and that "...the earth did quake, and the rocks rent" (Matthew 27:51). What tremendous powers were released through the death of Jesus—not only in nature, but above all in the spiritual realm! No other power than the blood of Jesus was able to separate you, who were a negative element with sin, death and Satan, from the power of darkness and to unite you with God. God's Son, Jesus Christ, accomplished this saving "nuclear fission" through His death on the cross, by being made to be sin Himself. Why does the blood of Jesus have such great power? Because in His blood Jesus poured out His eternal life. He gave it as an atonement on God's altar.

15 AUGUST

"And it came to pass, when they had brought them forth abroad, that he said, Escape for thy life; look not behind thee, neither stay thou in all the plain; escape to the mountain, lest thou be consumed" (Genesis 19:17).

The main sin of Sodom was devastating immorality: homosexuality, perversity, robbery, murder and greed. In our day we are living as the people lived in Sodom. Governments are losing more and more of their authority, and are becoming more and more helpless where increasing crime is concerned. For Lot at that time the command was, "Escape for thy life!" It is beyond doubt that this message of love was not proclaimed in an indifferent way but in a very earnest one. Lot was privileged by two angels coming to him personally. You are also privileged too, for God is speaking to your heart right now through His Word. Escape for your life; flee to Jesus! God Himself is turning to the people of today, with the very same message. It is because God loves you. So, flee for your life! God says, "I have no pleasure in the death of the wicked; but that the wicked turn from his way and live" (Ezekiel 33:11).

16 AUGUST

*"Knowing this first, that there shall come in the last days scoffers,
walking after their own lusts, and saying,
Where is the promise of his coming?" (2 Peter 3:3-4).*

With prophecy it is often similar to how it is with prayer: exactly the opposite of what we ask for takes place. Instead of being saved from our troubles, they become greater. But true children of God do not let themselves be discouraged. They know that when everything they see and experience contradicts their requests, God's answer is very near. Often the opposite of a certain prophecy takes place first, and the enemies of God mock us. Sanctified children of God, however, know, even see what is taking place in the invisible world, although it is not yet seen in the visible world. An example of this is the prophecy of the prophet Isaiah, that Babel and the glory of the Chaldees will be overturned by God like Sodom and Gomorrah. Or, as the prophet Jeremiah says, that Babel will become a pile of stone and a dwelling place of jackals. This prophecy is still yet to be fulfilled in its finality. But it is coming ever nearer; it is already within the realm of its fulfillment.

17 AUGUST

"We have also a more sure word of prophecy; whereunto ye do well that ye take heed, as unto a light that shineth in a dark place, until the day dawn, and the day star arise in your hearts" (2 Peter 1:19).

*T*o have means that we possess something. The Lord wants to say to us with these words, not that we will receive the prophetic Word, but that we already have it. It is a precious possession that we must take heed of, "as unto a light that shineth in a dark place," and that we should make use of. We are living in the dark night of the end times, "until the day dawn, and the day star arise in your hearts." It moves me deeply that Peter does not say, "until the day star arises in heaven and Jesus comes from the heavenly glory," but "until the day dawn, and the day star arise in your hearts." By this he testifies that the returning Jesus has something to do with our hearts. For this reason, at the moment He comes, a tremendous echo will resound in the hearts of the sanctified children of God. The light of the prophetic Word is all the more necessary because the fulfillment, the realization, of Biblical prophecy is being accelerated in our day. The time is not far off when the Lord will reveal Himself personally before the eyes of the whole world.

18 AUGUST

"And Elisha sent a messenger unto him, saying, Go and wash in Jordan seven times, and thy flesh shall come again to thee, and thou shalt be clean. But Naaman was wroth, and went away..." (2 Kings 5:10-11).

The Jordan is a strange and wonderful river. The leprous man is told to go and wash himself in it. Only there can he be healed of his leprosy. The natural man resists this, of course. The Jordan is a picture of Jesus Christ, the crucified One Himself. Jesus, the One who came from the Father, the sinless One, descended to the lowest depth. He debased Himself and became a cleansing river for all who want to wash themselves in it. The name Jordan means "the descender." In this is a picture of the humiliation of Jesus. He also descended. But through humbling Himself in this way, by descending, He opened up a river that will flow in all eternity. If you follow Jesus into this "Jordan" in His death, then you will also descend. He said, "If any man serve me, let him follow me" (John 12:26). Then it will be for you as with the Jordan, whose waters never dry up. Those who follow the Lamb in going downwards will become more and more deeply humbled. But for this very reason such a person is, according to the Scriptures, "...like a watered garden, and like a spring of water, whose waters fail not" (Isaiah 58:11).

19 AUGUST

"If any man come to me, and hate not his father, and mother, and wife, and children, and brethren, and sisters, yea, and his own life also, he cannot be my disciple" (Luke 14:26).

As we have already seen, the name Jordan means "the descender" or "going down." But it also has a second meaning, namely "divider." The Jordan divided the people of Israel from the wilderness. When Israel passed through the Jordan River, she left her old life behind in the wilderness. This is a picture of the cross. Nothing divides us so radically from our old life in the wilderness as passing through the Jordan of death. That is the sincere confession, "I am crucified with Christ" (Galatians 2:20). Paul testified that he was divided from everything by the cross, "God forbid that I should glory, save in the cross of our Lord Jesus Christ, by whom the world is crucified unto me, and I unto the world" (Galatians 6:14).

Those who do not accept the death of Jesus through consistent separation from all that is of this world, will not be capable of experiencing the fullness of God. It is shocking to see the incapability of many Christians. They stop at the Jordan. Dear reader, pass through the Jordan today; say "yes" to the way of the Lamb, the way of death. Say, "I have decided to follow Jesus...."

20 AUGUST

"Speak unto the children of Israel, and say unto them, When ye are passed over Jordan into the land of Canaan; then ye shall drive out all the inhabitants of the land from before you, and destroy all their pictures, and destroy all their molten images, and quite pluck down all their high places" (Numbers 33:51-52).

The river Jordan represents in a wonderful way the death of the Lord Jesus. We see it here as the only basis for victory over all the power of the enemy. The Lord commanded the children of Israel to drive out all the inhabitants of Canaan and to destroy all their idols. But first He says, "When ye are passed over Jordan...." From this we learn how to overcome: not toward the cross, toward victory, but from His cross, from His accomplished victory! Believe it, child of God, "It is finished!" (John 19:30). If you rest in this finished work, if you are united with Jesus on the cross, then your life of victory will begin, and not the other way around. You do not have to try to gradually be crucified with Him, but set your feet now in faith on this victorious ground. This is exactly what it says in Romans 6:6, "Knowing this, that our old man is crucified with him." Why? Paul continues, "...that henceforth we should not serve sin."

21 AUGUST

"And it shall come to pass, that every thing that liveth, which moveth, whithersoever the rivers shall come, shall live" (Ezekiel 47:9).

According to my knowledge, the Jordan is the only river that the triune God used to reveal Himself. We find this in Matthew 3:16-17, "And Jesus [God the Son], when he was baptized, went up straightway out of the water: and, lo, the heavens were opened unto him, and he saw the Spirit of God [God the Holy Spirit] descending like a dove, and lighting upon him: and lo a voice from heaven, saying, This is my beloved Son, in whom I [God the Father] am well pleased." Oh, that you would grasp this today! The triune God concentrates on Calvary: there where the blood of Jesus flowed, there where the death of the Lord Jesus became reality. The holy God only unites with a person who has passed through the "Jordan" with his sins. Those who say "Yes" to Jordan, those who say "Yes" to the death of Jesus, must reckon with great resistance, for the whole of hell will attack him. If you go through the "Jordan" today, if you take the crucified One seriously, then there will be war! But the enemy is overcome. You may rejoice with David, "Though an host should encamp against me, my heart shall not fear: though war should rise against me, in this will I be confident" (Psalm 27:3).

22 AUGUST

"Nay but, O man, who art thou that repliest against God? Shall the thing formed say to him that formed it, 'Why hast thou made me thus?'" (Romans 9:20).

These words tell us that it is presumptuous of us to ask the living God, our Creator, "Why?" There is only one justified "Why?" in the whole of human history, and that was when the Lord Jesus cried out on the cross, "My God, my God, **why** hast thou forsaken me?" (Matthew 27:46). There are mysteries and depths of God which we humans with our finite intellect can never fathom. All eternity will not be sufficient to search out or exhaust His being. As infinite and eternal as He is in His existence, so infinite and eternal He is in the glory of His being. This again means that we can never fully fathom the nature of God. For this very reason, however, the message of the Gospel is so precious. He sent Jesus, our Savior. Jesus said, "He that hath seen me hath seen the Father" in John 14:9. And through Jesus the possibility of victory is given us, "Thanks be to God, which giveth us the victory through our Lord Jesus Christ" (1 Corinthians 15:57).

23 AUGUST

"Redeeming the time . . . " (Ephesians 5:16).

*W*e must continually remind ourselves that time is a precious gift of God. He has given it to us so that we can redeem it. We must give the minutes, hours and days eternal value. If we do not do this and waste precious time, we are unthankful and despise a great gift of God. We must remember that lost time can never be replaced. Every minute that passes by is gone forever; it will never return in all eternity. Through the time that is given us, we have the possibility of working for God. As children of God, we are His coworkers, each one in the place where God has put us. No person on earth gave His time such eternal value as our Lord Jesus. John says at the end of his Gospel, "And there are also many other things which Jesus did, the which, if they should be written every one, I suppose that even the world itself could not contain the books that should be written" (John 21:25). Time is short and the king's business is urgent (cf. 1 Samuel 21:8). Be faithful, therefore, in the use of the brief time that is entrusted to you. Then it will be said to you one day, "Well done, thou good and faithful servant: thou hast been faithful over a few things, I will make thee ruler over many things: enter thou into the joy of thy lord" (Matthew 25:21).

24 AUGUST

"Abide in me, and I in you. As the branch cannot bear fruit of itself,
except it abide in the vine; no more can ye, except ye abide in me"
(John 15:4).

There is a saying which is also applicable to spiritual history, and that is "History repeats itself." That which Israel experienced in olden days, is taking place again today, though spiritually. Israel lived for over 400 years under foreign rule in Egypt. Then the Israelites were led, through the blood of a lamb, with a mighty hand out of Egypt through the Red Sea, "as by dry land" (Hebrews 11:29). Then they entered into the wilderness. There it became dark around them, because they had withdrawn themselves from the lordship of God over them. This was so at that time, and it is so today. I look at Israel as in the desert on their way to the Promised Land. Now read what Jesus says to us, "He that abideth in me, and I in him, the same bringeth forth much fruit: for without me ye can do nothing" (John 15:5). What did the Lord mean by this? Many people do much without Jesus. We can also do many things without Him, but if we do not live under the lordship of Jesus Christ, if we do not remain in Jesus in all that we do, and have no true fellowship with Him, it is all in vain. The greatest absurdity is a life without fellowship with Jesus.

25 AUGUST

"For he will finish the work, and cut it short in righteousness: because a short work will the Lord make upon the earth" (Romans 9:28).

We are already living in this period of "cutting short." We can see it with our own eyes and we can hear it with our own ears, for not a day goes by without some kind of catastrophe taking place. Why? Because man, in his presumption, has turned the sword against God. Almost everywhere we meet with degeneration today, an overturning of all values, whether it be in the field of music, art or morals. Faith in Christ has been undermined, and in its place we have self-life. This will all increase, up to the sudden return of the Lord. When we read in the last book of the Bible, we see clearly that the time is no longer far off when the Lord will reveal Himself personally, before the eyes of the whole world: "Behold, he cometh with clouds; and every eye shall see him…" (Revelation 1:7). The world has no more intervals. We see this daily. If you look at temporal values, your financial situation, and compare your salary with the world, you are on the wrong path. Turn your eyes away from the world and turn them consciously on Jesus. Do it now and you will hear His voice anew saying, "Follow me!"

26 AUGUST

"Behold, I give unto you power to tread on serpents and scorpions, and over all the power of the enemy: and nothing shall by any means hurt you"
(Luke 10:19).

With these words, the Lord gave His own unlimited authority over the whole destructive power of the enemy. We must be conscious of the fact that Satan's activity is a reality. The ignorance of a believer will not protect him from attacks; on the contrary, the enemy seeks the ignorant. The watchful, however, those who abide in the Lord, are untouchable. Therefore, the Lord reminds us so often that we should watch and pray, so that we do not come into temptation. Paul says, "We are not ignorant of his devices," when speaking of the devil. The enemy does indeed employ all his power against us. But when we stay close to Him, we can experience the whole victorious power of Jesus, for the Lord says to us, "I give unto you power…over all the power of the enemy." As seen globally, we are experiencing today an onslaught from hell, an invasion of spirits out of the abyss. Children of God are at the top of the enemy's blacklist, but they are the only ones who have the whole victory!

27 AUGUST

"Because I will publish the name of the Lord: ascribe ye greatness unto our God. He is the Rock" (Deuteronomy 32:3-4).

*M*oses, who had experienced the Lord as a safe refuge in many severe trials and temptations, testified to the people of Israel at the end of his life, "He is the Rock." Throughout the Bible, Jesus Christ reveals Himself as the "Rock of Ages," as the safe refuge. Do you believe that He is also your Rock? Or do you pass Christ by, the safe refuge for everyone, at this time when the need for safety and security is growing? We all have a desire for safety, security, protection and peace. And we seek it, but often not where we can find everything in abundance, namely in the one eternal Rock: Jesus Christ. What ground have you built your life upon? The foundation on which we stand determines victory or defeat in our daily lives, and is decisive for eternity. We are not anything in ourselves, but the Rock on which we stand is significant. Set your feet upon this "Rock of Ages"! Found your life anew or for the first time on Jesus Christ, the eternal Rock. Call upon Him with all your heart and pray, "Let me hide myself in Thee!" And He will do it, for God hears an earnest prayer.

28 AUGUST

"For the word of God is quick, and powerful, and sharper than any twoedged sword, piercing even to the dividing asunder of soul and spirit, and of the joints and marrow, and is a discerner of the thoughts and intents of the heart" (*Hebrews* 4:12).

The soul is the organ with which we feel emotion and grasp and deal with earthly things. The danger is great that we let ourselves be led by our emotions, and here the enemy finds a foothold. He clouds our view of Jesus. The confusing of the emotional and the spiritual means to confuse what is temporal with what is eternal. This confusion opens the door for the enemy in the life of a believer. It is easy for Satan to use sheer emotions or even wishes so that you think the Lord has said this or that to you. You may belong to the category of people who are so quick to say, "The Lord told me," but it proves not to be true in the long run. You can have power over all the power of the enemy only through the Word of God! Obey the Word and let the Word judge you, so that the emotional and the spiritual are divided in you. You must become a spiritual person. Then you will see clearly again. Then your spirit will be led by the Spirit of God on a straight path, and the "up in the clouds" to "down in the dumps" will cease. Your heart will be rooted in Jesus. This takes place through grace.

29 AUGUST

"I am crucified with Christ: nevertheless I live; yet not I, but Christ liveth in me" (Galatians 2:20).

A disfigured soul has a disfigured character. This is the sad picture of a believer over whom the enemy has power. Because such a person is negative emotionally, he has many troubles. He gets annoyed over this and that; he is offended by everything, just not about himself. Nothing seems to help, so finally he creeps back into his shell to sulk...and the whole of hell breaks out in laughter. Why? Because he was another one whom the Lord could have used wonderfully. But he is now paralyzed by the enemy. Such people are often very gifted people, who have good prospects of doing something in the kingdom of God to the glory of His grace. But there is no room in their hearts for others. The more this emotional character is disfigured, the smaller your radius of action will be. Go back to the starting point, therefore. This means, go back to being crucified with Christ. Those who take the words of Jesus seriously, "Behold, I give unto you power...over all the power of the enemy" (Luke 10:19), will also have victory in other spheres.

30 AUGUST

"Who is among you that feareth the Lord, that obeyeth the voice of his servant, that walketh in darkness, and hath no light? Let him trust in the name of the Lord, and stay upon his God" (Isaiah 50:10).

Our spiritual trials and temptations are very deep and severe. To have victory in them, we first need victory over our emotions. The human spirit is the seat of the Spirit of God. Our spirit grasps what is eternal. This is why it is the goal of the enemy to lead our spirit into darkness. The Lord allows these trials so that we can claim the authority of the victory of Jesus, "Behold, I give unto you power...over all the power of the enemy" (Luke 10:19). What can we do in practical terms when our spirit is led through unimagined depths of darkest night? Trust in the Lord—even when we feel nothing! When we receive no answer from above, when everything seems closed to us and we are led through an inner night, let us do what Isaiah said, "Trust in the name of the Lord, and stay upon [our] God." When we cling to the Lord, we come into the victorious attitude of Job, who cried, "I know that my Redeemer liveth!" (Job 19:25).

31 AUGUST

"And every man that hath this hope in him purifieth himself,
even as he is pure" (1 John 3:3).

The hope we have in Him necessitates an ever deeper purification. The person of Jesus, to whom we come ever nearer, obliges us to seek ever deeper cleansing. What does this mean in practical terms? The answer is, according to the decrease of the distance between Him and us timewise, we should become increasingly like Him. Why? Because it is the result of our progressive sanctification, "We shall be like him; for we shall see him as he is" (1 John 3:2). Now my earnest question to you is, is your spiritual life drawing nearer to the Lord in light of the fact that timewise we are drawing nearer? Is your heart becoming more and more fervent, more mild, more like Jesus? How is this progressive sanctification expressed? In the increase of the characteristics of Jesus in our nature. The clearer we see the goal and the nearer we come to Jesus, the more we will be able to hope in Him alone completely. This concentration on His person gives us ever stronger confidence, and our hope will become alive. Hope is an expression of faith.

Spiritual Strength
FOR EACH DAY

SEPTEMBER

1 SEPTEMBER

"...But ye are washed, but ye are sanctified, but ye are justified in the name of the Lord Jesus, and by the Spirit of our God"
(1 Corinthians 6:11).

A person who has received Jesus has become spotless and justified before Him; that's a fact. But the same Paul who wrote the above words also exclaims, "For I know that in me (that is, in my flesh,) dwelleth no good thing" (Romans 7:18). Is this a contradiction? No! Note the reason in 2 Corinthians 4:7, "...that the excellency of the power may be of God, and not of us." As children of God, we live continually in this conflict. On the one hand, we are confronted daily with the fact that there is no good in us. On the other hand, we have the excellency of the power of God at our disposal. How does this power of God become effectual in our lives? Through the obedience of faith! The more we are tried, and the more we claim His victory through faith, i.e. the obedience of faith, the more the Lord is praised and glorified. How could we prove the reality of the victory of Jesus otherwise, if the presence of sin was taken away? Now, however, we may rejoice in spite of our sinful flesh, in the face of the enemy, "Thanks be to God, which giveth us the victory through our Lord Jesus Christ" (1 Corinthians 15:57).

2 SEPTEMBER

*"Wherefore in all things it behoved him to be made like unto his brethren,
that he might be a merciful and faithful high priest in things pertaining to
God, to make reconciliation for the sins of the people. For in that he himself hath suffered being tempted, he is able to succour them that are
tempted"* (*Hebrews 2:17-18*).

Many people are seeking help in their desperation today. Some look for help from psychologists and psychiatrists, yet they do not find true help. Why not? Because outward help does not bring inward help. Your trouble is not outward but inward, in your heart, which is why only Jesus can help you. He can help you inwardly because He was made like you and me. He took your sin also upon Himself, "For he hath made him to be sin for us, who knew no sin; that we might be made the righteousness of God in him" (2 Corinthians 5:21). This means that Jesus Christ identified Himself completely with your and my sin, with our corrupt being, on the cross at Calvary.

Are you afraid of death? The Lord Jesus was made one with your fear of death, for when He, the Eternal One, died, He overcame the one who had the power of death, namely the devil. Therefore, only Jesus can help you.

3 SEPTEMBER

"For in that he himself hath suffered being tempted, he is able to succour them that are tempted" (Hebrews 2:18).

*A*re you inwardly discouraged? Only Jesus can help you, for He, the King of all kings, the highest Majesty, became inwardly one with your discouragement. He identified Himself with your fear.

Are you lonely? Only Jesus can help you, because He became one with your loneliness. He was forsaken by His best friends.

Do your find your afflictions too hard to bear? Only Jesus can help you, because He became one with your afflictions. He knows the subtle temptations that afflict you, and He has pity on you, not as an outsider, but as one who suffered more and deeper than you, yet who overcame.

Only Jesus can help you, because He became inwardly one with your shame. There are shameful things in your life, which you would hate to be discovered. But Jesus went to the uttermost and became one with your shame, "…despising the shame, and is set down at the right hand of the throne of God" (Hebrews 12:2).

4 SEPTEMBER

"...Lord, thou knowest all things; thou knowest that I love thee"
(John 21:17).

Jesus helps the disqualified. This means, He helps those who are stuck and feel they are a failure. Peter was just such a disqualified person; he had failed miserably. Before a girl, he denied His Lord with a curse. After the Lord's resurrection, Peter said to the other disciples, "I go a fishing" (John 21:3). We see in this his resignation; he is saying, "It's no use. I've failed in my discipleship!" He felt himself disqualified. But there was no blessing on his former occupation, for we read at the end of the same verse, "...and that night they caught nothing." Now, he is completely written off. But Jesus helps those who have failed, the disqualified, and in verse 4 we read, "But when the morning was now come, Jesus stood on the shore." We know how He helped Peter. He struck the chord in Peter's heart that made him exclaim, "Lord, thou knowest all things; thou knowest that I love thee." Has everything gone wrong for you in your life? Only Jesus can help you, and He wants to help you now!

5 SEPTEMBER

"Jesus . . . said unto him, Dost thou believe on the Son of God?
He answered and said, Who is he, Lord, that I might believe on him?"
(John 9:35-36).

*J*esus helps those who are not able to see Him, and those who, although they have sought Him, have not yet found Him. I am reminded of the man in the above text who was born blind. We see that he sought Him from the answer he gave Jesus to the question of whether he believed on Him, "Who is he, Lord, that I might believe on him?" What about you who are seeking Jesus? You do not see Him, you have not experienced His help yet, but you have the promise, "He that seeketh findeth" (Matthew 7:8). Only Jesus can help you! When the man who was born blind finds Jesus, the cause of his blindness is revealed by Jesus in a shocking way, "When he had thus spoken, he spat on the ground, and made clay of the spittle, and he anointed the eyes of the blind man with the clay, and said unto him, Go, wash in the pool of Siloam, (which is by interpretation, Sent.) He went his way therefore, and washed, and came seeing" (John 9:6-7). Here cause and effect, dirt and blindness, are brought together. The cause of your inner blindness is the dirt of sin in you. Only Jesus can help you! Let Him convict you of your impurity, like the man who was born blind, and be willing to do something about the root of all impurity.

6 SEPTEMBER

"Finally, my brethren, be strong in the Lord, and in the power of his might. Put on the whole armour of God, that ye may be able to stand against the wiles of the devil. For we wrestle not against flesh and blood, but against principalities, against powers, against the rulers of the darkness of this world, against spiritual wickedness in high places" (Ephesians 6:10-12).

We are told to "fight the good fight of faith" in 1 Timothy 6:12. Do not imagine, however, that it is *our* faith through which we fight; it is the faith of our Lord Jesus. Paul says this quite clearly in Galatians 2:20, "The life which I now live in the flesh I live by the faith of the Son of God." Jesus Christ is God's unspeakable gift to us, and in Him and through Him God has given us faith, His faith. The Scriptures testify of Him that He is the Author and Finisher of faith. For this reason, nobody can be proud of his or her strong faith, but those who glory should glory in the fact that they know the Lord. So thank God that in His unfathomable grace He has given you Jesus, and with Him all things. Those who have received Jesus may rejoice with Paul, "How shall he not with him also freely give us all things?" (Romans 8:32).

7 SEPTEMBER

"Thanks be to God, which giveth us the victory through our Lord Jesus Christ" (1 Corinthians 15:57).

What is the strategy of the battle of faith that we have to fight? It is not ours directly, but it is the battle of the highest Captain. And our Captain is Jesus Christ, as it is written in Exodus 15:3, "The Lord is a man of war: the Lord is his name." The question arises here, are we at war, then? Yes, as believers we are engaged in a war between life and death. The ignorance of many children of God where this is concerned is shocking. Let us remember, however, discipleship means involvement in the most severe and simultaneously most victorious war service. Many children of God do not recognize, however, that this war, this battle, is what they are appointed to. The Word of God says clearly that we are to "fight the good fight of faith" in 1 Timothy 6:12. Discipleship is not a war game but a serious battle. We are concerned with invisible, yet real and strong enemies who seek our downfall, but Jesus is Victor!

8 SEPTEMBER

"Wherefore lift up the hands which hang down, and the feeble knees; and make straight paths for your feet, lest that which is lame be turned out of the way; but let it rather be healed" (Hebrews 12:12-13).

*T*he strategy of the battle of faith is concerned with the execution of individual orders of the captain: march, reconnaissance, safety and shelter. As children of God, we must never retreat, but always go forwards. We cannot afford any cease-fire; we must continually hold up the banner. Reconnaissance means to recognize the intentions of the enemy. Why? "Lest Satan should get an advantage of us: for we are not ignorant of his devices" (2 Corinthians 2:11). Only those who have surrendered unconditionally to Jesus Christ can be His warriors, "...I was not rebellious, neither turned away back" (Isaiah 50:5). Those who, like Paul, however, walk with Jesus in absolute obedience, also recognize the reality and the tactics of the enemy. This is what Paul meant when he said, "We are not ignorant of his devices." Paul knew the subtlety of the enemy, but he also knew of the victory of Jesus. This is why he overcame in the fight of faith, and at the end of his life he could look back and testify, "I have fought a good fight, I have finished my course, I have kept the faith" (2 Timothy 4:7).

9 SEPTEMBER

"And no marvel; for Satan himself is transformed into an angel of light"
(2 Corinthians 11:14).

The Lamb of God conquered Satan on Calvary's cross. Not by might, nor by power, but by His Spirit, through His nature (cf. Zechariah 4:6). This is the strategy of Jesus Christ.

The most frequently employed tactic of the enemy is cunning camouflage. He pretends to be an angel of light, and so he is able to sit today in the midst of the Church of Jesus Christ. He wants to do away with the cross. Believers today act the same as the children of the world, and children of the world often look like "believers." There seems to be no difference between them. What tactics should we use to confront the enemy and avoid this trap? Do the opposite: instead of camouflage and lies, use truth! Let us consider here the divine armor: "Stand therefore, having your loins girt about with truth, and having on the breastplate of righteousness" (Ephesians 6:14). The truth always exposes lies. If we confront our opponent in disguise, that is, insincerely, our confession of the Lord has no effect, because our hearts are lying. This is the terrible spirit of disguise in the Church: sins are covered, camouflaged and the enmity of the cross is wrapped in a pious covering. But when you follow truth, you will experience Jesus as the Victor; then truth will be victorious. Gird your loins with truth!

10 SEPTEMBER

"And lest I should be exalted above measure through the abundance of the revelations, there was given to me a thorn in the flesh, the messenger of Satan to buffet me, lest I should be exalted above measure"
(2 Corinthians 12:7).

Another of Satan's hostile tactics is the frontal attack on the body, soul and spirit of children of God. That is war on all fronts. Paul knew this, as a servant of the Lord. The chronic satanic attack on his body also affected his spirit and his soul. What counter-tactics do we have to employ when the enemy attacks us frontally? How can we stand still? Our counter-tactics must be that we in no way launch a counter-attack, but that we seek counsel with our highest Authority, Jesus Christ. This is just what Paul did. When he saw others oppressed by Satan's servants, he commanded them to depart in the name of Jesus. When he was himself attacked, however, he turned to the Lord, "For this thing I besought the Lord thrice, that it might depart from me" (verse 8). And then the Lord Jesus Christ, the greatest Strategist, did a miraculous thing: He opened up new sources of grace to His servant and said, "My grace is sufficient for thee: for my strength is made perfect in weakness" (verse 9). In this way the devil's tactics rebounded off of Paul.

11 SEPTEMBER

"For the weapons of our warfare are not carnal, but mighty through God to the pulling down of strong holds" (2 Corinthians 10:4).

*E*verything depends on which direction we are looking! Joshua had the discouraging picture of Jericho before his eyes, but he directed his eyes upwards, "And it came to pass, when Joshua was by Jericho, that he lifted up his eyes and looked, and, behold, there stood a man over against him with his sword drawn in his hand" (Joshua 5:13). Through this meeting with the Victor, Joshua was victorious over Jericho. This was a pure victory of faith. The tactic of the people of Israel was only that they followed the strategy of God. The warfare of God was and is completely illogical for the human intellect. Israel did not wage war against Jericho, but simply surrounded the enemy through the presence of the Lord, for they bore the Ark of the Covenant in their midst. The prayerful surrounding of the enemy with the presence of the Lord made the power of the enemy collapse. From God's perspective, victory had already taken place. The presence of God was enough for victory at that time, and it is enough today! This is the secret of our heavenly Strategist: it is already finished! The victory is ours, and this assurance makes us strong in the fight of faith.

12 SEPTEMBER

"Be sober, be vigilant; because your adversary the devil, as a roaring lion, walketh about, seeking whom he may devour: whom resist stedfast in the faith" (1 Peter 5:8-9).

We must see clearly that we are organically one with Israel. This is the reason for the many attacks by the enemy. Israel is the side of God's people that is visible, and the Church is the other side, the inner spiritual side. We have, therefore, the same enemy and the same fight. This means that the enemy who wants to destroy Israel physically and who knows no mercy, also wants to destroy us, as children of God, spiritually. He wants to sow sin in your heart, sinful thoughts. The Scriptures say, "Keep thy heart" in Proverbs 4:23. Let the Word of God remain in your heart! Satan wants to control your thoughts, but think of your supreme Captain and Redeemer, Jesus Christ. The enemy wants to put your tongue to use negatively, but the Word of God admonishes you to be silent, "For he that will love life, and see good days, let him refrain his tongue from evil, and his lips that they speak no guile" (1 Peter 3:10). Many are falling away today, but we want to be on the offensive and claim the victory in the name of Jesus, for there is much land to be possessed, especially in these end times.

13 SEPTEMBER

"Behold the Lamb of God, which taketh away the sin of the world"
(John 1:29).

*W*hoever grasps these words in their whole extent knows the way to eternal life. The Lamb of God is the nucleus of the biblical message. Everywhere in the Bible we meet the Lamb, the perfect Lamb, "And Abraham set seven ewe lambs of the flock by themselves" (Genesis 21:28). Seven is the number of divine completion. The seven lambs of Abraham point to the complete gift of God, His Son, the Lamb of God.

David and the whole community sacrificed one thousand lambs. This is ten times ten times ten. The number ten represents the whole of humanity in the Scriptures. Jesus, the Lamb of God who bore the sins of the whole world, is also the Lamb for the individual sinner. I repeat, He is not only the Lamb of God for the whole world, but also for you who are conscious of your sinfulness and corruption. John the Baptist preached repentance and forgiveness of sins to a great crowd. And in the fullness of time, the day came when he suddenly stopped and pointed to a man in the midst of the listening crowds. All eyes were directed on Him, and John cried out, "Behold the Lamb of God, which taketh away the sin of the world."

14 SEPTEMBER

"He was led as a sheep to the slaughter; and like a lamb dumb before his shearer, so opened he not his mouth" (Acts 8:32).

*J*esus is called a Lamb to reveal His nature to the world. A lamb is a picture of innocence and purity. Jesus is true man in all things, "…but was in all points tempted like as we are, yet without sin" (Hebrews 4:15). We see that He really was a man made of flesh and blood from the revelation of His deep humanity: He shed tears, He was hungry, He was thirsty, He rejoiced, He was tired, He was tempted by Satan—but He did not sin! This is why He is called the Lamb of God. Jesus was pure; thus His blood, and His blood alone, cleanses us from all sin.

He was called the Lamb of God to show us His way. He came into this world with the clear aim of being slaughtered for our sins, "Worthy is the Lamb that was slain…" (Revelation 5:12). He was not taken by surprise by His executioners, but said in holy determination, "For this cause came I unto this hour" (John 12:27). He gave His life voluntarily, and thereby He revealed His nature as a lamb that knows before it is going to be slaughtered.

15 SEPTEMBER

"For though he was crucified through weakness, yet he liveth by the power of God" (2 Corinthians 13:4).

Jesus is also called the Lamb of God to reveal the nature of His victory, for the victory of Jesus is a victory of the Lamb. He won it completely apart from all human efforts, for "He was crucified through weakness." This is why these words are so mighty in their divine contradiction, "Behold the Lamb of God, which taketh away the sin of the world!" The weakest thing of all did the greatest thing of all! We see just how weak Jesus was on His way to Calvary when He collapsed under the burden of His cross. But when He hung on the cross before the amazed and trembling invisible powers of the world, the greatest revelation of power of all times began: the Lamb of God carried away the sins of the world! What power enabled the weak Lamb to bear all the sins of the world? Here is the answer: the world-embracing love of God was behind Him. It does not say, "Behold the Lamb," but "Behold the Lamb of God"! The Lamb is capable, through the power of the love of God, to accomplish what is eternally valid: to carry away the guilt and sin of all men. Those who follow the Lamb will experience the same thing: in the greatest weakness He accomplishes the most difficult. In this light the Word of the Bible, "My strength is made perfect in weakness" (2 Corinthians 12:9) gains greatest significance.

16 SEPTEMBER

"After this I beheld, and, lo, a great multitude, which no man could number, of all nations, and kindreds, and people, and tongues, stood before the throne, and before the Lamb, clothed with white robes, and palms in their hands" (Revelation 7:9).

The last book of the Bible, the Revelation, reveals the glory of the Lamb to us. There we see the position of the Lamb before God. The throne of God is seldom mentioned without the Lamb. We read in Revelation 7:10, "And cried with a loud voice, saying, Salvation to our God which sitteth upon the throne, and unto the Lamb." And in Revelation 22:1, "And he shewed me a pure river of water of life, clear as crystal, proceeding out of the throne of God and of the Lamb."

Then the Lamb is revealed to us as the center of the glory of God, and that in all eternity. There is no life, no eternal life, outside of the Lamb of God, "And there shall in no wise enter into it any thing that defileth, neither whatsoever worketh abomination, or maketh a lie: but they which are written in the Lamb's book of life" (Revelation 21:27). God has given the Lamb the task of the "registration" of the saved. Only those who have received the nature of the Lamb at the rebirth can see the Lamb one day, "We know that, when he shall appear, we shall be like him; for we shall see him as he is" (1 John 3:2).

17 SEPTEMBER

"I am come to send fire on the earth: and what will I, if it be already kindled?" (Luke 12:49).

Who is Jesus? He is the Lamb of God, the perfect sacrifice, the Good Shepherd. He is the door, the way to the Father.

Who was Jesus? Peter says that He was pure, unblemished and innocent. Paul testified that He knew of no sin. But the inner desire for the fire that was to burn was not ignited through the purity and sinless nature of Jesus alone. Many know that they have been cleansed through the blood of Jesus and have been justified through the name of our Lord Jesus. But this fact does not ignite the fire of the Holy Spirit, and thereby I come to a further important question.

How did Jesus live? In obedience! "He humbled himself, and became obedient unto death, even the death of the cross" (Philippians 2:8). Here we come nearer to the mystery of the ever-burning fire, the revelation of His commission, "I am come to send fire on the earth; and what will I, if it be already kindled? But I have a baptism to be baptized with; and how am I straitened till it be accomplished" (Luke 12:49-50). Jesus laid aside His rightful glory so that the fire could be ignited on earth through Him.

18 SEPTEMBER

"Not by might, nor by power, but by my spirit, saith the Lord of hosts"
(Zechariah 4:6).

The whole Bible is full of the testimonies of people who humbled themselves, who laid aside their glory and surrendered themselves. If you want to remain fervent in your love for the Lord, then renounce self-glory! "Let this mind be in you, which was also in Christ Jesus" (Philippians 2:5). The fire of the Holy Spirit begins to shine, to burn, to warm, as soon as a sinner humbles himself as Jesus humbled Himself and emptied Himself.

Samson, a figure from the Old Testament, is an example of this. In the midst of his enemies he humbled himself, and we hear the cry of repentance come from his heart in Judges 16:28, "O Lord God, remember me, I pray thee, and strengthen me, I pray thee, only this once, O God." With these few words, Samson humbled himself in his impotence, in his failure, under his sins. And after he had humbled himself, the dying Lamb who overcame death revealed Himself to him. The victory of the Lord through Samson was the most glorious when he surrendered his last strength in repentance. This obedience that was expressed prophetically through Samson in the presence of the enemy powers allowed the fire of the Holy Spirit to burn.

19 SEPTEMBER

"Then the fire of the Lord fell and consumed the burnt-sacrifice, and the wood, and the stones, and the dust, and licked up the water that was in the trench" (1 Kings 18:38).

*H*ere we see Elijah standing in the midst of the people on Mount Carmel, and hear him call to the people, "Come near unto me" (1 Kings 18:30). Not much is said about the burnt-offering on the altar and the fire that overcame all the obstacles that would normally resist it—the wood, stones, dust and water—because the whole offering was on the altar.

Today, the hindrances are great. Earthly attitudes, portrayed by the dust; stubbornness, portrayed by the stones; weakness, portrayed by the wood; even the water, the element opposite to fire, which in this case is unwillingness, is no obstacle for the fire from above, because the burnt-offering is there.

When the meal-offering (Numbers 5:15), willing surrender, is united with the burnt-offering, complete surrender, it is also capable of staying on the altar. The willing surrender and the whole surrender bind us fast to the altar of God: as it is written, "Bind the sacrifice with cords, even unto the horns of the altar" (Psalm 118:27). In this way we are bound to the Lord, bound to the place where He meets us.

20 SEPTEMBER

"Is not my word like as a fire? saith the Lord; and like a hammer that breaketh the rock in pieces? (Jeremiah 23:29).

What is this fire? It is the Word of God that lives and burns in us. Fire is also a symbol for the suffering of the Lamb. We are similarly led to what Jesus experienced and suffered. It is the way of humiliation. He so humbled Himself that He even took upon Himself the form of a servant. For this reason, God has given Him a name that is above all names (cf. Philippians 2:7-9). The fire is a fire of purification, which is a result of our willing and complete surrender, "That the trial of your faith, being much more precious than of gold that perisheth, though it be tried with fire, might be found unto praise and honour and glory at the appearing of Jesus Christ" (1 Peter 1:7).

The coming of the Lord Jesus Himself will be the last purification through fire for His children. All our works will be proved by fire when we stand before His judgment seat. Then, all that is earthly, all that is temporal, all that is sinful, will burn. Only the burnt-offering—complete surrender—that is not consumed by fire will remain, for that is "gold, silver and precious stones."

21 SEPTEMBER

"Verily, verily, I say unto thee, Except a man be born again, he cannot see the kingdom of God" (John 3:3).

There are true Christians and nominal Christians. Satan, the enemy of the soul of man, is the greatest author of confusion. He does this especially where crucial decisions are concerned. I can well understand when a person who does not know Jesus Christ as his Savior says, "Everyone has to find the way to heaven himself. There are so many churches, and nobody knows which one is telling the truth and which one is lying." This is the tactic of the enemy, who does not want us to have assurance of faith. But there is one point we can certainly agree on, namely that Jesus Christ, the Son of the living God, cannot lie! He claims that He Himself is the truth. Do you believe this? You may say, "I have lost my faith in people." You are not the first to do this. You may have a grudge against many people who have disappointed you. But what do you have against Jesus, the Son of God, who left His glory for your sake, became man and died a bloody death on the cross? He wants you too to see the Kingdom of God.

22 SEPTEMBER

"The Spirit itself beareth witness with our spirit,
that we are the children of God" (Romans 8:16).

Assurance of salvation is the joyful consequence of re-birth. A wonderful assurance floods through the sinner who has come to Jesus, who has received forgiveness of his sins at the cross. Simultaneously he received the Holy Spirit there, and now this rock-like assurance fills him: "I have become a child of God." Perhaps you are saying in surprise, "Can I know that?" We not only *can* know it, but we *must* know it, "...that ye may *know* that ye have eternal life" (1 John 5:13). Perhaps you have been on the "Christian" path for years, yet you have no assurance of salvation, no assurance of the forgiveness of your sins. How poor you are, in spite of everything!

Many people think it is Pharisaical when a person claims to be a child of God. We can only reply, "When I testify that I have assurance of salvation, I am only saying something that I cannot understand myself, for I was a miserable sinner. I have only one explanation for this assurance of salvation: God loved me and gave His Son for my sins on the accursed cross!"

23 SEPTEMBER

"He that hath the Son hath life; and he that hath not the Son of God hath not life" (1 John 5:12).

The fact that a person has been born again cannot remain hidden, for Jesus said, "Ye shall know them by their fruits" (Matthew 7:16). If you are a Christian in name only, this fruit will be lacking. You are ashamed of confessing Jesus, and when you have the chance, you take the way of least resistance. You "don't talk about things like that," it is said. Of course not, for how can you speak of a new life, how can you testify to Jesus, if you do not have Him? Just think for a moment. Are you born again, or are you merely following others? The truly born-again person must be a witness for Jesus, for he has experienced Him as the One who bore his sins. Through word and deed, through the whole life of a born again person, Jesus Christ is revealed. Why? Because Christ Himself lives in the heart of this person through His Spirit. Perhaps you are arguing now, "Well, I know Christians whose deeds speak so loudly that I can't hear their words!" Unfortunately, you are right. But these "Christians" will one day have to give account before the throne of God. Does this change your position, however? What will your religion profit you if you do not come to Christ today, if you do not venture to take the personal step of faith to Jesus?

24 SEPTEMBER

"Be strong and of a good courage, fear not, nor be afraid of them: for the Lord thy God, he it is that doth go with thee; he will not fail thee, nor forsake thee" (Deuteronomy 31:6).

How wonderful! He Himself, the eternal, almighty God, says to you that you need not fear, for He Himself will be with you. What does it mean to go with the Lord, with the eternal God? If He had not promised this Himself, that He will go with us, I would not dare to speak any further of this. But it is possible to walk with the eternal God. To walk not only means to go forwards, but also to keep in step with Him. This keeping in step with Him comes from inner peace, from resting in Him. If there is a disharmony between the living God and your soul, if there is sin between you and Him, then you cannot keep in step with Him. Then you will either walk too fast or too slow. In Amos 3:3 it says, "Can two walk together, except they be agreed?" In other words, the basic condition to be able to walk with the living God is that you have become one with Him, one with the Holy One—through the Lord Jesus Christ and His shed blood. Then you will let yourself be led by His steps alone.

25 SEPTEMBER

"As ye have therefore received Christ Jesus the Lord, so walk ye in him"
(Colossians 2:6).

What makes our walk with God unsure and faltering? There are so many children of God whose faith lives are a continual up and down. At times they are hastening forwards rejoicing, and at other times they are resigned and lie like Elijah "under a juniper tree." Is He, the Lord, unsure? Is He fearful? Is He powerless? No, never! The Scriptures tell us of Him, "He is the rock" (Deuteronomy 32:4). We are surrounded by the threatening power of darkness, but we do not need to be despondent for we are walking with the living God. It is not necessary for you to be oppressed by the menacing powers of darkness, the powers of blasphemy and weariness. David cried out in the face of such trials, "Though I walk through the valley of the shadow of death, I will fear no evil." The reason for his fearlessness was, "...for thou art with me" (Psalm 23:4). Walk with the living God as though only you and He were in this world. For Him even darkness is light, "...for thou art with me."

26 SEPTEMBER

"...For he endured, as seeing him who is invisible" (Hebrews 11:27).

*L*earn to walk with God in your daily life like Moses, "...for thou art with me" (Psalm 23:4). I cannot see Him, I do not feel His presence, but I know by faith that He is with me. Many children of God do not know this walk with God. The cause is not outward weariness, but rather inner weariness. When a child of God is inwardly resigned and weary, he or she is not keeping in step with God. They are lagging behind and no longer have fellowship with the Lord. Those who have become inwardly tired and weary, however, are missing the grace that God wants to give them daily. Yet it says in the last sentence of Isaiah 40, "...they shall run, and not be weary" (verse 31). What can you do about this fatal weariness in your walk with God? "They that wait upon the Lord shall renew their strength...." You will not grow weary when you learn to wait upon the Lord. This waiting upon the Lord is expressed in an intensive prayer life. He stands by His Word. He wants to renew your strength. He will let you walk with Him and not grow weary, if you want that with all your heart.

27 SEPTEMBER

"O Lord, I know that the way of man is not in himself: it is not in man that walketh to direct his steps" (Jeremiah 10:23).

We can never plan our way ourselves, but have to adapt to the steps of the Lord and to walk where He walks. The way with God is a clearly determined path. Jesus walked this way with His Father. The way that He trod with God, however, is against our will, against our nature, against our plans. Friendship with God means enmity against the flesh. There are many who wanted to follow the Lord, who had given up their jobs, maybe, yet they walk as they want to and not as Jesus walked. By nature we do not want to walk as He walked, for God begins at Calvary. Only there where you surrender yourself, where you remain in the death of Jesus, will you walk as He walked. Only when your old man has disappeared in the death of the Lord Jesus, will the new man be able to walk with God. The vital union with Him begins where our old lives die. "I live; yet not I, but Christ liveth in me" (Galatians 2:20). Only then will our new walk with the living God begin.

28 SEPTEMBER

*"He that saith he abideth in him ought himself also so to walk,
even as he walked" (1 John 2:6).*

I want to ask you in great earnest, are you abiding in Jesus, in His death; are you crucified with Him? I know that our flesh does not want this. I heard of a brother who was wronged by fellow Christians and continually prayed the one sentence, "Let the nails hold, Lord!" He wanted to say, "Lord, help me not to come down from the cross and justify myself!" Is not this the victory of Jesus, the Lamb of God, who could have exerted his majesty, because all power had been given unto Him, "If thou be the Son of God, come down from the cross" (Matthew 27:40)? Could He not have come down? Of course He could! But the Lamb overcame. He walked with God to the end. His walk with God was expressed in His absolute obedience unto death, even death on the cross. If you want to walk with God—and this is possible! —then Calvary is the starting point. There your proud nature will come to its end. Something completely new can begin in your life today, if you humble yourself before God and say, "My God, I will begin to walk with You now by letting myself be led where I do not want to go—starting at Calvary."

29 SEPTEMBER

"Ye are all the children of light, and the children of the day: we are not of the night, nor of darkness" (1 Thessalonians 5:5).

We can only be raptured before the judgment if we walk with God. A walk with God is a walk in judgment upon our old nature. Thus, as children of God, we must walk with Him in light, so that we can be raptured before the judgment. The Lord Jesus said, "Verily, verily, I say unto you, He that heareth my word, and believeth on him that sent me, hath everlasting life, and shall not come into condemnation; but is passed from death unto life" (John 5:24). Those who do not want to do the perfect will of God, however, who do not want to come to the light, are already under condemnation. A child of the light walks with God in the light. Whoever withdraws from the light, withdraws from the Rapture and will come into condemnation. That is why I am asking you, are there spheres of your life that are in darkness? If you have not kept in step with God, do you want to come to the light now? Break through to a perfect walk with Him, so that you—who knows how soon? —can suddenly be raptured into His presence.

30 SEPTEMBER

"Every good gift and every perfect gift is from above, and cometh down from the Father of lights, with whom is no variableness, neither shadow of turning" (James 1:17).

The eternal God is unchanging! The Scriptures teach us this very clearly. When we read that God repented of something, it is always connected with the sins of man, not with His failure. So, when it says, "And it repented the Lord that he had made man on the earth, and it grieved him at his heart" (Genesis 6:6), this means nothing other than that God regretted making man and was grieved. He grieved over the consequences of sin in the man that He had made perfect. He regretted it. It is clear that the Lord cannot repent of anything He has done. God did not change His plans, for His intentions have been perfect from eternity to eternity. We cannot change His plans or ways through our prayers, but exactly the opposite takes place. We are changed through intensive prayer. God can at last do what He always wanted to do: bless, save and liberate. He is always the one who blesses. Man can never change God.

293

Spiritual Strength
FOR EACH DAY

OCTOBER

1 OCTOBER

"But God commendeth his love toward us, in that,
while we were yet sinners, Christ died for us" (Romans 5:8).

The Holy Spirit continually points to Jesus, the living proof of God's love for us. When Joseph, Jacob's favorite son, was sold by his envious brothers to a caravan traveling to Egypt, he could hardly have imagined that God only had good and kind intentions with him. But God projected in Joseph, who was sold for 20 pieces of silver by Judah—Jesus Christ, who about 1,800 years later was sold by Judas for 30 pieces of silver. What a profound prophetic mystery: "For God so loved the world, that he gave his only begotten Son, that whosoever believeth in him should not perish, but have everlasting life." God wants to achieve His way through you too, by your acceptance of the way of the cross. In other words, He wants to point to Jesus Christ through you, and in this way reveal His unfathomable love. This is what Paul intended to say when he cried out: "My little children, of whom I travail in birth again until Christ be formed in you" (Galatians 4:19). He meant that we should become one with Jesus Christ and willingly and joyfully accept every way that God leads us, so that His love is revealed.

2 OCTOBER

"My little children, let us not love in word, neither in tongue;
but in deed and in truth"
(1 John 3:18).

To walk in love means nothing more and nothing less than to follow the Lamb, wherever He goes. The natural man does not want to do this. Peter, the most zealous and fiery of all the disciples, did not want to follow the Lord's way. When he followed Jesus to Calvary, it says that he "...followed him afar off" (Matthew 26:58). As long as we reject the way of the Lamb, as long as we "follow Him afar off" and avoid the sufferings of Christ, we will continue to have our shortsighted and rebellious attitude: Why me? With that question, we will not notice that the eternal God wants to reveal Himself to us through the very sufferings of Jesus Christ in our lives.

How can our love for God become deeper and more fervent, so that we are able to follow the Lamb wherever He goes? By contemplating anew the tremendous truth of Romans 8:32, "He that spared not his own Son, but delivered him up for us all, how shall he not with him also freely give us all things?" This is the infinite love of God, which He was only able to show us through the bitter sufferings and death of His Son. This love produces love in our hearts. God really has given us all things in Jesus, so we may experience the reality of Romans 5:5 continuously, "The love of God is shed abroad in our hearts by the Holy Ghost which is given unto us."

3 OCTOBER

*"Behold, I stand at the door, and knock: if any man hear my voice, and
open the door, I will come in to him, and will sup with him,
and he with me" (Revelation 3:20).*

Do you want the mind of Jesus Christ? Has not the
hour come for you today to begin to walk in His love?
Maybe you feel your complete inability to love your fellow
men. You may be consumed with hatred for your enemy. This
comes from the fact that Jesus Christ still has no room in
your heart. If He has begun to knock on the door of your
heart, it will cost you great strength to resist Him. But if you
receive Jesus into your heart, God will give you with Him all
that you so painfully lack. It even says, "The love of God is
shed abroad in our hearts by the Holy Ghost which is given
unto us" (Romans 5:5). Then hatred and irreconcilability will
depart from your heart and the nature of God flood it, because He has entered into your heart through Jesus Christ.
Then you will suddenly be able to love your worst enemy and
to bless him in prayer. You will walk in the love of God and
begin to understand how well He means with you. Then your
walk will become a walk on the high mountain, though you
may be in the deepest valley.

4 OCTOBER

"Men's hearts failing them for fear, and for looking after those things which are coming on the earth: for the powers of heaven shall be shaken" (*Luke 21:26*).

There is great tension among people today; everything is coming to a point of seeming confrontation. This tension not only lies over the nations, but also just as much over millions of individual people. Why are there so many people who are tired of life? Because all the decisions they have made in their lives have not brought them the solution to life's deepest problems. Make a decision for Jesus Christ! Give a clear answer to the question Pilate asked, "What shall I do then with Jesus which is called Christ?" Say "Yes" to the Son of God! For all those who have made this clear decision, all other decisions, however hard and difficult they may be, have already been made, because with the "Yes" of man to Jesus Christ, all other problems are wonderfully solved. Those who take refuge in Him will find their lives to be completely renewed. Those who make a decision for Jesus Christ will find their deepest hunger and thirst for true life to be eternally satisfied. Such a person has a clear course in his life and his walk has been given a decisive direction.

5 OCTOBER

"But God commendeth his love toward us, in that, while we were yet sinners, Christ died for us" (Romans 5:8).

*E*verywhere the Son of God comes, the spirits are exposed. The one says "Yes" to Him, the other says "No." But God takes this decision seriously. God takes you seriously because you are His creation. When the eternal God made the great masterpiece of creation, He made man after His own image "...of the dust of the ground," and "...breathed into his nostrils the breath of life" (Genesis 2:7). Therewith He gave us of His own nature. The nature of God is love. God wants people who love Him of their own free will, for love presupposes free will. This means that man could and can choose his way. But man chose, and he chose sin. We will never be able to fathom what the heart of God, which is perfect love, felt when man, whom God created in His own image, turned away from Him and turned to Satan deliberately. Only those who have recognized Jesus Christ as the gift of God begin to have an inkling of what John 3:16 says, "For God so loved the world, that he gave his only begotten Son...." This is the wonderful message of the second possibility of decision that God gave man in his now lost state.

6 OCTOBER

"For the good that I would I do not: but the evil which I would not, that I do" (Romans 7:19).

I s this a picture of you? You would like to have victory over your temper, your lust, your sins, and yet you do not have victory. Why not? Because your surrender is not complete. "I want to live for Jesus," you say, "but I don't have the strength!" God does not expect any strength of you. On the contrary, if you follow Jesus, you will not become strong but remain as weak as you were before. And yet it is possible to live a life of victory, for the victory of Jesus on Calvary's cross is a reality. There on the cross He cried out, "It is finished" (John 19:30)! At the moment you made your decision for Jesus, did you suddenly receive strength to overcome? No. You will remain as weak as before, in fact become even weaker. However, through your clear decision you appropriate strength you do not have in yourself; you now walk in the strength of the Lord. Beyond your "Yes" to Jesus, the whole victorious power of Jesus Christ is ready for you. Do not look at your sins; do not look at your weakness. God knows all that! He knows what feeble creatures we are. Do not look upon your cares and worries either, but take refuge in the strong arms of Jesus.

7 OCTOBER

"Behold the Lamb of God, which taketh away the sin of the world"
(John 1:29).

*D*id you know that this Jesus, who hung on the cross and died for you, is the Creator of all things? Did you know that the eternal God does not get tired or weary (Isaiah 40:28)? His understanding is unfathomable. He bears the whole universe. We hear much about the laws of nature, but there is only one, because everything is borne by one person: Jesus Christ. We read in Isaiah 9:6, "The government shall be upon his shoulder." It is as though the Holy Spirit would say, "This Jesus, the eternal Son of God, is so strong that He carries the whole of the universe on one shoulder." Now read Luke 15:4-5. There you see Him as the Good Shepherd. He has become man, and speaks here of the hundred sheep that He has; when He loses one, He goes and looks for it until He has found it, and then He lays it on His shoulders. Where the lost lamb is concerned, He needs two shoulders to carry it! Do you think these strong shoulders could ever collapse? Never! Why not? Because they collapsed under a burden that was heavier than the whole universe: "Behold the Lamb of God, which taketh away the sin of the world." He collapsed for the sake of our sins, but death could not keep Him. He rose and lives!

8 OCTOBER

"And thou shalt make a plate of pure gold, and grave upon it, like the engravings of a signet, HOLINESS TO THE LORD" *(Exodus 28:36).*

Here we have a moving chapter about separation. The Lord set Moses apart for holy service. If you read through this chapter, you will be gripped by the earnestness of the priesthood. But now, in the new covenant, every born-again believer is a king and a priest, "…Unto him that loved us, and washed us from our sins in his own blood, and hath made us kings and priests unto God and his Father; to him be glory and dominion for ever and ever" (Revelation 1:5-6). If we look at the Church today, however, we see a terrible vacuum before our eyes. Many are converted, and that is all. "…Ye turned to God" (1 Thessalonians 1:9)—this is redemption from the slavery of Egypt, the slavery of sin. But where is the solemn earnestness, the separation for service? What was the goal and climax of the service? Were the Levites priests for the sake of the priesthood? Did their service have a goal in itself? By no means! It was the means to the goal, "Holiness unto the Lord!" Such a person gives himself to the Lord and becomes His complete possession.

9 OCTOBER

"And ye shall be holy men unto me" (Exodus 22:31).

*L*et us consider this "Holiness unto the Lord" a little more closely. It had to be engraved upon a plate of gold. Gold symbolizes the glory of God in the Bible. Those who are holy and live holy lives reveal subconsciously the nature of God: glory.

The golden plate with the inscription, "Holiness unto the Lord" had to be upon Aaron's forehead, which represents the seat of human thought and from where commands proceed. There on the seat of personality, the Lord lays His hand and puts His seal, "Holiness unto the Lord." "Holiness unto the Lord" was engraved upon the plate "...like the engravings of a signet." Something that is engraved represents an unchanging and irrevocable fact. It is as though the Lord had sealed His servant with these words, and thus announced before the visible and invisible world, "He is Mine!" The plate on Aaron the High Priest's forehead was where everyone could see and read it. Aaron did not have to proclaim, "I belong to the Lord," because people could see it at first glance. Truly sanctified people speak through their nature louder than through their words; they are legible epistles of Christ, read of all men.

10 OCTOBER

"But as he which hath called you is holy, so be ye holy in all manner of conversation; because it is written, Be ye holy; for I am holy"
(1 Peter 1:15-16).

*W*hy "Holiness unto the Lord"?

1. Because He is holy! Who are you following if you are a follower of Jesus? The Holy Spirit. There is no other sphere of life that has more chance to sin than the sphere of our relationship with God. Here truth and lies lie very close together. Many bless with their tongues, but they curse with their hearts. Some have faith but no works of faith, while some have no faith but they have works. Aaron's wonderful high-priestly costume, the white mitre, the precious stones on his breastplate, the golden signet on his forehead, his presence in the sanctuary—all were the outward expression of his inner attitude of heart: "Holiness unto the Lord"!

2. Because you are His property. It is very moving how often the Lord repeats this in Exodus 28. In verse 1, "...that he may minister unto me"; verse 3, "...that he may minister unto me"; verse 4, "...that he may minister unto me"; and verse 41, "...that they may minister unto me." This clearly documents that "Holiness unto the Lord" is actually the expression of the love of the Lord: "You belong to Me!"

11 OCTOBER

"Therefore if any man be in Christ, he is a new creature: old things are passed away; behold, all things are become new" (2 Corinthians 5:17).

*D*oes a born-again Christian no longer sin? Has everything become new? The Bible does say clearly, "All things are become new." However, this means that the essential part of a person, the spirit that came from God, becomes alive at the moment of the new birth. This is the new creature, the new man. This new man can no longer sin; he is blameless, holy and righteous.

But the old man is still subject to sin—that which was executed in Jesus Christ on the cross, the old man, my ego, my flesh. This ego has no more right of existence in God's eyes. When the Bible says, "All things are become new," it requires the old to die. For this reason, we exclaim again and again the words of the apostle Paul, "I am crucified with Christ: nevertheless I live; yet not I, but Christ liveth in me: and the life which I now live in the flesh I live by the faith of the Son of God, who loved me, and gave himself for me" (Galatians 2:20).

306

12 OCTOBER

*"Thanks be to God, which giveth us the victory through our
Lord Jesus Christ" (1 Corinthians 15:57).*

"*H*ow can I make my old nature remain dead?" many people ask. We often see so little of this in our daily lives. But here too the question is, "Do you believe that Jesus Christ really died on the cross?" If so, then the words of Romans 6:6 apply, "Knowing this, that our old man is crucified with him, that the body of sin might be destroyed, that henceforth we should not serve sin." This is what I mean: the moment the enemy attempts to provoke us through people who insult us, slander us or wrong us in some other way, we have the chance to prove that we believe in the power of the death of Jesus. At that very moment, being crucified with Christ proves to be the mystery of victory over all that is negative. God makes sure that we are continually confronted in our daily lives with the crucified Lord. We meet the cross everywhere. If we did not have these trials, there would be no opportunity to practice the victory of the Lord Jesus Christ that He won on the cross. For this reason, we should love those the most who hurt us the worst, because in every affliction we have the opportunity of exclaiming what it says in 2 Corinthians 2:14, "Thanks be to God, which always causeth us to triumph in Christ."

13 OCTOBER

"Wherefore he is able also to save them to the uttermost that come unto God by him, seeing he ever liveth to make intercession for them"
(Hebrews 7:25).

*C*an a Christian be lost? Those who have come to believe in the Lord are sealed with the Holy Spirit of promise, which is a deposit, a down payment for the day of redemption. The Holy Spirit leads us into all truth. A person who has received the Holy Spirit is saved forever. The Lord Jesus says in John 10:28 that nobody will pluck His sheep out of His hand, and He confirms this in verse 29 with the words, "No man is able to pluck them out of my Father's hand." Now the question arises, what if I sin in spite of this wonderful position as a child of God? John answers in 1 John 2:1, "And if any man sin, we have an advocate with the Father, Jesus Christ the righteous." The born-again Christian is redeemed from the guilt and power of sin, but not from the presence of sin. The Bible warns us urgently that through our conscious disobedience, we can lose our reward. Our salvation we receive freely, but we receive the reward only if we are fully surrendered to Him. We can attain the reward only when we follow Jesus faithfully in all of our work and walk.

14 OCTOBER

"Be sober, be vigilant; because your adversary the devil, as a roaring lion, walketh about, seeking whom he may devour: whom resist stedfast in the faith" (1 Peter 5:8-9).

*T*his admonition says that we should be sober and vigilant, even while we continually claim the victory of Jesus. Paul says the same thing in Ephesians 6:10-11. He does not say that we have to fight against the cunning attacks of the devil, but rather that we must become strong in the Lord! Are we denying the fight of faith? No, but we are not fighting *toward* the victory of Jesus, but *from* the accomplished victory of Jesus. Somebody may protest, if Satan really is conquered, how can he still be active?

Because the victory of the Lord Jesus must be proved before the visible and invisible world through those who believe in Jesus Christ.

Because man can only be saved on the grounds of his free-will decision. He must choose between Jesus and Satan, between light and darkness, between life and death.

Because the sovereign, holy God does not need to suppress the darkness by force. God's presence in itself and the gift of His love, Jesus Christ, who as the light of the world reconciled the world with God, tore the power from Satan.

15 OCTOBER

"...He which hath begun a good work in you will perform it until the day of Jesus Christ" (Philippians 1:6).

When there are storms all around us, and the enemy attempts in all possible ways to make us fall, then we know that we are safe in Jesus and are able to react out of His given security. This is our fight of faith; we practice what we claim to believe. We are only able to do this when we have had a meeting with the Victor, Jesus Christ. In other words, those who want to have victory in their daily lives, must first have a meeting with the Victor. It is God who works in you "to will and to do of His good pleasure" (Philippians 2:13). He is able to do what we are not able to do in our own strength. "My grace is sufficient for thee: for my strength is made perfect in weakness" (2 Corinthians 12:9). And when we fail, do we have to be despondent? No. Those who confess their failure, their inability, and humble themselves over it may have the assurance of forgiveness through His precious blood. Resignation is a cunning tactic of the enemy that we must resist. Jesus Christ is the Author and Finisher of our faith, and He will also complete the good work He has begun in us.

16 OCTOBER

"If any man will come after me, let him deny himself, and take up his cross daily, and follow me" (Luke 9:23).

*D*oes the Church have to endure the same sufferings as the Lord Jesus? We are told in the Bible repeatedly that we:

- have to go the same way as the Lamb (Revelation 14:4),
- should follow in His footsteps (1 Peter 2:21),
- are destined to be partakers of His sufferings (1 Peter 4:13),
- are even conformed to His death in the fellowship of Jesus' sufferings (Philippians 3:10), and
- are not only conformed to His death but are planted with Christ in the same death (Romans 6:5).

We have to suffer persecution because, as born-again Christians, we are one body with Him. He is the Head, and we are the members of His body. It is not that we have to carry away the sins of the world, however. He did this once and for all. Also, we are not asked to bear His cross, which we would never be able to do anyway. We are not required to bear His cross, but our own. This willingness to bear my cross is part of my discipleship and leads to me being like Him in glory. This is God's great goal for each of us.

17 OCTOBER

"Whatsoever ye shall ask in my name, that will I do, that the Father may be glorified in the Son" (John 14:13).

Whom should we call upon in prayer? The Lord Jesus Himself said expressly that we should pray to the Father in His name. He pointed us to His Father again and again. God is the goal, and His Son is the way that leads us to this goal. This was the purpose of the sufferings of the Lord Jesus, "For Christ also hath once suffered for sins, the just for the unjust, that he might bring us to God" (1 Peter 3:18). We should tread this path also. There is no other way! We have boldness to enter into the sanctuary, that is, into the direct presence of God, through the blood of Jesus. And Jesus taught us to pray, "Our Father which art in heaven..." (Matthew 6:9). Paul also shows us this way, "I thank my God through Jesus Christ" (Romans 1:8).

We confess that Jesus Christ is the Lord. We wait for His appearing. In Jesus Christ, the grace of God has been given us. May we not pray directly to the Lord Jesus, then? Stephen did, "Lord Jesus, receive my spirit" (Acts 7:59). Jesus Himself said, "He that seeth me seeth him that sent me" (John 12:45).

18 OCTOBER

"Let him ask in faith, nothing wavering. For he that wavereth is like a wave of the sea driven with the wind and tossed. For let not that man think that he shall receive any thing of the Lord" (James 1:6-7).

What does it mean to pray in faith? It means to base my prayers on the promises of God. We cannot simply believe something will happen. There are people who say, "You only have to believe, and then you will receive it." They are wrong. We need a concrete promise of God on which we can base our faith in every situation. This is the wonderful thing: the promises are there! For the lonely, for instance, "I am with you always" (Matthew 28:20). For the weak, "My strength is made perfect in weakness" (2 Corinthians 12:9). For the worried, "Casting all your care upon him; for he careth for you" (1 Peter 5:7). For the weary, "The joy of the Lord is your strength" (Nehemiah 8:10). For the sick, "I am the Lord that healeth thee" (Exodus 15:26). God has given a promise for every situation, so that you can base your prayers in faith on these promises of God. Prayer is the highest expression of faith, so that you no longer depend on what is visible, but on what is invisible, the eternal God.

19 OCTOBER

"The effectual fervent prayer of a righteous man availeth much"
(James 5:16).

What should your attitude be before God in prayer? Miserable in yourself, yet perfect, just and blameless! How is this possible? Only through the blood of Jesus can we attain to the righteousness that counts with God. Consequently, we can only appear before the throne of God through the holy blood of Jesus, "Having therefore, brethren, boldness to enter into the holiest by the blood of Jesus..." (Hebrews 10:19). We can never speak with God, then, without first claiming cleansing in the blood of Jesus. This precondition is often ignored. That's why it is difficult for you to intercede. You have forgotten that you can only approach God through the blood of Jesus. This means that we cannot draw near to God without the Holy Spirit glorifying the Lamb. Without realizing something of what He suffered for our sakes, we are simply not partakers. Suffering drives us to worship, and worship is always the foundation for true intercession. Never come thoughtlessly, therefore, into the holy presence of God, for He will not hear you if you do not approach Him consciously through the blood of Jesus.

20 OCTOBER

"Verily, verily, I say unto thee, When thou wast young, thou girdedst thyself, and walkedst whither thou wouldest: but when thou shalt be old, thou shalt stretch forth thy hands, and another shall gird thee, and carry thee whither thou wouldest not" (John 21:18).

The Lord said to Peter, "You led yourself until now, but the time is coming when you will be led where you do not want to go." We may always be assured of the Lord's leading. We are also being led by Him when we do not notice it. We have many promises to that effect in the Bible. Think of Psalm 32:8, for instance, "I will instruct thee and teach thee in the way which thou shalt go: I will guide thee with mine eye." Yet there are many Christians who are misled instead of being led. What is the reason you cannot see the way? It is your accursed self-will, which darkens your view and brings you great distress. Reach out to Him anew today and say, "Take my life and let it be consecrated, Lord, to Thee." Then He will lead you where you do not want to go by nature—to Calvary—but He will lead you in paths of righteousness for His name's sake. It's no longer you trying to find the way, but His guiding. He promised to guide you with His eye!

21 OCTOBER

"And thine ears shall hear a word behind thee, saying, This is the way, walk ye in it, when ye turn to the right hand, and when you turn to the left" (Isaiah 30:21).

It is a sign of the end times that Christians who are on the last part of the way are losing their way. Does not the Lord lead His children clearly? Yes, He does lead us very clearly, but only few in our day are prepared to submit unconditionally to the leadership of the Lord. The leading of the Lord is under the condition that we are willing to let ourselves be led. The Lord always leads us where we do not want to go. He demands complete submission of our own will. We must be willing to be led where we do not want to go by nature. The Lord does not demand just a bit, but everything! "When thou shalt be old, thou shalt stretch forth thy hands, and another shall gird thee, and carry thee whither thou wouldest not." We do not necessarily have to become old first, for these words that were addressed to Peter apply to us all. Are you prepared—in whatever sphere of your life you may be—to submit your self-will unconditionally to the Lord? This means nothing other than that we let ourselves be conformed to the image of Jesus and allow ourselves to be led where we do not want to go.

22 OCTOBER

"And he saith unto them, Follow me, and I will make your fishers of men. And they straightway left their nets, and followed him"
(Matthew 4:19-20).

When the Lord says to Peter, "...and carry thee whither thou wouldest not," it was a new and deeper call to follow Him. Peter had heard the Lord's call once by the Sea of Galilee. But after the crucifixion and resurrection of Jesus, the Lord calls Peter to follow Him again, "Follow me" (John 21:19). Why does the Lord Jesus call him a second time? Because there are two kinds of following: an outward following and an inner following. There is an outward following of Jesus that does not lead to the renewal of our hearts as a consequence. Such a following never breaks through to a life of victory. Following Jesus inwardly, however, results in a radical renewal of our hearts. The reason why so many Christians are powerless today has its root in that they only follow the Lord outwardly. Let us examine ourselves thoroughly and ask the Lord to keep us from following Him outwardly. Those who do not know the inner following of Jesus bear already the consequences of their outward following: no power from above and no "Amen" from the sanctuary.

23 OCTOBER

"But when the morning was now come, Jesus stood on the shore: but the disciples knew not that it was Jesus. Then Jesus saith unto them, Children, have ye any meat? They answered him, No" (John 21:4-5).

One sign of a person who is only following Jesus outwardly is that they are affected by outward things and circumstances. This is why they are so inconsistent in their Christian lives; one day they are walking on air, and the next day they are down in the dumps. Although Peter was very near to the Lord Jesus in his first outward following of Him, he was far from Him in his heart. He had no true fellowship with the Lord. The Lord even had to call him "Satan" once. It was on account of the lack of this fellowship that he fell to such depths when he denied the Lord before the crucifixion. The wavering and defeats in your life—the power of the enemy—have their origin in your outward following. Are you one of those who has to answer "No" to the Lord's question, "Have you anything to eat?" There are people around you who are hungering for redemption, eternal life and peace with God. You have not been able to give the "hungry" anything. Why? Because you have failed on account of your outward following. The Lord is calling you to an inner, fruitful following today!

24 OCTOBER

*"Peter was grieved because he said unto him the third time, Lovest thou
me? And he said unto him, Lord, thou knowest all things;
thou knowest that I love thee" (John 21:17).*

If you are one of those who have to confess, "Lord, I have
failed to follow You. I am a miserable failure, but You
know that I love you with all my heart," then you are at the
point where a person is called to follow the Lord inwardly.
That is the point where the risen Lord is very near to you.
He is able to give such people a clear, concrete commission
before He tells them to follow Him. After the threefold as-
sertion of Peter, "Yea, Lord; thou knowest that I love thee,"
Jesus says to him three times, "Feed my lambs...feed my
sheep...feed my sheep" (John 21:15-17). Have you failed like
Peter, but you love the Lord? Then He also has a new definite
task for you: feed His lambs, His sheep! Let us seek together
the lost sheep who "are not of this fold" and serve the Lord
with all our might. The Lord's commission, "Feed My lambs"
is a message of hope for the disqualified, for those who are resigned because they have failed, but who truly love Jesus!

25 OCTOBER

"Jesus Christ the same yesterday, and to day, and for ever"
(Hebrews 13:8).

This irrefutable Bible verse is of great importance. It tells us that Jesus Christ, who shed His blood at Calvary for the forgiveness of your sins, never changes. He is the same as He always was, yesterday, today and in all eternity. He is the same in His unlimited victorious power over sin, death and the devil. Our troubles and fears come from the fact that we cannot deal with the powers of darkness around us. We become frustrated, confused and intimidated. Children of God certainly do not have to wrestle with "…flesh and blood, but against principalities, against powers, against the rulers of the darkness of this world, against spiritual wickedness in high places" (Ephesians 6:12). It is a spiritual battle. We should always be aware that the stronger one is on our side: Jesus Christ! He is the same today as He was long ago, greater than any power that may oppress us, and He will remain so in all eternity. The greatness of Jesus is so absolute that nothing surpasses Him. For those who believe, there is no power that can oppress them that Jesus has not long since overpowered through His accomplished work on Calvary's cross.

26 OCTOBER

*"Verily, verily, I say unto you, If a man keep my saying,
he shall never see death" (John 8:51).*

A person in his right mind does not want to die. You can see this in a newborn baby. It clenches its fists as though it wants to say, "I am never going to let go of the life that I have received." Modern man seeks desperately to escape death. The business connected with death is a very lucrative one. Yet, in spite of all attempts at rejuvenation and cell renewal, man has not been able to overcome death. Only one person achieved this: Jesus Christ. It says of Him in Hebrews 2:14, "Forasmuch then as the children are partakers of flesh and blood, he also himself likewise took part of the same; that through death he might destroy him that had the power of death, that is, the devil." This is the wonderful thing about the victory of Jesus. He overpowered the one who had the power of death. How? By dying Himself. Death could not hold Him. If you have this Jesus in your heart, who is greater than death, then you are saved from the fear and power of death. Then you will not see death any more, for He Himself said, "I am the resurrection, and the life: he that believeth in me, though he were dead, yet shall he live" (John 11:25).

27 OCTOBER

"In the world ye shall have tribulation: but be of good cheer;
I have overcome the world" (John 16:33).

How can you experience the Lord Jesus as the One who is greater than all your worries, fears and unsolvable problems in your present situation? By talking over everything with Him. You will experience Jesus as the One who is greater according to the measure in which you tell Him everything. When I tell Him in faith what is troubling me, He takes my problems in exchange for His joy and peace.

Are you in danger? Then tell Jesus. Do what the disciples once did. When they were in their boat on the lake and the Lord Jesus had fallen asleep, suddenly a storm began to rage. The waves tossed their boat to and fro so that the disciples could bear it no longer. What did they do? They awoke Jesus and told Him about it. Then He proved Himself to be the One who is greater than all the threatening waves and mightier than the most terrible storm. Jesus "...arose, and rebuked the winds and the sea; and there was a great calm" (Matthew 8:26). Tell Him about all the dangers around you and in you. Then the threatening waves that rage around you will grow calm and everything will become still.

28 OCTOBER

"And Jesus went out, and departed from the temple. . .and Jesus said
unto them, See ye not all these things? Verily I say unto you,
There shall not be left here one stone upon another,
that shall not be thrown down" (Matthew 24:1-2).

The disciples began to ponder these words, and questions arose among them. Many a thinking person concerns himself with the future today. If we want to know about the future, we must do as the disciples did. They asked Jesus about the future, not realizing that they were already in the future, for He is the Eternal One. Jesus is "...the same yesterday, and to day, and for ever" (Hebrews 13:8). If you really ask Him about the future, you will receive from Him a panoramic view that extends from Jerusalem over the entire earth, including the whole of humanity, even the universe, and then that panorama will lead you back to Jerusalem. It is not surprising that Jerusalem is the focus of the world today. Tell Him everything that worries you about the future. But don't try to understand everything. It is enough that He knows and understands everything. He says to you concerning that which you do not need to know, "I have yet many things to say unto you, but ye cannot bear them now" (John 16:12).

29 OCTOBER

" . . . Jesus, thou son of David, have mercy on me. And many charged him that he should hold his peace: but he cried the more a great deal, Thou son of David, have mercy on me. And Jesus stood still, and commanded him to be called. And they call the blind man, saying unto him, Be of good comfort, rise; he calleth thee. And he, casting away his garment, rose, and came to Jesus" (Mark 10:47-50).

Blind Bartimaeus hears that Jesus of Nazareth is passing by and begins to cry out, "Jesus, thou son of David, have mercy on me." This annoys the sanctimonious crowd. But Bartimaeus continues. What does this cry from the bottom of his heart produce? Jesus stands still! Does He heal him? Does He take away his blindness immediately? He first asks Bartimaeus, "What wilt thou that I should do unto thee?" (verse 51), although He knows that Bartimaeus is blind. This should teach us that we can also tell Jesus clearly what our wishes are. The Lord wants us to tell Him exactly what we desire of Him, although He knows everything about you. When Bartimaeus tells Him his wish, "Lord, that I might receive my sight," Jesus immediately intervenes and says to him, "Go thy way; thy faith hath made thee whole. And immediately he received his sight, and followed Jesus in the way" (verse 52).

30 OCTOBER

*"Master, I beseech thee, look upon my son: for he is mine only child.
And, lo, a spirit taketh him, and he suddenly crieth out; and it teareth
him that he foameth again, and bruising him hardly departeth from him"*
(Luke 9:38-39).

There are various kinds of family problems. But Jesus, as He was during His time on earth, is still greater than all the family problems today. The father of that poor boy knew this, and this is why he told Jesus his troubles. Nobody was capable of solving this family problem; only Jesus could help. And He did it! He "...rebuked the unclean spirit, and healed the child, and delivered him again to his father" (verse 42). Jesus wants to help us with our family problems today, whether they are our own fault or that of others.

Whatever your case may be, tell it to Jesus. Tell your troubles to Him, as that father did. Even if He does not intervene immediately, do not be discouraged. Go on talking to Jesus about your family problems. He will hear you and, full of compassion, reveal Himself as the One who is greater than everything. He will not turn you away, for He Himself said, "Him that cometh to me I will in no wise cast out" (John 6:37).

31 OCTOBER

"And they said one to another, Did not our heart burn within us, while he talked with us by the way, and while he opened to us the scriptures?"
(Luke 24:32).

The hardest thing for a child of God is when he no longer understands the ways of the Lord. This is what happened to those two disciples who walked together from Jerusalem to Emmaus. They were deeply shocked. Jesus had disappointed them. They had thought He was Israel's Messiah, but now He had let Himself be crucified. Why did He do that? Why didn't He prove His omnipotence? As they discussed this together, a stranger joined them. They poured out their disappointed and sorrowful hearts to Him, the stranger whom they did not know. But what did they hear from the mouth of this stranger? Pretentious words? No, it says, "And beginning at Moses and all the prophets, he expounded unto them in all the scriptures the things concerning himself" (Luke 24:27). Even now, they did not know that it was Jesus Himself speaking to them. Only later on, when He ate with them, did they recognize Him. The two disciples who had lost their faith in the Lord experienced that He was nearest to them in their terrible disappointment. Jesus was and is today greater than everything. He wants to transform your disappointment into wonderful joy!

Spiritual Strength
FOR EACH DAY

NOVEMBER

1 NOVEMBER

"Call unto me, and I will answer thee, and shew thee great and mighty things, which thou knowest not" (Jeremiah 33:3).

What a mystery the unlimited power of prayer is! I am almost afraid to speak of this, because I feel incapable of putting into words the infinite omnipotence of God that is revealed to the one who prays.

Why should we pray? First, because God the Father tells us to, "Call upon me in the day of trouble: I will deliver thee, and thou shalt glorify me" (Psalm 50:15). Apart from the fact that the Lord takes our cries concerning our outward troubles to heart, the one who begins to read His Word with an open heart inevitably finds himself in inward trouble. And then the command of the Father comes, "Call upon me in the day of trouble." Secondly, because God the Son urges us to pray, "Ask, and it shall be given you; seek, and ye shall find; knock, and it shall be opened unto you" (Matthew 7:7). He, the Son of God, urges us to intensify our prayers. "To ask" is passive, "to seek" is earnest perseverance, and "to knock" means to make our way into the presence of God until He opens the door to the inner sanctuary.

2 NOVEMBER

"...I will love him, and will manifest myself to him" (John 14:21).

Whatever may have happened in your life, whatever sins you may have committed, if you, like Peter, say to your Lord today, "Lord, Thou knowest all things; thou knowest that I love thee" (John 21:17), He will reveal Himself to you. The reason that you, as a child of God, are not filled with the Holy Spirit is that the Lord Jesus has not been able to reveal Himself to you. There are many people who sincerely believe in Jesus Christ, but lack the revelation of Him up to the present day. One thing is sure: those who believe in Him experience His victorious power. But here we come to the point where it goes much deeper. To those who testify of their love through obedience to His Word, He will reveal Himself. And when He reveals Himself to you, this is never an end in itself. Rather, the Lord has given you the task of passing on this revelation. Peter was told, "Feed my lambs...feed my sheep" (John 21:15-17). With Peter, we see how love germinates and grows. The love of God is eternal, however, for God Himself is love. When we are filled with the Holy Spirit, He unites us through Jesus Christ with the Father, so that His love is planted in us and begins to grow.

3 NOVEMBER

"Lord, thou knowest all things; thou knowest that I love thee"
(John 21:17).

The Lord's questions always reveal our innermost feelings. If the Lord asks you today, "Lovest thou me?" and you ponder on this question, you will suddenly notice how He has touched a part of you that has long since been forgotten, and you are moved. Then the actual truth, which has been covered for so long, breaks out of the depths of your heart, "Yes, Lord, I love You because You first loved me!" Peter also began to notice how he loved Jesus when he was asked this question. It was a revelation to realize how much he loved the Lord, and he said full of amazement, "Lord, thou knowest all things...."

With what patience, determination and wisdom the Lord dealt with Peter, who had denied and cursed Him out of sheer fear and cowardice! The Lord never asks questions before the right time has come. Very likely, He will one day take you aside, perhaps today, and, without speaking of your sins, ask you, "Lovest thou me?"

4 NOVEMBER

"For, brethren, ye have been called unto liberty;
only use not liberty for an occasion to the flesh, but by love
serve one another" (Galatians 5:13).

If we read the above verse carefully, the question of our calling is already answered. To what are we, as children of God, called? To liberty! Paul also says this in Romans 8:21, "Because the creature itself also shall be delivered from the bondage of corruption into the glorious liberty of the children of God." A person who is born again comes out of the slavery of sin and attains to the glorious liberty of the children of God. Such people are free of guilt; they are free sons and daughters of the living God. Paul also pointed out the danger, for this liberty in Christ Jesus can be abused, "...only use not liberty for an occasion to the flesh" (Galatians 5:13). What should we do with this wonderful liberty in the Lord Jesus Christ, then? Can we simply live for ourselves? No, the liberty that we have through the Lord should be subordinated to the Spirit of God. We cannot dispose of our liberty at our own discretion, but the Spirit of God must be in charge of our life.

5 NOVEMBER

The heart is deceitful above all things, and desperately wicked: who can know it? I the Lord search the heart. . ." (Jeremiah 17:9-10).

The question of the condition of our hearts is decisive where the effect of the Word of God in us is concerned. Often we do not know our own hearts, but the Lord knows! Now comes the question of how we receive the Word of God. Have you, have I, removed all defiance, despondency and sin out of our hearts before we begin to read the Word of God? James 4:7-8 tells us, "Submit yourselves therefore to God. Resist the devil, and he will flee from you. Draw nigh to God, and he will draw nigh to you. Cleanse your hands, ye sinners; and purify your hearts, ye double minded." These are the four things that the Lord requires of us. Notice the sequence and obey them, or you will be deceiving yourself when you read the Word of God. First, resist the enemy in the name of Jesus; second, draw near to God; third, cleanse yourself in the precious blood of the Lamb; and fourth, purify your deceitful heart.

If you do this, the field of your heart will be prepared, just as the Lord Jesus says in the parable of the sower. If you refuse to do it, you are deceiving yourself. James 1:26 warns us, "...this man's religion is [in] vain."

6 NOVEMBER

"Fight the good fight of faith" (1 Timothy 6:12).

The fight of faith is understood and practiced by very few. The majority of believers fight but do not fight lawfully, according to the rules. Paul explains in 2 Timothy 2:5, "And if a man also strive for masteries, yet is he not crowned, except he strive lawfully." It is not the fact that we fight that is decisive, but that we fight according to the rules. This means that we fight with the goal in view. In order to fight the good fight of faith effectively and victoriously, we must first of all know our enemy. Our real enemies are not people of flesh and blood. Ephesians 6:12 tells us, "For we wrestle not against flesh and blood, but against principalities, against powers, against the rulers of the darkness of this world, against spiritual wickedness in high places." It is very shortsighted of us, therefore, to regard people as our actual enemies. The driving force behind human deceit, cunning and hatred is always the powers of darkness. Jesus has conquered the enemies of man on Calvary's cross and overpowered them. His victory is our victory! To fight the good fight of faith, then, means that we no longer have to fight alone toward victory, but we fight from the accomplished victory of Jesus.

7 NOVEMBER

"So God created man in his own image, in the image of God created he him; male and female created he them" (Genesis 1:27).

God wants man to go the way of perfection, so that he can be returned to the image of God again. When God had finished making man with His master hands, He saw Himself in these first people, "And God saw every thing that he had made, and, behold, it was very good" (Genesis 1:31). The first people must have been extraordinarily beautiful, but through sin they lost this image of God. This is why God sent His only-begotten Son, to redeem fallen man from sin and to transform hiim into His image again. When a person comes to recognize his sins, he receives Jesus Christ in his heart. Such a person understands that Jesus carried away all his sins on Calvary's cross, reconciling the sinner with God. Then the wonderful thing that is described in John 1:12 takes place, "As many as received him, to them gave he power to become the sons of God, even to them that believe on his name." From this moment on, the Holy Spirit works in the person concerned the ever-growing desire to be like Jesus. This is the way to perfection. When we arrive at the goal and are with Him as we long for, "…we shall be like him; for we shall see him as he is" (1 John 3:2).

8 NOVEMBER

"Jesus answered and said unto him, If a man love me, he will keep my words: and my father will love him, and we will come unto him, and make our abode with him" (John 14:23).

*H*ere the Lord speaks of the greatest and deepest mystery: the Father and the Son come and dwell in a person who loves God, through the Holy Spirit. When you open the door of your heart, you suddenly discover that the Lord Himself lives in you. This is surely what the profound words of Proverbs 8:17 mean, "I love them that love me; and those that seek me early shall find me." This "seeking Him early" speaks of the fact that He wants to have first place in your life and highest priority in your heart. "Those that seek me early" also means, simply put, those who first seek Him every morning. Just imagine, the triune God, the Father and the Son, want to dwell in mortal man through the Holy Spirit! The urgent question for you who love Him and keep His Word is, are you really a dwelling place for Him? The Lord rejoices when He can say to those who love Him, "Come and see: this is where I live!" Can He point to you and say that He lives in you? Does He feel at home in your heart?

9 NOVEMBER

"I in them, and thou in me, that they may be made perfect in one; and that the world may know that thou hast sent me, and hast loved them, as thou hast loved me" (John 17:23).

Just how much importance our Lord Jesus Christ attached to the indwelling of the Father and the Son through the Holy Spirit is shown us in the high-priestly prayer, as also His command in Matthew 5:48, "Be ye therefore perfect, even as your Father which is in heaven is perfect." When we are one with the Lord Jesus, we will be conformed to His image, just as Paul said so majestically in 1 Corinthians 6:17, "He that is joined unto the Lord is one spirit." Thus, the Father and the Son are completely one with those who love Him and are loved of Him through the Holy Spirit. "That they all may be one; as thou, Father, art in me, and I in thee, that they also may be one in us: that the world may believe that thou hast sent me. And the glory which thou gavest me I have given them; that they may be one, even as we are one" (John 17:21-22). Here the Lord is speaking of the organic unity with His own: the Father and the Son in His own, and they in Him through the Holy Spirit. Thus, as born-again Christians, we are the temple of the Holy Spirit.

10 NOVEMBER

"Who is among you that feareth the Lord, that obeyeth the voice of his servant, that walketh in darkness, and hath no light? Let him trust in the name of the Lord, and stay upon his God"
(Isaiah 50:10).

*H*ere is described the experience of a person who fears the Lord and obeys the voice of His servant—Jesus Christ. All those who truly follow the Lord will inevitably have the genuine nature of their discipleship tested, in that they are led through stretches of darkness. He, the Good Shepherd, says of His sheep, "And when he putteth forth his own sheep, he goeth before them, and the sheep follow him: for they know his voice" (John 10:4). Of those who heard Him with their physical ears, however, it says, "…but they understood not what things they were which he spake unto them" (John 10:6). Today also, many people do not understand what wonderful depths our Good Shepherd opens us to us when He speaks in this way. It is a mystery. If you adopt the attitude of faith and say, "However dark it is around me and in me, I will listen to His voice and trust in His leading," then you will be able to exclaim with the Psalmist, "Yea, though I walk through the valley of the shadow of death, I will fear no evil: for thou art with me; thy rod and thy staff they comfort me" (Psalm 23:4).

11 NOVEMBER

"Though he were a Son, yet learned he obedience by the things which he suffered" (Hebrews 5:8).

*I*f we want to experience victory in our daily lives, we must be willing to be obedient. A definite inner decision has to precede this. If I have an inner "Yes" to the Lord, if I want to do what He requires at all costs, then He can reveal His will to me and through me. Let us consider the Lord Jesus. What was the foundation of His unconditional victory? His secret was His obedience. Many people do not become completely obedient outwardly because they have not yet become obedient inwardly. You must consider before the Lord, do I want to do what He wants at all costs? Then obedience will be followed by victory. Obedience is an inward decision that has outward results. What did the Lord Jesus say before He went to the cross, even before He became flesh, from eternity? "Lo, I come...I delight to do thy will, O my God" (Psalm 40:7-8). In eternity, before the foundation of the world, the decision had already been made by the Son of God. His coming to this earth was implementing the will of God. It is important for us to see clearly what obedience is. Obedience means doing the will of God, and then God can work through us unhindered.

12 NOVEMBER

"Ye know that your labour is not in vain in the Lord"
(1 Corinthians 15:58).

*W*e must go much deeper into this labor; it must be "...in the Lord." Only then will our work for Him be of eternal value. To work "in the Lord" does not simply mean to run the course and endure hardship, but to maintain our lifelong fellowship with Him under all circumstances. This passivity in Jesus is the highest divine activity. How often do the Scriptures tell us that the Lord will work for us? What do you have to do then? Simply trust in Him: "Commit thy way unto the Lord; trust also in him; and he shall bring it to pass" (Psalm 37:5).

He, the Lord, wants to guide you clearly and unmistakably in all things. Once again, what do you have to do? The answer: "Trust in the Lord with all thine heart; and lean not unto thine own understanding. In all thy ways acknowledge him, and he shall direct thy paths" (Proverbs 3:5-6).

He wants to fight for you against your enemies who threaten you. What do you have to do? "The Lord shall fight for you, and ye shall hold your peace" (Exodus 14:14). When will you learn to be still? Only then will you experience His strength, "In quietness and in confidence shall be your strength" (Isaiah 30:15).

13 NOVEMBER

"Behold, I have refined thee, but not with silver; I have chosen thee in the furnace of affliction" (Isaiah 48:10).

God often lets His saints here on earth experience inconceivable hardships. The explanation for this is given us by the prophet Isaiah. From my personal life, I could tell of inexplicable hardships and afflictions that nobody could understand. But our faithful Lord has continually comforted, strengthened and given new courage. Through all the darkness, He continually let His radiant glory shine, as He did with His servants whom we can read about in the gallery of the heroes of faith in Hebrews 11.

In the above Bible verse, we have an explanation for why children of God often have to go through deep sorrow. Why? To hold on in faith, as Job once did, and thereby others are also made perfect. We must prove through faith that we have everything we need in Him. The Psalmist says in chapter 73:25-26, "Whom have I in heaven but thee? And there is none upon earth that I desire beside thee. My flesh and my heart faileth: but God is the strength of my heart, and my portion for ever." In this way, you will be filled with deep joy and peace in the midst of the trials, hardships and tribulations you are led through.

14 NOVEMBER

"... Mattaniah, which was over the thanksgiving, he and his brethren"
(Nehemiah 12:8).

Is it important to give thanks? There are so many offices in the world today, but here in the Bible a particular office is mentioned: that of thanksgiving. We do not know why this is only mentioned once in the whole of the Bible. Out of the men returning from Babylon (present-day Iraq), Nehemiah appointed Mattaniah for this office. We know that giving thanks is an expression of faith. Yet we have no idea how much the Lord is waiting for our thanks. The Lord God reacts immediately, visibly, perceptibly and mightily when we thank Him with all our hearts, because then we prove that we believe Him. That is why lamenting over being overburdened or mistreated is sheer unbelief, for we have a source whose streams of strength never cease. I want to emphasize again that the Lord reacts immediately, and things take place in the invisible world, when we begin to give thanks in our situation. Then something "clicks" and the power of the enemy is broken. The enemy threatens, oppresses and torments us, but he is also overcome in your life when you dare to give thanks. Psalm 92:1 says, "It is a good thing to give thanks unto the Lord."

15 NOVEMBER

"We give thanks to God always for you all,
making mention of you in our prayers" (1 Thessalonians 1:2).

Many believers waste their energy in prayer by telling the Lord how difficult it is to live with this or that person, even tell Him all the negative things about that person. But when you learn to give thanks to the Lord instead, you will give thanks for all people. Paul wrote to the Philippians, "I thank my God upon every remembrance of you" (Philippians 1:3). The Philippians were wonderful and faithful children of God, who were also loyal to Paul. We could, therefore, say it was easy to give thanks for them, according to the principle: if you are nice to me, I will be nice to you! But Paul also gave thanks for the difficult and annoying people. We see this in 1 Corinthians 1:4, "I thank my God always on your behalf, for the grace of God which is given you by Jesus Christ." The Corinthians had hardly grown in their faith lives. They gave Paul a lot of trouble, and he had to earnestly admonish them. But he began to give thanks for them. What could he give thanks for? There was so much strife, envy and slander in the church at Corinth, and they had attacked him. What could Paul give thanks for, then? "For the grace of God." Even in the most difficult believers, we can still find the best of all: "the grace of God."

16 NOVEMBER

"...I am exceeding joyful in all our tribulation" (2 Corinthians 7:4).

*T*his great joy was not based on anything temporal, but on the eternal love of God, which nothing can change and which exalts us in Christ, "And hath raised us up together, and made us sit together in heavenly places" (Ephesians 2:6). How highly we have been exalted!

However terrible or monotonous our experiences may be, they have no power to attack the love of God in Jesus Christ, if we are in Him and remain in Him. The Lord said of our earthly existence, "...and I in you" (John 15:4). Our Lord Jesus is at the right hand of the majesty of God in heaven, and simultaneously He lives through the Holy Spirit in each believer's heart. What a miracle of the grace of Jesus! Paul makes it clear when he says, "Christ is dwelling in you so that you may understand with all the saints, "...what is the breadth, and length, and depth, and height; and to know the love of Christ, which passeth knowledge, that ye might be filled with all the fullness of God" (Ephesians 3:18-19). Four dimensions of the divine love! How exalted you are, child of God! You have been raised with Him and seated with Him in heavenly places—infinitely high! Now we are able to understand what it means when the Bible says our conversation or citizenship is in heaven during our time on earth.

17 NOVEMBER

"Abide in me, and I in you" (John 15:4).

The Lord is speaking here of the vital organic union with Him. Christ in me is the guarantee of victory over my flesh and blood. I in Christ is the realization of the victory of Jesus Christ through me, and over all the dark powers of the enemy around me.

If this organic union with Jesus is a reality in your life, however, then the enemy will try by all means to interrupt this wonderful cycle. Keep this blessed cycle all the more in your sights: Christ in you and you in Him. His love is your love, His power is your power, His victory is your victory, His patience is your patience. Let me emphasize this once more: the enemy will try with all his might to interrupt this blessed cycle. Many children of God who are not watchful succumb to the cunning attempts of the devil. Not in vain does Peter warn us, "Be sober, be vigilant; because your adversary the devil, as a roaring lion, walketh about, seeking whom he may devour: whom resist stedfast in the faith" (1 Peter 5:8-9). If you do not resist temptation in faith, you will sin in thought, word and deed, and then spiritual circulation problems will arise.

18 NOVEMBER

"For our conversation [citizenship] is in heaven"
(Philippians 3:20).

When Paul says here, "Our citizenship is in heaven," he names in the same breath our goal, "...from whence also we look for the Saviour, the Lord Jesus Christ." Having our citizenship in heaven here on earth is the first step to the Rapture. "Who shall change our vile body, that it may be fashioned like unto his glorious body, according to the working whereby he is able even to subdue all things unto himself" (verse 21). As we know, Jesus took us with Him when He ascended into heaven. None of His blood-bought ones will remain behind, for we are members of His body; we form the body of Jesus Christ. This is why it says in Colossians 3:4, "When Christ, who is our life, shall appear, then shall ye also appear with him in glory." This event of transformation in the Rapture is very near. If your spiritual circulation is weak or even interrupted, then go now to your Savior and Lord, so that you can find cleansing in His blood and are able to hasten toward Him with joy when He returns.

19 NOVEMBER

"For I know the thoughts that I think toward you, saith the Lord, thoughts of peace, and not of evil, to give you an expected end"
(Jeremiah 29:11).

Those whose citizenship is in heaven will inevitably come within the magnetic field of the love of God. God is not loving, He *is* love, and all His intents and ways with His children are motivated by His wonderful love. The fact that you often do not understand His thoughts, ways and guidance makes no difference, for the Lord says through Isaiah, "For my thoughts are not your thoughts, neither are your ways my ways, saith the Lord. For as the heavens are higher than the earth, so are my ways higher than your ways, and my thoughts than your thoughts" (Isaiah 55:8-9).

The Lord Jesus has great understanding when you do not understand the heavenly side, which you do not see in your life. For this reason He says to you, "What I do thou knowest not now; but thou shalt know hereafter" (John 13:7). Then you will confess in amazement through your tears, "Lord, You meant so well with me, but I didn't understand."

20 NOVEMBER

"He shall call upon me, and I will answer him: I will be with him in trouble; I will deliver him, and honour him" (Psalm 91:15).

Why does prayer have such power? Because the Eternal God goes into action when we pray. He has solemnly promised to answer the prayers of His own, because:

• He hears, "…The Lord will hear when I call unto him" (Psalm 4:3).

• He responds, "…I will surely hear their cry" (Exodus 22:23).

• He gives strength, "They that wait upon the Lord shall renew their strength" (Isaiah 40:31).

• He is active, "He will fulfill the desire of them that fear him" (Psalm 145:19).

• He answers, "Before they call, I will answer" (Isaiah 65:24).

• He reveals, "I will…shew thee great and mighty things" (Jeremiah 33:3).

This is why it is immensely more important to find Him in prayer than to present Him with a lot of requests. If you find Him, you have already found the answer to your prayers.

21 NOVEMBER

"...He that loveth me shall be loved of my Father, and I will love him,
and will manifest myself to him" (John 14:21).

*S*uch a doer of the Word not only comes into the wonderful cycle of the love of the Father and the Son, but the
Father and the Son will also come to him and dwell in him!
This promise, that the Lord Jesus will reveal Himself to those
who keep His Word and thereby prove that they love Him,
was fulfilled for the first time after the resurrection of Jesus.
Something very moving took place then. Jesus revealed Himself in a special way to the disciple who had failed the most
through his threefold denial of the Lord, but who loved Him
the most! The Lord wanted to lead to perfection this very disciple, Peter. For this reason, He asked him three times the all-
important question, "He saith unto him the third time,
Simon, son of Jonas, lovest thou me? Peter was grieved because he said unto him the third time, Lovest thou me? And
he said unto him, Lord, thou knowest all things; thou knowest that I love thee" (John 21:17). As often as we speak about
this verse, we cannot say plainly enough that the Lord does
not mention Peter's sins, but only asks him whether he loves
Him.

22 NOVEMBER

"But if ye be led of the Spirit, ye are not under the law"
(Galatians 5:18).

*W*hy does it take so long for many children of God to come to a clear relinquishing to the power of the Holy Spirit? In politics, we have an object lesson that helps us to understand it better. Many a government is not capable of governing because there is no political party that has the majority. In the lives of many children of God, there is also no handing over of power to the Holy Spirit because there is no "majority vote" for the Spirit of God. Inner conflict arises because different powers such as pride, envy, bigotry, gossip, or other dark passions are continually attempting to take over the rule of your heart. The Holy Spirit is not a despot! He wants to rule, but if we doubt, He withdraws. When the Holy Spirit cannot rule in the heart of a child of God, the result is not only inner conflict, but also outer. Thus, the life of faith is a continual battle. We see this with many children of God. Discipleship is a great effort, and this is exactly the opposite of what the Lord wants to give. When the Spirit of God can rule in us, there is no compulsion in our discipleship but glorious bliss expressed in unconditional surrender to Him.

23 NOVEMBER

"Likewise the Spirit also helpeth our infirmities: for we know not what we should pray for as we ought: but the Spirit itself maketh intercession for us with groanings which cannot be uttered" (Romans 8:26).

If it really is so that the Holy Spirit prays through us, then it is not our requests but the requests of God that He wants to realize. When the Holy Spirit can pray through us, then the answer is guaranteed. Let us consider six aspects of prayer.

1. Be prepared to receive.

The Holy Spirit mediates to us that which God wants to give us. Consequently, we must be prepared to receive the Holy Spirit. Many will object and say, we already have the Holy Spirit. This is true if we are born again, for, "...no man can say that Jesus is the Lord, but by the Holy Ghost" (1 Corinthians 12:3). But we are not full of the Holy Spirit. This is why we need to be prepared to receive a new fullness of the Holy Spirit in us. How can we be prepared? "These all continued with one accord in prayer and supplication" (Acts 1:14). This is the foundation, i.e. precondition to be able to receive the Holy Spirit. To be inwardly prepared is thus the most important thing.

24 NOVEMBER

"Let us draw near with a true heart..." (Hebrews 10:22).

2. Be prepared to be completely truthful.

It is senseless to hold prayer meetings if we do not want the truth. The apostle John also mentions this in 1 John 3:18-19, "My little children, let us not love in word, neither in tongue; but in deed and in truth. And hereby we know that we are of the truth, and shall assure our hearts before him." The apostle wants to say with these words, "If we are completely truthful and do what we profess to believe, then we can rest our hearts in prayer before Him." We will then be able to rest in Him who is the truth, and are able to pray until we are sure we have been heard. Many children of God, however, do not penetrate to the innermost sanctuary because the door is closed. They pray halfheartedly, and are relieved when they can say "Amen." Is anything in you blocking the way because you are not prepared to be completely truthful? There are many prayer meetings in our land, and yet there is no revival, no breakthrough, because we are not prepared to receive and to be completely truthful.

25 NOVEMBER

"But without faith it is impossible to please him: for he that cometh to God must believe that he is, and that he is a rewarder of them that diligently seek him" (Hebrews 11:6).

3. Be prepared to believe.

"Faith" is a term today that sounds very trite, because so few people have faith. And yet it is something alive, for through faith we can have everything. This is closely connected with being prepared to be truthful. If we are not prepared to be truthful in our hearts, we have correspondingly little faith, for faith in my heart is as strong as the truth in me. We see these connections in Hebrews 10:22, "Let us draw near with a true heart in full assurance of faith...." In other words, we are incapable of believing if we are not truthful. If I seek the Lord and really want to find Him, but my heart is clinging to other things, then my prayer has no power, because that which I say in my prayer is not really true. If I am a liar, I cannot believe. We pray for revival and all sorts of things, and then when the answer comes, we are still unbelieving. There are great areas before us that remain to be possessed, for everything is possible to those who believe!

26 NOVEMBER

"And the Lord said unto Joshua, Get thee up; wherefore liest thou thus upon thy face?" (Joshua 7:10).

4. Be prepared to be judged.

This is a sore point. There is nothing that searches our hearts more than prayer. When we pray, we come into the holy presence of God and the depths of our being are brought to light. Everything is revealed, and if there is a hindrance to our prayer, it is futile to say, "Lord, if there is anything in me, take it away...." This is a cheap excuse. If there is anything there, the Lord points His finger at it and shows us why it is that we do not experience a breakthrough in prayer. We see this with Joshua, "And Joshua rent his clothes, and fell to the earth upon his face before the ark of the Lord until the eventide..." (Joshua 7:6). We must be prepared to be judged! "And the Lord said unto Joshua, Get thee up; wherefore liest thou thus upon thy face?" (Joshua 7:10). Once we do away with pious phrases, pious talk and break through, then we will be prepared to be judged. There is no point in going to a prayer meeting if we are not prepared for this. True prayer is being prepared to be judged.

27 NOVEMBER

"And when ye stand praying, forgive, if ye have ought against any: that your Father also which is in heaven forgive your trespasses"
(Mark 11:25).

5. Be prepared to be reconciled.

One sign of the end-times Christian is his unwillingness to be reconciled. If we do not forgive with all our hearts those who have something against us, then the Lord will close the heavens over us. We must be conscious of the fact that the measure with which we measure others will also be applied to us. "And forgive us our debts, as we forgive our debtors" (Matthew 6:12). There is no point in praying for revival if we are not prepared to penetrate to the core. Only when we break through will the living Lord reveal Himself, pour out His Spirit and give revival. We must go all the way, or we will become lukewarm and our prayer meetings will become "religious activity." Our Lord seeks people today who, like the disciples, are full of the Holy Spirit, clear and true, firm in their faith and reconciled. Then we can pray and the Lord will answer, as it says in Isaiah 58:9, "Then shalt thou call, and the Lord shall answer; thou shalt cry, and he shall say, Here I am." Here the way to revival is shown us. Are we willing to go this way?

28 NOVEMBER

"And whatsoever we ask, we receive of him, because we keep
his commandments, and do those things that are pleasing in his sight"
(1 John 3:22).

6. Be prepared to receive.
We cannot simply take, however. John says, "...we...do those things that are pleasing in his sight." Here he is saying nothing other than that it has to do with obedience. We ask for much, but we do not receive. Why do we not have the power to receive? Is God so hard, is His arm too short, that He is not able to help? No! But we don't do what He says. The truth is, we do not want to obey, we do not want to be fully truthful, we do not want to forgive, and therefore we cannot stand fast in faith. These different aspects are closely connected; they are actually an entity: to be prepared to receive, prepared to be truthful, prepared to believe, prepared to be judged, prepared to be reconciled. Then we are also prepared to receive what we ask for, because we do what He requires of us. The life of a person who is obedient and prays in this way becomes unspeakably rich. Such a person will say with David, "My cup runneth over" (Psalm 23). And he will rejoice with Paul, "Blessed be the God and Father of our Lord Jesus Christ, who hath blessed us with all spiritual blessings in heavenly places in Christ" (Ephesians 1:3).

29 NOVEMBER

"...Behold, he prayeth" (Acts 9:11).

These three words are very important. The Lord Himself addresses them to Ananias when He tells him to go to Saul of Tarsus. The Lord also describes where he is to be found, namely in the street called "Straight." There he finds the blind Saul, of whom the Lord says, "Behold, he prayeth." The Lord knows that Ananias and all the Christians in Damascus fear Saul, but He sees more than this: "Behold, he prayeth." Ananias is in consternation when he receives the order to go to Saul of Tarsus because Saul is praying, and he objects, "Lord, I have heard by many of this man, how much evil he hath done to thy saints at Jerusalem" (verse 13). Ananias is so intimidated by Saul that he even contradicts the Lord. When the Lord says, however, "Behold, he prayeth," this means that everything has changed in Saul's life. It is not only about our praying, but that we pray in such a way that our prayers really do reach God's ear. Only then will they have power. Prayer changes everything, but the one who prays is also changed. Saul of Tarsus was originally spiritually dead, but his testimony later reveals to us the way to victorious prayer.

30 NOVEMBER

"But what things were gain to me, those I counted loss for Christ"
(Philippians 3:7).

What Paul writes to the Philippians about himself explains why he was such a man of prayer. Directly after his conversion, Paul prayed and the Lord Himself went into action. On various occasions, Paul repeats that he counts everything loss so that he can gain Christ. From this position he could pray with authority. He had given up his own being, his religiosity. I am convinced that in the same moment as Paul prayed, thousands of others also prayed. But the Lord said of Paul alone to Ananias, "Behold, he prayeth." Why? Why does He mention no other? What was so special about Paul's prayer that he was heard? The answer is, his prayer came from the bottom of his heart. "For the eyes of the Lord run to and fro throughout the whole earth, to shew himself strong in the behold of them whose heart is perfect toward him" (2 Chronicles 16:9). This means in practical terms that God's eyes watch all praying Christians and seek those whose hearts are perfect toward Him, "And ye shall seek me, and find me, when ye shall search for me with all your heart. And I will be found of you…" (Jeremiah 29:13-14).

Spiritual
Strength
FOR EACH DAY

DECEMBER

359

1 DECEMBER

"As it is written, Eye hath not seen, nor ear heard, neither have entered into the heart of man, the things which God hath prepared for them that love him" (1 Corinthians 2:9).

The Church of Jesus Christ is portrayed in the Scriptures in twofold glory: the body of Christ and the temple of God. The true glory of the incorporated member of the Church is so great, so infinite, that we can only imagine it by means of a picture: that we are His body, His temple. The glory itself cannot be described. In the New Testament, there are seven parables of the Lord about a wedding. The Bride is neither visible nor mentioned in any of them. She is still veiled. Why? Because the Bride of the Lamb will only be revealed after the Rapture, when the complete Church stands before the throne of Christ. This great moment will reveal the true Bride. All will have eternal life, but some will "suffer loss." What loss? The loss of a yet undisclosed position in relationship to the Lord. The Bride is revealed as "His wife" for the first time in the last book of the Bible, "...and his wife hath made herself ready" (Revelation 19:7). How zealous we should be, in view of such glory, to strive for this indescribable honor of belonging to His Bride!

2 DECEMBER

"Behold, I shew you a mystery; We shall not all sleep, but we shall all be changed, in a moment, in the twinkling of an eye, at the last trump"
(1 Corinthians 15:51-52).

*H*ave you ever noticed how little the Bible says about the Rapture? Why does it speak so little of it? Because the Rapture, as Paul says here, is a mystery. What is the nature of the mystery of the Rapture, for we who are children of God? The Lord Jesus Himself reveals it to us in John 16:22-23, "And ye now therefore have sorrow: but I will see you again, and your heart shall rejoice, and your joy no man taketh from you. And in that day ye shall ask me nothing." The Lord is saying that in the moment we see Him, all mysteries will be solved and all our questions will be answered. We notice too that the Lord Jesus not only says that He will see us, but that He will see us again. How can we see Him again at the Rapture? Have we ever seen Him? Yes, we see Him now and recognize Him in the Word of God. Then, however, when He comes in the clouds of heaven, we shall see Him as He is. This is a great mystery!

3 DECEMBER

"...For the trumpet shall sound, and the dead shall be raised incorruptible, and we shall be changed" (1 Corinthians 15:52).

When Paul writes to the Thessalonians about the Rapture, although he was inspired by the Holy Spirit, he interrupts himself to emphasize, "For this we say unto you by the word of the Lord" (1 Thessalonians 4:15). In His prophetic speech in Matthew 24, the Lord Jesus Himself mentions various events as signs of His return (wars and rumors of wars, for instance), which are meant for the people of Israel. For the Church of Jesus Christ, however, there is only one great sign by which she can see that the Rapture is imminent: it is Israel! The increasing troubles in Israel, therefore, are a sign of the Rapture of the Church. Parallel to this, the trials of children of God are increasing, in which they—we—need to become more persevering in our faith. We cannot get away from the fact that in recent times, we are experiencing an increase in trials and temptations that we had no idea of ten years ago. They are things that we cannot even define sometimes, but if we are persevering and stand the test, they will mean judgment for the world, but serve to prepare us for the Rapture!

362

4 DECEMBER

"For the Lord himself shall descend from heaven with a shout, with the voice of the archangel, and with the trump of God"
(1 Thessalonians 4:16).

This unique and tremendous event in the history of the Church will be preceded by a unique event: the conversion of one single person. The conversion of this one soul who will be added to the Church, will initiate the Rapture. We know that not all people will be converted; the prophetic Word clearly documents that fact, but when the last from the Gentiles is converted, the Church is complete, "...until the fullness of the Gentiles be come in" (Romans 11:25). Every addition to the Church is registered in heaven and, when the last one is converted, the Rapture will take place. This could be today. The Rapture is also a spiritual mystery from another point of view. In the Old Testament, we read of two prophetic examples of the Rapture who did not see death but were taken away: Enoch and Elijah. Neither of these men died. They are examples of the Church. We, as members of His body, hope that we will not have to die. Paul says, "We shall not all sleep, but we shall all be changed" (1 Corinthians 15:51).

5 DECEMBER

"For if we believe that Jesus died and rose again, even so them also which sleep in Jesus will God bring with him" (1 Thessalonians 4:14).

How is it possible for all born-again Christians to be gathered from among billions of people? What power is able to distinguish between those who will remain behind and those who will take part in the Rapture? This question was once put to Edison, the famous inventor of the electric light bulb. His learned colleagues asked him, "How can it be that only believers will go to meet the Lord?" He answered this with a simple illustration. He took a box with fine sand in it, added some iron particles and mixed them with the sand. Then he held a powerful magnet over the sandbox. The sand moved, but only the iron particles attached to the magnet. This is how it will be at the Rapture. All those who have the inner disposition, the connection with the Lamb of God, will be raptured. All others will be left behind on earth. What is the power behind this? The Rapture that we await will be a demonstration of the resurrection power of Jesus Christ. Those who do not believe in the resurrection cannot be raptured.

6 DECEMBER

"For we know that if our earthly house of this tabernacle were dissolved,
we have a building of God, an house not made with hands,
eternal in the heavens" (2 Corinthians 5:1).

It must be absolutely clear to us that only those who inwardly accept the dying and the resurrection of Jesus Christ will appear with Him in the clouds. The Rapture, which proceeds from the risen Lord, is an ignoring of death. In other words, when the risen Lord appears in the clouds of heaven, His victory over death will be revealed immediately. Where are our departed loved ones? The moment a child of God is called to be with the Lord—and this only applies to those who are born again—the spirit and soul are in the presence of the Lord, but the body must wait for the resurrection, to receive a glorified body. At that moment, the marriage of the Lamb has not yet taken place. Therefore, the child of God who has died will be first at the Rapture, "...The dead in Christ shall rise first: then we which are alive" (1 Thessalonians 4:16-17). The dead in Christ will receive their glorious bodies first. However, their spirit-soul is with the Lord, and they are unspeakably blessed. Paul reveals his desire "rather to be absent from the body" (2 Corinthians 5:8). At the Rapture, we all will receive a body that is like His glorious body.

7 DECEMBER

"For in this we groan, earnestly desiring to be clothed upon with our house which is from heaven" (2 Corinthians 5:2).

If we are born-again children of God, then our lives should be a continual demonstration of the events of the Rapture. What will happen when Jesus Christ, the risen Lord, reveals Himself visibly to His own? We read the answer in 1 Corinthians 15:51, "Behold, I shew you a mystery; we shall not all sleep, but we shall all be changed." Then the law of gravity, the law of death which pulls us down, will be abolished. Sicknesses will fall from us like a garment, and we will be "clothed." We will be redeemed from the earth in an instant and raptured to meet the Lord Jesus. We will be in His presence forevermore.

Now I would like to ask you the direct question, are you practicing this transformation in your daily life? Are other people being changed and renewed by your life? A ready life is a person ready for the Rapture. Is the life of Jesus being revealed through you? Romans 6 emphasizes that we have died and are risen again with Christ, so that other people are being redeemed, saved and transformed through this. Is this possible? Yes, it is our holy task!

8 DECEMBER

"For if we believe that Jesus died and rose again, even so them also which sleep in Jesus will God bring with him" (1 Thessalonians 4:14).

*T*his faith should rule our lives today. How will the Rapture take place? What will happen? Paul says, "Then we which are alive and remain shall be caught up together with them in the clouds, to meet the Lord in the air" (1 Thessalonians 4:17). Just imagine that quite practically! From all four corners of the earth people will be raptured, in the same direction: toward Jesus, who is coming in the clouds of heaven! "And so shall we ever be with the Lord" (verse 17). The Rapture will start with Him. He is the source of the power. He ignores death. We will be changed because we are in Him and will hasten toward Him. The center of the Rapture will be the risen Lord and Him alone! Is your life ruled and filled by Jesus alone? Can you testify with Paul that you are consciously dying to yourself so that life is manifested in you? Are you able to be transformed? Paul forms it like this in his letter to the Corinthians, "Always bearing about in the body the dying of the Lord Jesus, that the life also of Jesus might be made manifest in our body" (2 Corinthians 4:10).

9 DECEMBER

"Nevertheless I have somewhat against thee,
because thou hast left thy first love" (Revelation 2:4).

The Rapture is also the meeting of the Bridegroom with His Bride in the clouds of heaven. The Bride has a bridal love for the Bridegroom and waits longingly for Him. She has adorned herself for Him and is ready for His coming. But listen to what the coming Bridegroom said to the believing Christians in Ephesus, "Nevertheless I have somewhat against thee, because thou hast left thy first love." This is the terrible thing in our day. We see many around us falling because they no longer have this fervent first love, this bridal love and devotion to Jesus Christ, because they have no more spirit of prayer and no longer give their lives for the lost. They have become indifferent. Dare we pose the question resulting from this fact: who will participate in the event of the Rapture? Will the whole Church be raptured or only an elite few? The answer is that the Church of Jesus Christ is an elite in itself. Therefore, the whole Church will be raptured, but not all belong to the Church who think they do. Who is ready to meet the Lord? It is almost too simple to say: those who are waiting for Him. Such people are living in their first love for the Lord.

10 DECEMBER

*"Wherefore doth a living man complain,
a man for the punishment of his sins?" (Lamentations 3:39).*

*I*t is a small step from lamenting to complaining. It is fateful when we as believers complain just because we are experiencing hardship, and go from lamenting to complaining. When we do this, we are denying clear statements of Scripture, such as Romans 8:28, "We know that all things work together for good to them that love God...," or 2 Corinthians 4:17, "For our light affliction, which is but for a moment...." When you begin to see the blessings in your life that come from apparent hardships, even catastrophes, gratitude to the Lord will flow from your lips. We ask the Lord to let streams of living water flow from us, but we are not willing to accept the fact that the bed of our stream must be dug deep and wide. The depressing situation that you may find yourself in now will turn into glorious streams of blessing when you begin to thank the Lord. If you have to go through a period of deep despondency, an increasing of your spiritual personality is in the plans ahead of you. Learn, therefore, to practice the words of the Holy Scriptures, "Giving thanks always for all things unto God and the Father in the name of our Lord Jesus Christ" (Ephesians 5:20).

11 DECEMBER

"Yea, in the way of thy judgments, O Lord, have we waited for thee"
(Isaiah 26:8).

We have need of power and inner strength. This lies in waiting, as we read in Isaiah 30:15, "In quietness and in confidence shall be your strength." This quiet, confident waiting is not ours by nature. We find it difficult. Why? Because we are simultaneously waiting for many other things, and when our expectations are not immediately fulfilled, we are disappointed. We must learn to wait for one person alone: Jesus! It is not the waiting in itself, but waiting for the Lord that will not be put to shame. This waiting for God is uninterrupted expectation. The words of the Psalmist have deep significance, "On thee do I wait all the day" (Psalm 25:5). In other words, waiting unceasingly. Outwardly we have good and bad days, but constant waiting for the Lord makes our hearts free from the ebb and flow of our emotions. The Bible says, "It is a good thing that the heart be established with grace" (Hebrews 13:9). This establishing grace is only made available to us, however, in constant waiting for Him, "But I will hope continually" (Psalm 71:14).

12 DECEMBER

"Let your loins be girded about, and your lights burning; and ye your-selves like unto men that wait for their lord, when he will return from the wedding; that when he cometh and knocketh, they may open unto him immediately" (Luke 12:35-36).

To be waiting for Jesus also means being watchful. We can only wait for Him if we are watchful. I remember that years ago I often came home very late from preaching assignments, sometimes at two or three in the morning, but my wife was always waiting for me. I saw from afar that the light was on in the house. A person who is waiting for Jesus is simultaneously a fervent missionary. Therefore, the Lord says, "Let your...lights [be] burning." Be ready to leave, let your loins be girded about, the Bible says. In waiting for Him, we will be safe in His wonderful work of salvation, "So Christ was once offered to bear the sins of many; and unto them that look for him shall he appear the second time without sin unto salvation" (Hebrews 9:28). Waiting for Jesus is closely connected with His first coming, when He carried away our sins, and with His second coming, to take us unto Himself. The more we are one with Him in His death on the cross, the more we live in the hope that He will come soon. The cross and the crown belong together.

13 DECEMBER

"...So that ye come behind in no gift; waiting for the coming of our Lord Jesus Christ" (1 Corinthians 1:7).

When we are waiting for Him, He takes away our worries and we receive grace to concentrate on Him alone. Those who are solely waiting for Him have no lack of any gift, physical or spiritual, but are showered with blessing because their lives are concentrated on Jesus alone.

Through waiting for Jesus, we are increasingly liberated from all earthly things, that "we should live soberly, righteously, and godly, in this present world" (Titus 2:12). Therefore, only those who have found grace can wait for Jesus. Grace is not an umbrella, however, beneath which we can promenade our old nature and say, "We are all under grace! Sin is not so serious." On the contrary! The grace of God teaches us to deny ungodliness and worldly lusts. Only then have we the right to wait for the blessed hope and appearing of our Savior, Jesus Christ.

14 DECEMBER

"But they that wait upon the Lord shall renew their strength; they shall mount up with wings as eagles; they shall run, and not be weary; and they shall walk, and not faint" (Isaiah 40:31).

In waiting for Jesus, we receive what we so badly need in these days: new strength. Do you know that the Lord is waiting for you to wait for Him? It says this in Isaiah 30:18, "Therefore will the Lord wait, that he may be gracious unto you, and therefore will he be exalted, that he may have mercy upon you." He wants to be one with you! In waiting for Him, we not only come nearer to Him timewise, but also in our nature, so that we become increasingly one with Jesus. In waiting for Him, your eyes will be opened to a new and glorious truth: I belong to His Church. I can rest in Him because I am one with Jesus, a member of His body. Those who are waiting for Jesus begin to understand that they no longer need to try to abide in Him, but that they are already in Jesus. You are in Him, and as a branch you no longer need to draw the sap out of the vine, but His life continually flows through you, whether you feel it or not. In this way, the waiting and expectation of Jesus becomes wonderful fulfillment even right now.

15 DECEMBER

"They return, but not to the most High" (Hosea 7:16).

This is the Lord's lament over His people through the mouth of the prophet Hosea. When a person truly turns to God, it is always followed by revival. Revival means new life, and such life is visible to others. Conversions cause living chain reactions; that's the norm for the Church. Of the first Church we read, "And the Lord added to the church daily such as should be saved" (Acts 2:47). When such a process does not take place, it is because the hearts of believers are divided. This is the greatest enemy of revival. The power of God, on the other hand, is always there where divided hearts turn to Him. In 2 Chronicles 16:9, it is written, "For the eyes of the Lord run to and fro throughout the whole earth, to shew himself strong in the behalf of them whose heart is perfect toward him." Those who are completely devoted to the Lord experience the strength of the Lord. Divided hearts are not only divided where the Lord is concerned, but also where their surroundings are concerned. This is why we have so many broken marriages and families. Therefore today, seek Him who is able to mend that which is broken by a divided heart.

16 DECEMBER

"...And the voice of weeping shall be no more heard in her"
(Isaiah 65:19).

What a wonderful, glorious promise! You, child of God, will weep no more in heaven, for there will be no more reason for sadness. In heaven, there will be no broken friendships and no thwarted hopes. Physical and mental diseases, misunderstandings, danger and death are completely unknown there. You may be sure, no suffering will grieve you there, and no thoughts of death or loss will depress you. All the tears shed here on earth will be wiped away by God Himself. You will no longer weep in heaven, because all your deepest longings and desires will be fulfilled. The "desperately wicked" heart the Bible speaks of in Jeremiah 17:9 will be replaced by a new one. You will stand before the throne of His Son without spot or blemish and will have become like the image of His Son. Be of good cheer, therefore, for "God shall wipe away all tears from their eyes; and there shall be no more death, neither sorrow, nor crying, neither shall there be any more pain: for the former things are passed away" (Revelation 21:4).

17 DECEMBER

"As it is written, Eye hath not seen, nor ear heard, neither have entered into the heart of man, the things which God hath prepared for them that love him" (1 Corinthians 2:9).

Our present knowledge about what God, whom we love, has prepared for us is incomplete, but through the revelation of the Spirit we sense many of the unspeakable things that await us. There is, for instance, a deeper reason why you will no longer weep there. It is because there is no fear of change; you will be eternally safe in Him. Sin is excluded and you are included in His presence. You will live in a city that can never be destroyed. You will be refreshed by a river that never dries up, and you will pick fruit from a tree that never loses its leaves. All temporal things will disappear, but eternity will remain. Your immortality and bliss will last for as long as eternity lasts. You will then be with the Lord forever. A glorious, unspeakably blissful future awaits the sanctified. Cling all the more, then, to the One whom you do not yet see, but on whom you believe, and over whom you will rejoice unspeakably when you see Him as He is.

18 DECEMBER

*"Surely I have behaved and quieted myself,
as a child that is weaned of his mother" (Psalm 131:2).*

*Y*ou can find everything you need in the Lord. He is perfect love. He loves you more than your father and mother together are able to love you. David knew what he was talking about when, inspired by the Holy Spirit, he said, "Truly my soul waiteth upon God: from him cometh my salvation" (Psalm 62:1). Do you understand now why a spirit of haste makes you inwardly restless, especially before the Christmas holidays? You say you believe in Jesus, and yet you let yourself be pursued through life like a hunted deer. When you sing, "Silent night, holy night" in a few days, do not rest until your heart has become still in Him. Do not flee into activity, but let the reason for your inability to be still be revealed in His holy presence. Sin is the cause, but Jesus is the remedy. That's why Jesus was born in Bethlehem, and afterwards went to Calvary. Did He do everything in vain for you? Jesus embraced the children. Become like a child. Flee through the Lord Jesus to the heart of God, and you will be renewed in the stillness of His presence. These words are addressed especially to children of God who have been made new through faith, but continually need to be renewed through obedience of faith.

19 DECEMBER

*"And the Lord spake unto Moses face to face,
as a man speaketh unto his friend" (Exodus 33:11).*

Of Moses we read so simply, "And Moses brought forth the people out of the camp to meet with God" (Exodus 19:17). What gave Moses such authority? The answer is simple: Moses lived in the direct presence of God. Moses had found grace in the eyes of the Lord. I want to emphasize that you can only lead a person to the Lord so far as you yourself live in the presence of God. Your spiritual children are what you are spiritually. The Lord wants to draw you to Himself with cords of love today. When we sank into sin and corruption, Jesus went much deeper. He caught us there to draw us to His Father's heart again. Therefore, the question is of such eminent importance: how far have you come to the Lord inwardly? If you are far from Him, then hear now what He is calling to you, "Yea, I have loved thee with an everlasting love: therefore with lovingkindness have I drawn thee" (Jeremiah 31:3). The drawing of God to Himself takes place via Calvary. The overpowering love of God, which drew Him to the cross, wants to draw us to the cross. There we are nearest to God, for there we are hidden with Christ in God; there we are one with Him.

20 DECEMBER

"Shew me thy ways, O Lord; teach me thy paths. Lead me in thy truth, and teach me: for thou art the God of my salvation; on thee do I wait all the day" (Psalm 25:4-5).

*H*ere we have the so necessary prayer for leading. Why is this so necessary? Because only God's ways are perfect, and therefore only His way for you is blessed. Between God's ways and your own, there is a great chasm. The Scriptures say clearly where our own ways lead us, "There is a way which seemeth right unto a man, but the end thereof are the ways of death" (Proverbs 14:12). It is a great tragedy when it says in Isaiah 53:6, "We have turned every one to his own way." Therefore, the question is all the more urgent, namely, what is the Lord's way for you? We read in Psalm 77:13, "Thy way, O God, is in the sanctuary." His way is holy, but this is the very reason that so few find this wonderful way, for "narrow is the way, which leadeth unto life" (Matthew 7:14). On this holy, narrow way, there is no room for our ego. The adjectives "holy" and "narrow" also emphasize the unique nature of His way for you. There is no other way, and on this way there is only room for two: the Lamb and you.

21 DECEMBER

"And the angel of the Lord came again the second time,
and touched him, and said, Arise and eat;
because the journey is too great for thee" (1 Kings 19:7).

Where does the Lord's way lead? I can tell all of you who are reading this now with great certainty: you have a great journey ahead of you. Come and go His way. Where to? Revelation 14:4 tells us this, "These are they which follow the Lamb whithersoever he goeth." I can also tell you with great certainty where this way does not lead: where the flesh wants to go. I ask you now to examine the measure of your willingness. Are you willing to follow the Lamb wherever He goes? This way means the surrender of your own will. The only right way for you is the way in which the Lord has wanted to lead you for a long while, but you did not want to follow. The starting point of your way up till now has always been in your own self. The starting point of the Lord's way, however, is Calvary. There He is waiting for you. You must return to where the crucified Lamb of God is waiting for you. Only from Calvary can you follow the Lord's way.

22 DECEMBER

"And I will make all my mountains a way, and my highways shall be exalted" (Isaiah 49:11).

What does this way look like? It is a prepared, paved way. Even if you cannot see it, you will still be able to walk it in peace and assurance. We are also being led by the Lord when we do not notice it. We are walking in the works that God prepared for us. The Lord says with emphasis that He Himself will prepare the way ahead of you, "I will go before thee, and make the crooked places straight" (Isaiah 45:2). I ask you, is it dry in your heart? Is it like a desert where no fruit grows, no fruit of the Spirit, which you need so desperately? Then hear the Word of the Lord for you, "Remember ye not the former things, neither consider the things of old. Behold, I will do a new thing; now it shall spring forth; shall ye not know it? I will even make a way in the wilderness, and rivers in the desert" (Isaiah 43:18-19). What a wonderful, comforting promise! The Lord legitimizes Himself simultaneously when He says in Isaiah 43:16, "Thus saith the Lord, which maketh a way in the sea, and a path in the mighty waters." He wants to give revival in your life! He wants to make a way in your desert—what a promise! Thank Him for this now and say, "Lord, I thank You that You have unlimited ways and means!"

23 DECEMBER

"Thanks be unto God for his unspeakable gift" (2 Corinthians 9:15).

*I*ngratitude toward the Lord is a great sin. How many reasons do we have to thank Him? Most of all, however, we need to thank Him for His beloved Son, whom He gave for our sakes on the accursed cross. Gratitude to the Lord is pleasing to Him, for it says in 1 Thessalonians 5:18, "In every thing give thanks; for this is the will of God in Christ Jesus concerning you." Have you thanked the Lord today? The measure of your gratitude determines the measure of the victory of Jesus in your life and through your life. To give thanks is the highest expression of faith, "Be careful [anxious] for nothing; but in every thing by prayer and supplication with thanksgiving let your requests be made known unto God" (Philippians 4:6). So few children of God, however, practice thanking the Lord first before they bring Him their requests. Thank Him first with all your heart for your redemption! Thank Him that He has carried you through up to the present day. Thank Him that you were able to become a child of God, that He gave you the new birth out of grace. The Lord loves to hear this, because you are doing His will when you do it. He is honored through this, and you yourself become inwardly happy and free to intercede for others in the right way before the throne of grace.

24 DECEMBER

"And they said unto him, In Bethlehem of Judaea;
for thus it is written by the prophet"
(Matthew 2:5).

*I*n these days around Christmas, it seems strange that millions of people believe in the fulfillment of the biblical
prophecy historically. Why is this strange? Because only a
small minority of these people believe in the current fulfillment of biblical prophecy. Many people believe in the Word,
but not in its fulfillment. Look at history; on the one hand,
the high priests and scribes believed in the Word implicitly. At
the fearful question of the worried King Herod as to where
the Messiah had to be born, they quoted Scripture, "In Bethlehem of Judaea." Yet they did not believe in the fact of the
fulfillment that had already taken place. On the other hand,
we see the wise men from the East who did not know the
Word, but they had seen the light. With great inner assurance, they followed the light, the star, and when they finally
arrived in Jerusalem they asked, "Where is he that is born
King of the Jews? For we have seen his star in the east"
(Matthew 2:2). The "believers" of that time believed in the
Word but not in its fulfillment; the ignorant Gentiles, on the
other hand, had the light, believed it, followed it, and found
Jesus. Just as it was at the first coming of the Lord, so it is
today, "...The last shall be first" (Matthew 19:30).

25 DECEMBER

"And thou Bethlehem, in the land of Juda, art not the least among the princes of Juda: for out of thee shall come a Governor, that shall rule my people Israel" (Matthew 2:6).

While the "believers," the theologians in the neighborhood of Bethlehem discussed the Word—Gentiles who possessed a simple faith, the wise men from the East, were blessed through the wonderful fulfillment of the Word. It is not much different today. While Christians squabble among themselves, and theologians publish their disputes, a little host out of the whole of Christianity believes in the biblical prophecy that has already been fulfilled and is currently being fulfilled, and they are blessed by God beyond measure. Because these believers not only believe in the Word but also in the fulfillment of the Word in our day, they have light. Of such the Lord Jesus said, "Ye are the light of the world" (Matthew 5:14). What a tremendous task! Hold fast, therefore, to the prophetic Word that is being fulfilled today before all eyes. Truly, we may now say, "We have seen His star! The King is coming!" The festival of Christmas is the festival of living hope. He who came will soon return!

26 DECEMBER

"For other foundation can no man lay than that is laid, which is Jesus Christ" (1 Corinthians 3:11).

The Bible is exclusive and complete. For this reason, nobody can lay any other foundation upon which a human soul can build for eternity.

Jesus Christ is the immoveable foundation. The lust and pleasure the world offers is vain because it is temporary. The Holy Scriptures teach us, "The world passeth away, and the lust thereof" (1 John 2:17).

Jesus Christ is the eternal foundation. He is the eternal Son of God. The Bible says that He obtained eternal redemption for us (Hebrews 9:12). Jesus said, "I give unto them eternal life" (John 10:28).

Jesus Christ is the reason for atonement. He laid the foundation for atonement with the holy God, "God was in Christ, reconciling the world unto himself, not imputing their trespasses unto them" (2 Corinthians 5:19).

Jesus Christ is the sure and proven foundation. Can you find security anywhere else? Nowhere! No matter how much insurance you may have, your insecurity, your restlessness and lack of peace, are not removed. Take refuge in Him! In the words of the old hymn, you will be "Safe in the arms of Jesus."

27 DECEMBER

"For he hath put all things under his feet" (1 Corinthians 15:27).

Wherever Satan's power rages, the name of Jesus alone has greater power. Why? Because behind this precious name is His blood, which He shed on Calvary when He poured out His life. Through this blood, Satan is overcome. The blood of the Lamb makes the believer invincible. You who are depressed, do not deny the name of Jesus by believing that the spirit of depression is stronger than the name of Jesus! Call upon this wonderful name, and you will find an open door. Where did the Lord put this door? Before you! "Behold, I have set before thee an open door, and no man can shut it: for thou hast a little strength..." (Revelation 3:8). This door is always before you, never behind you. Never go back! You must go through this open door, despite tribulation, into the blissful presence of God. The twofold guarantee that this door will remain open before you lies in His omnipotence and your impotence. "I have," He says. He has everything you lack. And what do you have? Nothing! You are miserable, poor and empty in yourself. Between His "I" and your "you" are the words, "have set before." "I have set before thee an open door."

28 DECEMBER

"It is of the Lord's mercies that we are not consumed, because his com-passions fail not. They are new every morning: great is thy faithfulness"
(Lamentations 3:22-23).

*L*et us always remember that it is of the Lord's mercy that we are even alive. Another translation reads, "Because of the Lord's great love we are not consumed." We will soon begin a new year; therefore, learn to live out of the fullness of divine mercy and love. Unfortunately, most Christians find this very hard. Why? Because grace is undeserved favor, and who wants to live out of undeserved favor? Only a child of God who is growing in self-recognition is able to. We actually have to learn to hate ourselves; only then are we capable of receiving the fullness of the grace of Jesus Christ, as John 1:16 says, "Of his fullness have all we received, and grace for grace." When we receive this grace, then, we are living in inner and outer peace and serenity. Then you will say thankfully, "It is of the Lord's grace that I am still here, that I am alive, that I know Jesus and can follow Him!"

29 DECEMBER

". . . All things are become new" (2 Corinthians 5:17).

*T*hese are precious words, particularly now as we approach the beginning of a new year. The Lord has not only made all things new, but He is continually making all things new, ever deeper, ever clearer. God accomplishes this miracle of inner renewal in the crucible of our suffering and misery, as it says in Isaiah 48:10, "Behold, I have refined thee, but not with silver; I have chosen thee in the furnace of affliction." When we begin to see all dark and negative things in this light, we receive a glorious perspective. Of course we feel surrounded by hostile powers, but they are all overcome at Calvary's cross. Think of our highly exalted Lord and Savior! With what sovereignty and inner peace did He react to the hostile powers surrounding Him—they could not touch Him! Let us learn from the Lord Jesus how we can remain untouched by the enemy powers. What was His secret? He was in the Father, and the Father was in Him. In this way He was invincible. The invincibility of a child of God who abides in his Lord is a wonderful reality, "...That wicked one toucheth him not" (1 John 5:18).

30 DECEMBER

"There is a way which seemeth right unto a man, but the end thereof are the ways of death" (Proverbs 14:12).

O n the border between the old and the New Year, many people become contemplative. Their thoughts can be quite depressing, because they are always about the things of this earth. There is the thought, for instance, "How quickly I am getting old!" This is true. If you do not have Jesus, you go downhill rapidly. It really is true that a life without "the life" is meaningless and a great tragedy because, in spite of all your seeking and creating, your deepest longings are never stilled. This is why you see with fear the dark night of death approaching, without hope and without comfort. You have reason to be more sorrowful every year, for you have an uncertain future ahead of you. Blessed are those, however, who have Christ in their hearts. Such people have the hope of glory! It is not the case, then, that growing old is "getting older," but you are actually "getting younger." Yes, we can even say, the older the better! This is not an empty phrase, my friend, but a wonderful fact, for "…though our outward man perish, yet the inward man is renewed day by day" (2 Corinthians 4:16).

31 DECEMBER

"The grass withereth, the flower fadeth: but the word of our God shall stand for ever" (Isaiah 40:8).

The promises of God remain valid in the New Year! Circumstances may toss you to and fro, time may fly, but the Word remains! How many people have attacked the Bible over the centuries? Enemy powers attempted to do their work of destruction, but the Bible remained! The Word belongs to you! The Word and you, you and the Word, should become one. Was not Jesus Christ inseparably one with the eternal Word of God? David said, "Thy word have I hid in mine heart, that I might not sin against thee" in Psalm 119:11. The Bible remains! The Word remains, because it is sure and reliable, because it is stronger than all else, stronger than human doctrine and destructive powers. Therefore, I wish all of you who are standing on the border of the new year the Lord's richest blessing with Psalm 33:4, "The word of the Lord is right; and all his works are done in truth." The Bible remains. This also applies to all who are in the Lord's service: the Bible remains. And it also applies to you who are sick or otherwise oppressed: the Word remains!

NOTES

NOTES

NOTES

NOTES

NOTES

NOTES

NOTES